Praise for *The Story Y[...]*

"Sandra Marinella uses her own story as t[...]
insurmountable odds to rise up to their ch[...]
them. Thoughtfully written, deeply enco[...]
— **Laurie Notaro**, *New York [...]*
The Idiot Girls' Action-Adventure Club and *Autobiography of a Fat Bride*

"Sandra Marinella's passion and enthusiasm for writing shine throughout
this poignant and insightful book. With the skills and experience of a sea-
soned writing teacher, she shares with us the tools to tell the stories we
need to tell and reminds us of the healing power of writing."
— **Michael Ferguson**, postdoctoral fellow, cognitive neuroscience,
Cornell University

"Both Sandra Marinella's writing and her workshops are filled with inspira-
tion and love. Her words truly touch her audience."
— **Dale Yavitt, RRT, MPH,** the Body, Mind, and Spirit
Program Coordinator, Piper Cancer Center, Scottsdale, Arizona

"In *The Story You Need to Tell*, Sandra Marinella inspires the vulnerable in all
of us to be the strength in each of us. She has a unique form, transforming
a sentiment of safety and empowerment through writing into healing. Her
own story highlights the power of the written word and provides a guide
to healing through writing. Her book and her work are transformational."
— **Courtney Klein**, cofounder and CEO of SEED SPOT

"Sandra Marinella's *The Story You Need to Tell* is a collection of illuminating
stories that shows us the power of writing to transform our lives."
— **Ellen Bass**, poet and bestselling author of
The Courage to Heal, Beginning to Heal, Like a Beggar,
Mules of Love, The Human Line, and *Free Your Mind*

"Marinella's practical direction and inspiring narrative invite readers to become writers. 'Our stories create us,' she writes. '*And our writing can re-
create us.*' *The Story You Need to Tell* is an important and beautiful book
that I cannot wait to share with my students and others whose stories are
aching to be told."
— **Judy Reeves**, author of *A Writer's Book of Days* and
Wild Women, Wild Voices

"In *The Story You Need to Tell*, Sandra Marinella does just that — recounting
her own personal and professional experiences with skill, wit, and bravery.

She reaches out and tells the stories of others, too, weaving a strong safety net for any of us who need a nudge toward paper and pen. This book is a testament to the author's courage, strength, and heart and a love letter to the power of words."

— **Amy Silverman**, author of *My Heart Can't Even Believe It: A Story of Science, Love, and Down Syndrome*

"Using her work with cancer patients and veterans, as well as her own experience, Sandra Marinella guides you through the dark and lonely times of illness, trauma, and loss to the healing power of writing. With writing prompts designed to lead you deeper into self-reflection, she shows how you can discover your own strength through writing the story you need to tell. And — most important of all — she offers the empowering realization that you can choose how you tell the story and what it means."

— **Barbara Abercrombie**, author of *A Year of Writing Dangerously* and *Courage & Craft*

"Sandra Marinella brings keen research skills, a brilliant storytelling voice, and a distinguished teaching career to this cohesive guide for writing the unspeakable. Her vivid prose twines her own powerful cancer story with dozens of other courageous voices, each writing the road from devastation to reclamation. User-friendly writing prompts and affecting case studies offer accessible portals for the safe expression of stories of woundedness and ultimate triumph."

— **Kathleen Adams**, LPC, director of the Center for Journal Therapy, author of *Journal to the Self*, and coauthor (with Deborah Ross) of *Your Brain on Ink*

"*The Story You Need to Tell* inspires, uplifts, and teaches people who need to address the power of their memories and their stories how to stand in their truth and how to find words to express what is often inexpressible. Words heal, and Sandra Marinella will help you find yours."

— **Linda Joy Myers**, president of the National Association of Memoir Writers and author of *The Power of Memoir* and *Don't Call Me Mother*

"Sandra Marinella has empowered us to take charge of our life story and to turn challenges into meaning and purpose. Telling our stories not only helps us heal from trauma but allows us to craft a beautiful life out of the ashes."

— **Dr. Norma Bowe**, professor at Kean University, author of *Perspectives on Community Mental Health*, and subject of *The Death Class: A True Story about Life*

THE STORY
YOU NEED
TO TELL

THE STORY
YOU NEED
TO TELL

WRITING TO HEAL FROM
TRAUMA, ILLNESS, OR LOSS

SANDRA MARINELLA, MA, MEd

Foreword by Christina Baldwin

New World Library
Novato, California

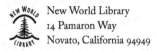 New World Library
14 Pamaron Way
Novato, California 94949

The material in this book is intended for education. It is not meant to take the place of diagnosis and treatment by a qualified medical practitioner or therapist. No expressed or implied guarantee of the effects of the use of the recommendations can be given or liability taken.

Text design by Tona Pearce Myers

Library of Congress Cataloging-in-Publication Data
Names: Marinella, Sandra, [date]– author.
Title: The story you need to tell : writing to heal from trauma, illness, or loss / Sandra Marinella, MA, MEd ; foreword by Christina Baldwin.
Description: Novato, California : New World Library, [2017] | Includes bibliographical references and index.
Identifiers: LCCN 2016056886 (print) | LCCN 2017008876 (ebook) | ISBN 9781608684830 (paperback) | ISBN 9781608684847 (ebook) | ISBN 9781608684847 (Ebook)
Subjects: LCSH: Marinella, Sandra, [date]—Health. | Breast cancer—Patients—Biography. | Postpartum depression—Patients—Biography. | Narrative therapy. | Self-care, Health. | BISAC: LANGUAGE ARTS & DISCIPLINES / Composition & Creative Writing. | SELF-HELP / Death, Grief, Bereavement. | BIOGRAPHY & AUTOBIOGRAPHY / Personal Memoirs. | SELF-HELP / Creativity.
Classification: LCC RC280.B8 M3445 2017 (print) | LCC RC280.B8 (ebook) | DDC 362.19699/4490092 [B]—dc23
LC record available at https://lccn.loc.gov/2016056886

First printing, May 2017
ISBN 978-1-60868-483-0
Ebook ISBN 978-1-60868-484-7
Printed in Canada on 100% postconsumer-waste recycled paper

 New World Library is proud to be a Gold Certified Environmentally Responsible Publisher. Publisher certification awarded by Green Press Initiative. www.greenpressinitiative.org

10   9   8   7   6   5   4   3   2

I am thankful —
For writers and students who inspire me.
For family and friends who love and encourage me.
And for Steve, who has always believed in me.

The greatest glory in living lies not in never falling,
but in rising every time we fall.

— **Nelson Mandela**

Contents

Part Four. Rewriting Our Shattered Stories

Part Five. Writing to Heal

Part Six. Writing to Transform

Foreword

This book makes a promise to its readers.

It promises that *you* are the author of your life story.

It promises that by understanding the power of story, you can change the way you carry your life circumstances, no matter what has happened to you. It promises that you have the power to shift your perspective from victim to victor, from survivor to thriver, from loser to winner.

It promises to show you the story you have to tell.

You cannot go back and change your life history. This is not about lying or self-delusion. Becoming the author of your story is about claiming the power to define what something means and to take charge of the ways your life events impact you and influence how you move forward.

Once there was a little girl who loved to dance. She danced as soon as she could walk. She took dance lessons from the time she was three. When she was six years old, she started ballet lessons. When she was eight years old, she was riding her bicycle to her dance class when she was hit by a car. Her leg was crushed and had to be amputated. After her hospitalization and physical therapy, she learned to dance again, sometimes with her prosthetic leg and sometimes one-legged. She says about herself, "The accident changed my life, but it didn't change who I am — a dancer."

This book makes that promise to its readers: the power is in you to shape how you will live with whatever happens. The power is in the stories you tell to encourage you to take the next risk, to make the next move, to keep saying yes to life.

Author Sandra Marinella is your guide, teacher, and friend in this process. She has watched the power of story release people's capacities to live through life challenges, losses, and tragedies. She shares their stories to illustrate how story making is map making, a pattern you can follow. She has researched the brain science and psychology to provide a strong foundation for the journey she invites you on. Chapter by chapter, she helps you get stronger and more informed and more excited about these possibilities.

Once in the height of her career as a college writing teacher, Sandra was diagnosed with breast cancer. She had been on a trajectory of service and work and suddenly had to stop and turn all her attention to working with the medical system to save her own life. A woman who had been busy, distracted, and carrying multitudes of responsibility fell to the floor, her sense-of-self story shattered at her feet. As she researched her life through the journals she had kept over the years, she realized she had been building up story reserves to help her come through this crisis.

When we talk about and write about ourselves differently, we change our sense of who we are and what we are capable of. We can recite tales of woe, or we can communicate resilience, confidence, insight, strength.

People navigate life through the stories we tell ourselves and each other about what just happened, what is happening, or what we expect to have happen. Story is the medium we use to make sense of experience.

Most days, we tell stories about weather and sports and family, about what we did with friends and our summer vacations and the birthday parties we've attended and our hopes for next week or next year. However, when something happens that shakes us out of the day-to-day storytelling we count on, we are propelled into new territory, where we have to articulate a new story in order to make a new life.

Once, several years ago, my partner and I faced the sudden death of our thirty-three-year-old son. We made it through this horrible and miraculous moment, handled those things that had to be handled, flew on to a Thanksgiving family reunion that now included fresh collective grief, then flew back to Denver for his memorial service. On the plane home, I wrote compulsively in my journal for four hours. I was determined to grab the string of events, detail after detail, knowing I would want to remember exactly what happened, no matter how painful. It was a story I had to tell — like the stories in this book. Now this survivor's tale is the basis for an integration story, for the perspective gained, for the hard beauties of grief.

When things happen that are unexpected, unwelcome, challenging, disorienting, or traumatic, we survive, but the storyline we were following is shattered. Untold stories don't go away; they morph into volatile emotions, into flashbacks and anxiety, into behaviors we don't understand in ourselves, things we wish we didn't do — lash out, hide, avoid, get depressed, become lethargic, unable to go on. Untold stories cause ruptures in relationships, ill health, and spiritual or religious crisis, and contribute to a growing sense that our lives are disintegrating into chaos.

People full of untold stories — people like you and me — are the ones whom author Sandra Marinella has taught and mentored as she fashioned this helpful book. *The Story You Need to Tell* is full of tools to fully restory your life; and even more, it is full of Sandra's understanding, compassion, and guidance.

So maybe you're not a writer.

You don't have to ever show anyone this writing, and it will still work on your heart and mind to reorganize your life.

So maybe you don't have time for this.

Ten minutes a day? Really? That's way shorter than a Facebook minute.

So maybe it's scary to think of putting your life-breaking moments into words.

This book provides you with a safety net.

So maybe with a little help you're ready to live a more resilient story.

You can dance on one leg.

You can get through a crisis.

You can survive grief.

That is the promise the book makes to you.

Now make a promise to yourself — to tell the story you have to tell!

— Christina Baldwin

Christina Baldwin is a lifelong journal writer and the author of *Life's Companion: Journal Writing as a Spiritual Practice*, and *Storycatcher: Making Sense of Our Lives through the Power and Practice of Story*, among many others. She is an international writing teacher emeritus.

Author's Note

This book is based on true stories. I have spent five years interviewing and taping people and researching, writing, rewriting, and editing this work. More than a hundred individuals — veterans, cancer patients, writers, and students — stepped forward with "the story they needed to tell." I am grateful for their wisdom and insights. They helped me to learn the power of writing and how our myths, metaphors, and meaning are born of the stories we choose. Out of respect for their privacy, I have changed names and identifying details, whether or not noted on these pages. For the sake of story, certain characters and events have been compressed and reordered.

Introduction

All the world is full of suffering.
— Helen Keller

At some point you will be *knocked to the ground*. Every one of us will.

I learned this as I sat on the edge of the black velvet chair in the chalk-white, sterile office. My heart clenched as I waited for a doctor I did not want to meet. The door swung open, and a chalk-white radiologist entered and motioned me to sit back. I began to choke, and tears of nervous anticipation flooded my eyes. And then it seemed as if we were trapped in a black-and-white 16mm movie of my life, a scary, surreal film — the kind of strange avant-garde ones Andy Warhol used to make in the '60s. There was no sound but the ghostly doctor mouthing the words, *"You have cancer."* In Warhol style the film, appropriately titled *Cancer*, was projected onto dark walls — and it was showing my story. Then the projector clicked and sputtered and went silent. Suddenly my story seemed to have slipped off the spool and was cascading to the basement of my mind as ribbons of unwound, damaged film. Could this film — my story — be repaired?

1

One week later I entered the office of a highly recommended, highly rated surgeon. I trusted she could surgically remove a small lump from the depths of my left breast in short order. It was, after all, early-stage cancer. Short, petite, well coiffed, the doctor entered the room with her assistant, a girl half her age but twice her size. The surgeon peered at my scans for a long time before turning to me. "I think it would be best if we popped that left puppy off — and I want you to seriously consider popping both those puppies off."

"Are we talking about my breasts?" I asked.

An hour later I was curled up in the fetal position on the cold tile of my kitchen floor, rocking back and forth and feeling caught in the undertow of my mind. Thoughts swirling out of control. Drowning. My arms began to flail, for I was uncertain that I could swim past a flood of questions and fears, uncertain that I would make it. Unprepared, jolted by surprise, I had joined the approximately 230,000 women in the United States who each year learn they have breast cancer. My husband was a thousand miles away on a business trip. It was after 6:00 PM, and the last rays of sun were disappearing from the winter sky. Darkness engulfed me.

Have you ever been there — knocked to the ground by a traumatic event? Woken up one morning as someone you knew and in the midst of your busy day had it all suddenly change? In my case, I was a college writing teacher with a load of papers to grade and a birthday party to plan for my dad, but unexpectedly I had joined the tribe of the traumatized — women facing cancer. How could I handle this change? With pills? With a few glasses of wine? Could I pull a plug and let the air out so I could deflate and start all over? Could I flip a switch and simply reboot?

Do you have your own I-don't-believe-this-is-happening-to-me story? I bet you do.

After walking around dazed for a few weeks, I began talking with other survivors of trauma — veterans, cancer patients, students, writers, and friends who have faced stories that have sucked the air out of their lungs and left them feeling trapped in the undertow. Stories that made them feel as if they were drowning, not even sure they would survive. There was the story of a baby born with a deformed, oversize head. The story of a husband who left without a word. The story of a best buddy who stepped on an explosive in Afghanistan and lost his limbs. The story of the young woman who learned she had advanced breast cancer as she held her newborn in her arms. The story of a coworker who entered a home as a friend and left as a rapist. The story of a husband who went into the ocean and never came out. The story of a first-grader who hid in a closet with his peers and teachers, only to be brutally shot to death by a teenager gone mad. I ended up interviewing more than a hundred writers — some famous, most not.

And I learned we all have difficult stories — tragic, traumatic, and stress filled. At times our pain erupts from the sum total of emotional hits we take daily: the alarm that didn't ring, the overdrawn check, the lost assignment, the broken glasses, the blue screen on the computer, and the wrecked bumper. If you have a story that has sucked the air out of you and made you feel as if you're going under, this book was written for you. In it we will explore how to write our way up and out of a heart-ripping trauma or the avalanche of little challenges that face us daily and threaten our well-being.

When I first learned I had cancer, I knew I was facing a life-threatening situation, and I made the decision — as many folks knocked out by trauma do — to rewrite my life. Change it all. I was about to face my first surgery, and radiation would follow. I would not be the same person I had been before this experience. With both a teacher's pension and a supportive husband, I decided to leave full-time work and remake myself. I did this by reading, researching, thinking, meditating, connecting, talking to friends, walking, listening to music, praying, embracing my family, and by writing — in a bright red I HAVE CANCER journal.

Every piece of this journey mattered, but my writing saved me. We are going to explore how.

After years of teaching and decades of facing life's challenges, I left my old path and found a new one, a path I would begin to walk down when I awoke groggy the morning after my second surgery, the one during which I lost both my breasts. A double mastectomy. On that morning, with anesthesia still pulsing through my veins, I found myself scribbling in my red journal, but I had the strange sense that I was outside myself, looking down *at me* writing.

The surreal nature of this image captivated me, for this woman's words — *my words* — were gushing from the deepest place in me. From this distance I could see that I was a woman who had been writing copious notes in recent months to lift herself up, to rise above the trials that cancer had given her. And it struck me my words had an unmatched power to heal me. *To change me.* A gentle wave seemed to wash over me. A wave of awe. For the universe was handing me a *glimmer*, an insight. It whispered, *"Our writing can transform us."*

And in that moment, I knew I had to listen to my intuition, run with my words, and write from my heart to catch the wisdom this glimmer offered.

And so this book was born. Born of my belief that our personal writing, often called "expressive writing," can heal and change us. Born of the knowledge that 81 percent of us believe we have a book in us. A story to tell.

Initially this journey led me to my personal journals, where I examined the power of my own writing. Here my life was spelled out in detail, and I saw time and time again, story after story, that writing had grounded me. Had made me whole.

After thirty years of teaching writing to high school and college students, I knew that when we find and write our stories from the heart, as truth seekers, we change ourselves. And this change comes not simply from personal journal writing. I had seen it in hundreds of student essays and stories and poems and scripts and articles and blog entries and memoirs and books, both fiction and nonfiction. Our expressive writing — writing about our thoughts, feelings, and experiences — defines us. Our words create us. Our stories create us.

And our writing can re-create us.

Veterans, cancer patients, students, and writers from all walks of life stepped forward to share with me "the story they needed to tell." These unsung heroes reconstructed the stories that shattered their lives. And they will teach us how to do this by breaking our silence, finding our voices, and editing our personal stories. In working with them I created and tested the writing prompts and suggestions that will help us write our way forward. I crafted the writing activities in this book to fit your unique time constraints and experiences. It does not matter if you have *never* explored writing or picked up a journal. Even a limited amount of personal writing can guide you toward personal change. Simply *telling* your story helps.

The stories I share of how writing brought about positive change are backed up by solid research. These findings were culled from more than two hundred studies that show how our expressive writing offers us physical, psychological, social, and spiritual benefits. And this research, coupled with my work with writing groups, helped me to identify an amazing process — the stages of writing to heal.

As I worked with individuals caught in the throes of a trauma, illness, or loss, it became apparent there were five stages of writing to heal and change. This book will guide you through these stages and help you explore how writing can lead to your personal change — *your story transformation*. While there is no definitive order to these steps, a pattern usually surfaces:

1. Experience your pain and grief.
2. Break your silence and find your voice.
3. Accept and piece together a difficult or broken story.

4.   Find meaning or make sense of this event or story.
5.   Rewrite your story and find ways to reconnect with your
     well-being.

Our life journey will be filled with challenges. The goal of this book is to teach you how to find and use your stories and your writing to make your difficulties not only manageable but meaningful. Even amid our problems we can find words that will help us explore, be mindful, grow, and create a better way of living.

In part 1, "Writing: Not Drowning," I share some personal experiences that taught me how we can face shock and trauma, embrace our silence, and find our way back to our words. Here we will meet two brave young men who will introduce us to the power of using our words and our writing to find a path through our difficulties.

Part 2, "Writing Down the Self," examines the benefits of writing and explores the stages of writing that lead to healing and transforming our lives. We will explore story transformation and the ways that anyone, even those who have never written, can embark on a writing practice or story-sharing practice.

Part 3, "Finding Meaning through Story," uses powerful true stories to unveil current neuroscience demonstrating how our brains efficiently run on our stories. We will examine how stories help us create our identities, create our character, and learn to solve our problems. Throughout this journey, we will be discovering how our personal stories and writing lead to personal change.

Part 4, "Rewriting Our Shattered Stories," demonstrates how to navigate traumatic events by breaking our silence, keeping our thoughts from getting stuck, embracing other perspectives, and editing our difficult experiences to create new ways of understanding ourselves. We will learn how each of these pieces can empower us to experience profound personal growth.

Part 5, "Writing to Heal," delves into the personal stories of three veterans torn by war experiences, a young woman destroyed by physical abuse, a young mother trying to live with her stage four cancer diagnosis, and a partner who has lost her lover to death. These individuals show how our personal writing can work to help us move forward in the most difficult of circumstances, including trauma, illness, and death.

And finally, part 6, "Writing to Transform," focuses on a young man who has lost his sister and turns to his writing — even amid his tragedy — to find a new path and create a better story. We will find that as the storytellers in this book transformed their stories — and often their lives — they tapped into their resilience and often experienced a burst of personal creativity. We will explore what makes this possible.

These are the gifts I hope this book gives to you — the power to find your voice, the ability to transform your story when needed, and the well-being that comes from renewed meaning, resilience, and creative living.

Let's begin our journey together.

Your personal writing can heal, grow,
and transform your life.
Give your words permission to change you.

PART ONE

WRITING:
NOT DROWNING

CHAPTER ONE

Waving
Not Drowning

All the world is full of suffering.
It is also full of overcoming.
— Helen Keller

Three weeks after my cancer diagnosis, I lay flat-stomached on the gurney. Scared. Vulnerable. I was shaking from the chilling temperatures inside the clinic. This tomb-like room was packed with medical machines. My left breast hung down perilously through a hole designed to trap and explore it. For days I had been poring over information on cancer websites while medical staff had been busy photographing and now prodding my left breast to determine her fate. I had affectionately nicknamed her "my celebrity breast."

This was my third or fourth biopsy. You begin to lose track. It was the nipple biopsy. I wished I could forget that.

Two women dressed in blue scrubs helped strap me into place. They could see me, shaking from fear and the Siberia-like temps. But I could not see them. The women in blue had slipped behind a door to another room with a one-way mirror. Still I heard them. The door was slightly ajar. The punk-haired petite one giggled. "What a party! Look at Dr. Venn!" she exclaimed. "I

11

posted it on Facebook." More laughter. I coughed, and the technicians realized I could hear them. The door softly clicked shut and a loud speaker above my head started blasting Dido's "Thank You" song. I wanted to feel grateful. But I didn't.

My mind flickered to the film I had watched on Netflix when I couldn't sleep the night before. It was a Glenda Jackson classic, *Stevie*, about the English poet and novelist Stevie Smith. "Life is like a railway station," Smith wrote. "The train of birth brings us in; the train of death will carry us away."

Since my diagnosis, I had been thinking a lot about death, wondering if I would have to face it. Wondering *if I could face it*. I realized Stevie's poems were obsessed with death. I used to teach one of her poems, and it popped into my head now. "Not Waving but Drowning" captured the shocking misfortune of a man who is swimming and starts to drown. He signals to those onshore that he is going under, but they think he is waving and ignore him. Tragically, he dies.

Nobody heard him, the dead man.
But still he lay moaning:
I was much further out than you thought
And not waving but drowning.

"Am I drowning?" I wondered. Then I twisted around in an attempt to free myself from the strap on the gurney. I glanced up at the clock. The doctor was twenty minutes late. I eyed an intimidating tray of meticulously aligned needles. "Am I drowning?" I said it out loud this time, before remembering I had a behind-the-mirror audience.

The image of drowning flooded my mind, and God knows I didn't want that picture stuck there like a catchy song I couldn't forget. Could I edit this image? I had been helping students edit their stories in my high school and college English classes for years. Maybe it was time to edit my own story. As I lay shivering on that gurney, I began to explore that possibility.

In recent weeks my bright-red journal and I had become inseparable. I had begun frantically listing my questions about cancer. And I read and researched voraciously, looking for strategies for handling this disease. I twisted around, looking for my journal. I had it with me in my book bag, but then I realized it was locked in the closet where I had stripped and donned this flimsy blue hospital gown. No wonder I was shivering.

Mentally I searched for a term I had scribbled somewhere in that red journal. I felt as if cancer were trying to suck me under. I didn't want it at all, but since I had it, I had to make room for it in my life. But at that moment I made a promise to myself. Cancer would not own me. It would not. And then I remembered the term — the *tragic gap*.

Facing Our Tragic Gap

Educator Parker Palmer named the strange space that lies between our hopes and our reality the "tragic gap." It is a tough place to stand because we have to balance two opposites: *what we have* and *what we dream*. I was dreaming of building an incredible creative writing program at my college and finishing a novel I had begun. My dream. But I had cancer, and I had to figure out how to survive it. My painful reality.

My journal was helping me reflect on my story. I was toying with ways to rewrite it. I could leave the college. I could embrace my writing full-time. And in that moment I had an insight: My journal writing *mattered*. It was my lifeline, the way I would maneuver my tragic gap. By writing I could reflect on and experiment with the changes I might make. Then I could make a plan and move forward.

I spun the word *reflection* around like a Rubik's Cube in my head. We need reflection in order to learn from, rebound from, and redefine our experiences. Reflection can calm our feelings of panic when we are caught up in a crisis. It allows the body and mind to float until we can catch the next wave or gather the strength to swim forward. Reflection helps us to manage our tragic gap by inviting us to rewrite our story, and by doing so, to remake ourselves, to incorporate even unwanted life events into the narrative that makes up "who I think I am: the story of myself."

If we do not reflect on our experiences, we stand in danger of losing ourselves. Our pain can claim our narratives and lead us into rocky terrain. Perhaps our suffering can even erupt in creative works — a Van Gogh painting of sunflowers or a manically funny riff by Robin Williams — but if we cannot edit our painful life stories and move forward, we will face an ongoing war with our ruminations and our demons, and we may fall prey to depression or other illnesses. Caught in this seemingly endless struggle, we are torn between choosing to fight on or to surrender, to live or to die. This is one reason a number of writers and creative artists' lives are associated with tragedy: Michael Jackson, River Phoenix, Heath Ledger, Janis Joplin, Philip Seymour Hoffman, Vincent van Gogh, Frida Kahlo, Ernest Hemingway, F. Scott Fitzgerald, Kurt Cobain, Jimi Hendrix, Sylvia Plath, Virginia Woolf, Ann Sexton, David Foster Wallace, Marilyn Monroe, and Robin Williams — and the list goes on. In the words of Stevie Smith, these artists were "much further out" than the people around them knew. While we admired their genius, they were drowning, not waving. I did not want this to be the end to my story — and I do not want it to be the end of yours.

Waving: Not Drowning

Our lives can read like soap operas. I started writing this book when I found out I had breast cancer. As I neared the end of the first draft, I learned my son had cancer. As I inched toward the end, my father fell ill, and after a hospital stay I brought him home to die. There are thorny, unfinished chapters being written in our lives all the time.

Many years ago Paul McCartney must have had this in mind when he wrote "Hey Jude." Divorce proceedings had started for John and Cynthia Lennon. Worried about how this split would affect their five-year-old son, Paul drove out to visit the boy. On the way Paul wrote a song to comfort the young Julian. The words still remind us how to handle a difficult experience: we have to take a sad song and make it better.

McCartney was wise to advise Julian to take his sad story and rework it. Make it better. We must face the hard realities of our lives, but we can *choose* how we face them. What if we took Stevie's poem and changed the title? If we reframed this metaphorical look at our souls, the story could be "Waving Not Drowning." We can choose to wave instead of drown. This book is about making that shift: discovering our strength by holding onto and sharing the story we have to tell.

Sitting on this little blue planet in the middle of our universe, we vacillate between fantasies of control over our lives and fears of no control. What we do have is a certain amount of control over *our choices*. Choices matter. Together we can choose to make our stories better. Perhaps I am crazy — both my sons tease me that I am — but I think we have that kind of power over our stories. We may exist within the tragic gap of life, but we can also "mind the gap." We can drown in our difficulties, we can struggle to tread water, and we can learn to swim, perhaps even splash in the waves, possibly surf the rollers to shore. Why not wave back at the unknown craziness of this universe? At the possibilities that are out there? Or at the possibilities that we can create?

Back at the breast clinic, the door creaked open, and the punk-haired technician quietly slipped into the room. "The doctor had an emergency at the hospital, but she is on her way," she said softly. Then she wrapped a nice warm blanket around me. I twisted my neck around just enough so I could smile up at her in appreciation. As I settled in, warm and cozy on my gurney, another memory popped into my head.

In the metro area where I live, fourteen or more children drown in family swimming pools every year. Like many parents who live in the Phoenix area, I have spent countless hours hauling my kids to and from swim lessons. The image etched in my mind came from a hot July day, a you-could-fry-an-egg-on-the-sidewalk day. The sun was jacking up the temperature to three digits as my son Zach and I arrived at the pool for his swimming lessons. Six four-year-olds began each day donning their inflatable armband floaties, sucking in the smell of chlorine, and jumping into the water for a ten-minute free swim. Zach loved his swim lessons. He also loved Heather, his beautifully sculpted and bronzed Red Cross–certified swim instructor. He waved at her gleefully as we entered the iron gates. We might have been the last to arrive, but Zach was always the first to don his floaties and line up for the jump into the pool.

On this particular day, Ally, a small redhead and a play buddy of Zach's, started to whimper. She wrapped her thin arms around Heather's long legs. "Not today," sulked Ally fearfully. "No swimming today."

Before Heather could respond to the little redhead's pleas, Zach had spun around, and even before Heather blew the whistle, he jumped into the water, surfaced, and threw his arms upward. "Ally!" Zach called out with his sock-it-to-the-world joy. "It's free swim. Get your butt in here!" For Zach there was no time for tears or whimpering. No wasting the time they had to play. Heather nodded down at Ally. Then she blew her whistle, and five kids jumped into the water like little sea urchins, laughing and squealing as they leaped. A transformed Ally joined in, squealing with delight. I was a bit anxious that Zach had overstepped his bounds by jumping in ahead of the whistle. But before Heather dove into the pool to play with the children, she turned back to me and mouthed, "I simply love your kid." In that moment I realized yet again how amazing he is. There he was in the water — laughing, wiggling around like a dolphin, popping up — and waving wildly to me.

If my son at age four could embrace the water and come up waving, I could do it. I could find a way to get out of this sinkhole called cancer. I was going to tread water, swim, or do whatever I had to do to find my way out.

Choosing Waving, Not Drowning

Waving, not drowning seems an apt metaphor for reaching past a bad story. For Zach there was no time to sulk or "drown" in the hard part of lessons. We have to swim in the other direction, as he did. By waving we are reaching out emotionally to others. We are reaching past the tragic gap and accepting hope and the possibility of finding joy. By writing to make better sense of our story, we can avoid drowning in our ruminations and painful emotions. We can take a shattered story and remake ourselves. We cannot change the facts, but we can change how we interpret those facts, how they affect us, and eventually how they teach us about our vulnerabilities and strengths.

In this book we are going to examine how the act of writing helps people deal with difficult setbacks and trauma. We are going to meet individuals who floated, swam, or grabbed a raft to get through them. We are going to learn how to take our sad song and make it better by using our words, our stories, our writing.

Back on the Gurney

The blanket that had warmed me had gone cold. I checked the clock. Nearly forty minutes late. But it no longer mattered. I didn't care. I knew something had changed inside me.

"I am going to make it," I announced to the sterile room and the world's most wicked-looking needles. "*I am going to be waving when this is over... not drowning... did you hear me, universe?*" I practically shouted now. "*Waving — not drowning!*" And I set out on the story of my own survival.

Dr. Venn, her thick, dark hair pulled back in a bouncy ponytail, entered the room. Immediately she picked up a needle. "Are you ready?" she asked, all businesslike. I nodded. "Now I am going to insert something. It might pinch for a moment, but the procedure won't hurt."

It did hurt. It hurt like hell — but it no longer mattered. A new voice had erupted from deep inside me. I had tapped into a new understanding of who I was — and who I could become. I could rewrite my story. *I could survive this.*

In facing our shattered life stories, we must reach deep inside our pain — for it is here that we can break our silence and find our new voice.

Personal Writing Guidelines

At the end of each chapter, you will find writing prompts. These are suggestions or ideas that can guide your writing. Choose the ones that sound like a good fit for you. If you are new to personal writing, begin by committing to *five minutes of writing at a time.* Additional ideas will be shared in coming chapters, but if you are ready to write, here are some guidelines to help you get started:

- Begin by finding a comfortable spot to write. If you want, bring your water bottle, coffee, or tea.
  Choose a journal, notebook, or computer.
- Forget about rules — grammar, punctuation, and spelling. Just plan to write.
- Choose a prompt, put your pen to paper (or your fingers on your keyboard), and write for at least five minutes. If you write more, congratulate yourself! If a prompt fails to connect with you, try the next one.
- Write as often and as much as you dare. Give it your best.
- Then reread and reflect on what you have written. You may be surprised at the stories or thoughts you hold within.

- Work to develop a personal writing practice that works *for you*. Every writer is unique, and by finding how you write best, you will grow your words and your voice.

All the best as you begin this amazing life journey!

Writing Prompts and Suggestions

Using these prompts, we will start to learn how to unleash our inner stories.

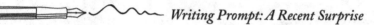 *Writing Prompt: A Recent Surprise*

For a minute or two make a list of some surprises, good and bad, that you have had. Then put a star by a recent and difficult surprise. Explore this event. What happened? How did you face it, or how will you face it? If it is too painful to explore at this point, let it go for now.

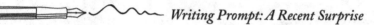 *Writing Prompt: Waving, Not Drowning*

Have you ever chosen to make the best of a bad situation? Describe this experience. What happened? Did you turn to others for help? Were you able to find a positive way of looking at it all? How did it work out?

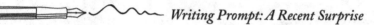 *Writing Prompt: The Tragic Gap*

Start by creating "tragic gap statements." Do this by writing one or more statements that follow this form: "I want to…but I can't because…"

Here are some examples:

I want to move, but I can't because I don't make enough money.

I want to be an actor, but I can't because I suffer from anxiety when I try to perform.

I want to undertake a new challenge, but I can't because I believe I am too old.

Now either choose a statement you have written or create a new one. This tragic gap statement needs to connect to a dilemma you are facing. After you write this statement, answer these questions as best you can: What is your dream? What obstacles are making it hard to accomplish your dream? How can you face this challenge? If you are not ready to explore this dilemma, come back to it later.

CHAPTER TWO

Facing Trauma
When There Are No Words

*I've begun to realize that you can listen to silence
and learn from it. It has a quality
and a dimension all its own.*

— Chaim Potok

The sun and the fragrance of orange blossoms belied the day. On this morning I hit the traffic lights — all eleven — with perfect timing. I arrived early at my high school and dashed up the front steps, past the imposing metal gates, and headed toward the teachers' mailboxes. When I heard the clinking bangles of Faye, a school counselor, I turned to greet her smile. Instead, her face was etched with tears. "Did you hear about the kid who was shot and killed by the Walmart thief yesterday?" she asked. I nodded. "It was Lucas," she blurted, and instinctively reached out to steady me.

But it was no use. My legs buckled beneath me. I dropped my stack of books, my essays scattered across the linoleum, and I landed, legs splayed, like a crumpled piece of paper.

"Not...not Lucas," I stuttered. Not the energetic, light-hearted, joy-filled student who lit up my class each day with his dark-green T-shirt sporting a German phrase I didn't understand. He was always the first student to bound into room 221 for

21

second period. He repeatedly teased me about my beat-up car, and I believe he was pretty certain I could be talked into selling it to him when he graduated in a few months. He was funny and personable, and while he enjoyed learning, he was completely unconcerned with grades, even proud of his C average. Still, most teachers wished they had someone with his lightbulb personality in their classes.

That morning my high school found itself unexpectedly knuckled under with the weight of shock. Two counselors came into my classroom and as gently and calmly as possible, they told his heart-ripping story. Lucas worked at a nearby Walmart. That Sunday afternoon, a security guard had caught someone walking out the front door of the store with a TV. On a whim the guard asked Lucas if he wanted to ride along as he tracked down the thief. All those Hollywood chase scenes must have flickered through their minds. And as one would expect, Lucas said, "Sure."

The two justice seekers jumped into an aging Chevy, completely unsuited for chase scenes, and followed the robber several miles until he pulled into an empty church parking lot. The chase car also pulled in and stopped. Then the thief pulled a gun out of his glove compartment, approached their car, and shot first the guard and then Lucas in the head. Both died instantly.

After long moments of silence, a few students haltingly asked questions. "What...what can we do?" sputtered Kara, tears inching their way down her cheeks.

"Why?" asked Ian. And in a few moments he asked it again, *"Why?"* But the only answer was stunned silence.

While we often wrote in class, we did not write that day. Or the next. We had trouble even talking. When a tragedy happens, it takes a while for our minds to absorb it and learn to live with it. We embraced our silence because we had to, and much later, I learned this was the best thing to do. Recent studies support the fact that silence lowers our stress and allows us to internalize and reflect on new and difficult information. In room 221 we had to edit our stories to include Lucas's death before we could move forward. We were accustomed to seeing the upbeat boy in the crazy green T-shirt, hearing his who-would-have-thought-that comments, and feeling the wonderful energy he brought into our room. Now his desk was empty. And at first his death was too mind-numbingly crushing to explore. In the coming days we practiced a reverential silence. We didn't write because we simply couldn't. There were no words.

Time Is on Your Side

Elie Wiesel lost his voice, too. After being liberated from a concentration camp at the end of World War II, Wiesel made a vow not to speak of the nightmare he had experienced for ten years. He kept his promise. It was not until 1960 that he published his renowned memoir, *Night*. In it Wiesel recounted how his parents, sisters, and entire community were crammed into cattle cars and shipped off to German concentration camps. He saw babies tossed into fires and innocent people hanged, and he watched his father die of starvation and dysentery. After the liberation, Wiesel waded through years of grief until he eventually rediscovered his voice. After breaking his silence, Wiesel wrote more than forty books and became a well-known speaker against repression, violence, and racism.

After her mother died of lung cancer at age forty-five, author Cheryl Strayed struggled with an unfathomable grief. Initially Strayed floundered with promiscuity and drugs, causing her young marriage to disintegrate. In 1995 she decided to hike the Pacific Crest Trail with the hope of finding herself. And she did, but it was not until 2008 that she began to write her memoir, *Wild: From Lost to Found on the Pacific Crest Trail*, about this transformative experience. "I gained perspective," said Strayed, "that I wouldn't have had if I'd written about it immediately." With difficult and traumatic experiences, we often need space and time before we can assimilate the events into our stories and understand what has happened.

Once we've reached an understanding of our trauma, we can write about it. At that juncture writing can give us the insights to find a resolution for our pain and perhaps an end to our story. At the very least, writing will grant us a framework for living with our pain and a roadmap to guide us forward.

The Silence of Trauma and Grief

Although I have been a writing teacher for thirty years, I am the first to acknowledge that there are times when it is okay *not to write*. Both trauma and grief can silence us. When we are faced with unbearable pain, we can get stuck in a hole, and at those moments we may not be able to dig out. Sometimes our brains are raining torrents of uncontrollable emotions or flooding with stories and memories that could sink anyone. At those times our job becomes to wait out the storm. To weather our pain. To lie at the bottom of the trough until a wave picks us up again. Judy Brown said it beautifully in her poem "Trough":

> There is a trough in waves,
> a low spot
> where horizon disappears
> and only sky
> and water
> are our company.
>
> And there we lose our way
> unless
> we rest, knowing the wave will bring us
> to its crest again.
>
> There we may drown
> if we let fear

hold us within its grip and shake us
side to side,
and leave us flailing, torn, disoriented.

But if we rest there
in the trough,
in silence,
being with
the low part of the wave,
keeping
our energy and
noticing the shape of things,
the flow,
then time alone
will bring us to another
place
where we can see
horizon, see the land again,
regain our sense
of where
we are,
and where we need to swim.

Breaking the Silence

While we should never force ourselves to write, there comes a point when we will surface from our pain. In that moment we will find we *need* our words again. Cheryl Strayed did. Elie Wiesel did. And after Lucas's death my class and I began to grope our way through the darkness in an effort to find our voices again.

It began with an all-school memorial for Lucas shortly after his death. Inspired by the speeches honoring our friend, I wanted my students to have time to share their thoughts, too. After we wrote in our journals, one student suggested that we create a gift for Lucas's family. We debated what to send and eventually agreed that I would buy a nice tribute journal. In it each student would place a page, and on their page they would find their personal way of honoring Lucas. In our book we compiled poems, songs, and stories. There were pictures, drawings, and even a beloved watercolor piece showing the boy in the green T-shirt. It became the book's cover.

It was hard to do this writing at first. Through the years I have witnessed this struggle — the first attempts to write about a traumatic event. But while painful, it is a critical step toward healing. Words allow us to unravel the knot inside and to make sense of our loss, not bury it within. For in our sadness and pain, we can be remade. We can learn how to understand our trauma and give it a container — a story — to hold it.

One way to rediscover your voice is to stay present in the experience, feeling your sadness and allowing it to move through you. I asked my students to do this and to listen carefully to those around them who were also caught in the eye of this storm. *To listen and to rediscover our voices.* This is what we did. And in the end what we created was a book filled with charming, heartfelt pieces. Lucas's mother was touched, and she wrote us, thanking the class for this lovely gift.

Ultimately this project, a lesson that reached outside the daily curriculum, lifted us up. I have never forgotten the pain of losing a young, vibrant voice in my classroom. Writing about this loss helped my students, as well as me. But also it taught us to write in our own words, in our own time. We should never punish ourselves with our writing. But eventually our words should give us a voice and help set us free.

Experience your pain. Embrace your silence.
When the time feels right,
find your way back to your words — and write.

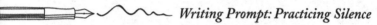

Writing Prompts and Suggestions

After a trauma it takes a while to find your voice, to break your silence. But you will. If you feel ready to write, pick up your pen, your tablet, or your laptop computer. If you need them, use the Personal Writing Guidelines on pages 18–19 to help you find your words. If you are not ready to write, accept and engage your silence. You will know when you are ready. Trust your inner voice.

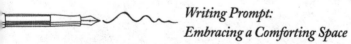 *Writing Prompt: Practicing Silence*

If trauma has left you without words, try to embrace and practice silence for several hours. (Even if you are not faced with a difficult experience, this is a valuable exercise.) Often the world is cluttered with noise and social media messages. Often we need silence to realign our story. Find a comfortable place to explore silence. Turn off your cell phone and shut down all social media. Perhaps you want to meditate or pray. Perhaps you want to be closer to nature and the beauty of the earth. Maybe you want to hike. Whatever you choose to do, for one or several hours, practice silence. When you finish, take up your pen and see if you are inspired to write about the experience. How was it? What did you learn? You may want to repeat this exercise whenever you feel you need the calm and quiet to center you.

Writing Prompt:
Embracing a Comforting Space

Whether or not you have faced a traumatic experience, it is comforting to find a space in the world that can comfort us. Pick out such a place — a garden, a mountain trail, a bedroom, the loft in your barn where you love to hide. Imagine or visit this place. Now write about it. What is the history of this place? Can you describe this space in detail? How does it look? Feel? Smell? Sound? How does this place make you feel when you are there? Can you go there when you need to? Can you reflect there? Can you write there? What do you love most about this space?

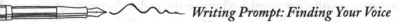 *Writing Prompt: Finding Your Voice*

Do you recall a time when you were so shocked you had no words? When was this? Can you describe what happened? When did it happen? How did you regain your voice? What did this experience teach you? Is it still hard to think or write about this experience?

CHAPTER THREE

Writing
Finding Our Words

I have not had an easy life.
I started out writing to save my life.
— Alice Walker

As the weeks stumbled by after my cancer diagnosis, I plodded to doctors' offices, where I continued to have my breasts examined, mashed, photographed, scanned, biopsied, and finally debated by a board of six medical professionals. All the while, I carried my bright-red journal in my book bag. And as I waited I scrawled notes and reflected. Sometimes about my cancer. Sometimes about my writing. "Words. What is the magic behind them?" I asked in those pages. I began to hatch a plan to answer that question.

As a result of that plan, I began to work with other cancer patients and veterans — anyone who wanted to write. I met Robert Serocki Jr. when he spoke to the veterans' writing group downtown, where I had begun volunteering. A week after his talk, we sat on a sun-drenched patio beside a golf course in Ahwatukee, Arizona. The former marine wanted to talk to me about his writing.

On that March day, as the smell of honeysuckle hung in the

air and we sipped iced tea, Robert transported me into his past with stories of his stint in Saudi Arabia and Kuwait in 1990–1991, during the Gulf War. He described digging the holes in the sand where he would sleep each night. He ate dried-up MREs or "meals ready to eat," and suffered from ongoing ant bites, scorpion stings, and visits from dung beetles and rats. A bout with dysentery and food poisoning led him to be seriously dehydrated. His fellow marines suffered the same nausea and malnutrition.

After a long and trying wait in the desert, the fighting erupted. During this intense period, Robert's squad faced minefields, bombing raids, firefights, and the unbearable — the reality of dead bodies littering their landscape. This trauma often left Robert sick to his stomach. While at war, he was encouraged by his superiors to buck up and hold in all his frustrations. And he did. "I felt I had lost all control of my life. It was like I was at the whim of the universe," he said.

After he returned home from Saudi Arabia, the war remained on unending replay in his mind. "I remember being scared of the dark at age twenty-six and not being able to sleep because there was no one on fire watch to guard me at night. I remember lying in bed sweating and trembling. I remember replaying the war in my mind like a tape while I slept. I would wake up in a pool of my own sweat, and I would shake. I would cry. I could not go back to sleep."

To cope, Robert began to drink. He drank beer. He drank martinis. He drank wine. At the time Robert's boss suggested he think about writing, a possibility he toyed with. As luck would have it, his folks had saved all the letters he had written home from the war. "I just began to type them all up, and before I knew it I was actually writing a book." It took Robert six years to complete *A Line in the Sand.*

"But I still had PTSD," Robert admitted. "And then I lost my job. That was a bad time for me. I wanted to end my life. I was on five medications and so sick I ended up in a wheelchair. I had to file for bankruptcy, and I was on a complete downward spiral. Twice I wanted to end my life — with a gun."

Many vets who suffer from PTSD have faced this sandstorm of bad memories when they returned home. Many vets, over half the ones I have interviewed, have contemplated suicide. And recently one tried to commit it. While Robert decided to forgo the gun and seek help, initially the counseling backfired. "When my doctor brought up the war, I always became nauseous. All I could do was get sick — or drink. Finally they put me in the hospital for a couple of weeks. There I began to talk to people, and the talking made a difference. I started to feel better." Robert admitted that it helped to break his silence. To share his story. Counseling, like writing, can help us lay out a broken experience and begin to piece it back together again.

Eventually, after being released from the hospital, Robert returned to his writing. "I realized I didn't want to live like this anymore, so I took the next step." He began work on his second book, *Chrysalis: A Metamorphosis Has Begun.* He admitted that writing about difficult subjects was not easy. "I had to relive it all again. Often that was painful." But then he sat back and smiled. At that moment, and perhaps it was no more than a slice of the Arizona sun cutting across the patio as we talked, a brilliant light pierced Robert's dark eyes.

"Writing is a beautiful way to let all your pain out," he said. "You put your story out there, and when you do, you release it. It is no longer buried and stuck inside. You are free. It is like saying good-bye to a monster that has been living in you." He paused and sipped his tea before looking at me. "And I *am* free."

Breaking Our Silence with Writing

All our minds run on our stories, as Robert's was doing. Unfortunately, sometimes our mental tapes break. Even writing does not always work. The words we write can slip down the same rabbit hole found in our brains. They can become equally trapped in an ongoing loop, repeating a broken story over and over.

Remember the story of Hamlet? He was stuck in a loop with his own nightmare. Over and over Hamlet replayed the story of his father's death, but mainly the young prince ruminated without coming to any resolution. If a story becomes stuck in our minds and continues to play out, it can become harmful, even dangerous, as it proved to be for Hamlet.

But our writing can lead us out of the hole where we are stuck. With the right prompts, we can find our way by making sense of the chaos unfolding within us. Words can ground us by helping us reach an understanding of what is happening, and we can rewrite the events we must live with. While we cannot change what happened, we can revise our interpretation of a painful experience and allow it to fit into the framework of who we are.

One lovely young woman I know did this. Paige had worked for years to edit the films of sexual abuse out of her life. As a child she had been repeatedly abused by her father, her brother, and her uncle — a priest. Once she found the courage to reveal her traumatic story and accept it, she reframed the story by taking positive action. She began by writing a book to help other abuse victims. Eventually her work led to the opening of a healing center in California for women who had been traumatized by severe child abuse.

The Power of Revealing Our Stories

Ten years ago, at the beginning of his senior year, Ben sat in the back of my high school classroom. Against the wall. Over his head was an imaginary sign that read "Leave me alone." But my job as a teacher was to knock down that sign. And while it took a few weeks, I did.

Ben's writing class met right before lunch. When the bell rang, seniors shot out the door and across campus like an atom splitting apart. But in contrast to the warp-speed movement of his peers, Ben traveled tortoise-like toward the exit, and I could always catch him. On my third or possibly fourth attempt at a conversation with him, there was a breakthrough. Although he had few words for what had happened, he had a story stuck inside. It had shattered his life. He had scrawled bits of it in his classroom journal, but now he would tell me. "Last summer…my uncle…my best friend…died."

Working with Ben was like taming an elusive squirrel hiding in the branches of a tree. You could see him but not reach him. While he kept his distance, Ben began to inch forward by joining classroom discussions and by acknowledging in his journal more of what had happened. Still, it would be several weeks before he would share it. Even then his story bobbed up unexpectedly.

It was near the end of class on the day narrative essays were due. As students finished with small writing groups, they moved their desks back into our circle. There were a few minutes left before the bell and the ensuing lunch-bound scramble, so I asked if any students wanted to read their work aloud. Ben's hand shot up — probably as much to his surprise as to his classmates'.

For a few seconds he sat staring at his essay, stunned that he had volunteered. As I prepared to intervene, Ben miraculously found his voice. He read haltingly at first about "his lost friend." But then he found his rhythm and read about the good times with his uncle — reading *Rolling Stone*, riding bikes, listening to U2, especially "Beautiful Day." Then he read about a visit to a memorial in Washington, DC, where he watched his uncle cry for the one and only time ever as he rubbed his fingers across a name. And he noted that Uncle Mark could neither forget this war nor talk about it. Then his voice softened, and Ben ended by describing a not-so-beautiful day when he opened the garage door to find his uncle shot to death. "Self-inflicted wound," he read. "A suicide." There was silence.

In a few moments the bell rang, but no one moved. Ben's story had pulled us beneath the surface of his loss and left us trapped there with his pain. When I found my voice, I thanked him for sharing his story — a powerful personal narrative. Then my students began to move in slow motion. As they left, a few complimented Ben on his piece or said they were sorry for his loss. "It's okay," he said. Some thanked him for having the courage to read it. Others paused to pat him on the back, and two girls hugged him.

While this story would never be okay, on that day, Ben began accepting his uncle's death and integrating it into his life story.

Some Groundbreaking Research

While my students were engaged in teaching me the power of expressive writing, James W. Pennebaker was engaged in a series of research projects and discoveries that would establish the power of writing to heal. Early in his career as a research psychologist, Pennebaker found that people who experienced a trauma — such as divorce, sexual or physical abuse, or the death of a family member — were much worse off if they kept these experiences to themselves. Trauma victims who did not talk to others were at a much higher risk for illness. This discovery reinforced the belief that "talk therapy," or talking to friends or counselors about troubling experiences, was helpful.

Pennebaker was intrigued; in the right place with the right person, talking about our troubles was clearly a healthy thing. He wondered what would happen if research participants wrote about emotional upheavals such as war, rape, divorce, illness, loss, and so on. Would writing be as effective as talking? In the mid-1980s, Pennebaker and his graduate students began a series of studies to test the power of writing. They called in healthy young adults, most of them new to college, and asked them to write for fifteen minutes for four consecutive days. Half of the group was asked to write about emotional or traumatic events, while students in the control group wrote on superficial, unemotional topics. The results were stunning.

Most students who wrote about difficult experiences noted they had never been asked to write about some of the most significant experiences in their lives. Since I was a writing teacher, that finding hit hard.

The students in this study embraced the opportunity to write expressively, and many of them had left behind heartfelt episodes covering parental divorce, suicide, abuse, loss, rape, and other difficult moments in their young lives. Initially the writing was painful for most students in the trauma group. But they came back all four days, and at the end of the experiment, they reported that the writing had been "profoundly important for them."

Across the first four studies, researchers were able to track visits to doctors due to illness before and after the writing exercises. Students in the expressive writing groups made 43 percent fewer visits to a physician for illness than the students in the control groups who wrote about insignificant topics. In sum, by writing about emotionally difficult experiences, students visited the campus health center at half the normal rate.

Expressive writing bestowed an array of psychological benefits as well. While writers might feel sad immediately after writing, if they had time to reflect, their emotional state would shift. "People who engage in expressive writing report feeling happier and less negative than before writing," explains Pennebaker. General anxiety, depressive symptoms, and the recurring-nightmare brain tapes, such as Robert experienced, dissipated after the writing.

Since Pennebaker's breakthrough work, more than two hundred studies have confirmed that personal writing can serve as a life raft for people facing a difficult event. The compulsion to write can be nearly overwhelming, a sense like Robert had: "I will write or die." He chose to write. So did Ben. So can we.

Expressive writing allows us to break our silence
and offers us many physical and psychological benefits.

Writing Prompts and Suggestions

While we are working together, you may be in search of the story you need to tell. Remember, there are significant physical and psychological rewards for doing this work. Follow your instincts about when and how much to write. But please — *write*. If you need them, the Personal Writing Guidelines can be found on pages 18–19.

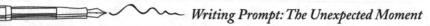 *Writing Prompt: The Unexpected Moment*

Choose a moment that caught you off guard. Perhaps you had an unwanted visitor, received a bad grade, or were dropped from a team or rejected for a job. Or perhaps you received an unwanted diagnosis or marriage proposal. What happened? What was difficult? Do you recall your emotions during this time? How did you manage it? What helped or could have helped? Did anything good result from this unexpected experience? Explore.

Writing Prompt: Changes

Make a list of the changes you have had to make (a job, a school, a home, a relationship). Describe one of these changes. What did you think? What did you feel while undergoing this transition? What was hard about this change? What was positive in this experience?

Writing Prompt: Challenges

What difficult challenge have you faced? Describe what happened. Explore your emotions as you faced this challenge. Have you been on a military assignment overseas and had to face a battle? Does a familial death haunt you or others in your family? Were you or someone you love in an accident? Have you faced injuries or trauma? How might you break your silence and explore this challenge? Later reflect on this story. How can it be reframed to fit your life?

PART TWO

WRITING DOWN
THE SELF

CHAPTER FOUR

A Room of Your Own
A Journal

I can shake off everything as I write;
my sorrows disappear, my courage is reborn.
— **Anne Frank**

A couple of days after my first cancer surgery, a lumpectomy, I awoke tangled in the surgical drain that looked like a grenade and dangled awkwardly from my left breast. Beside my bed on the nightstand sat a full bottle of Percocet — but I hadn't touched it. Adrenaline flushed through my body as I realized I had no pain. I had a joyful, albeit illusory, sense that I was knocking cancer out in round one.

I had not yet received the follow-up phone call from Dr. Liu informing me that my lumpectomy surgery had failed. The margins had not been met. But at this moment it did not matter, for I was focused on peering out my window into my garden, where I could see and smell the earthy, linen-like aroma of yellow spring daisies. One friend had planted them throughout my garden and hung pots of them over my patio. It was like waking up in Monet's Garden, but better. For another friend had made her vegetarian lasagna in my kitchen while I slept, and I could smell the aroma of fresh tomatoes and garlic and onion mingling in the air. And under the bottle of unused Percocet on my nightstand was a note scrawled in the handwriting of my best friend. It contained a list of the meals that would be magically appearing at my doorstep for a week. All I had to do in the coming days was heal. Writing and a stack of *Downton Abbey* DVDs were a part of that plan. With a light breeze directing the orchestra of my patio chimes, I felt flooded with hope — and joy.

One expects cancer surgery to be a nightmare. And for many it is. I was still haunted by the memory of the young voice behind the curtain in the pre-op room next to mine right before they rolled me into surgery. As my anesthesiologist tinkered with a tube that released anesthesia to drip into my veins, I heard a woman's voice explain, "Oh, no. My husband could not come today. He had to watch the kids. Yes — a mastectomy." She paused and her voice went to a near whisper. "Yes. Stage four, and this has messed up our lives. Yes. I'm alone." Then a technician yanked open the curtain, greeted me, and flipped the brakes off my gurney, shoving it forward.

"No!" I said as I began to fade. I wanted to talk to the woman on the other side of the curtain. Did she say *alone?*...But under the pull of the drugs, I blanked out.

Two days later I awoke in my bed and thought of her. I felt refreshed. Blanketed in love. But I also felt guilty.

Partly buried under my covers was my bright-red journal. I had fallen asleep while writing about my concern for this mystery woman. Untangling my drain tubes, I pulled the journal out and began flipping through the pages. The words on these pages had helped me juggle my cancer fears, and I wondered if expressive writing could help others, too. "Is there magic in this writing?" I asked myself once again. I wondered if writing could help the woman who faced her surgery alone. I wondered if writing could help women — as well as men — who were faced with trauma.

Suddenly I recalled an image of an independent suit-and-tied Virginia Woolf sitting on her desk. This was a throwback to a film I had taught years ago in high school. In the film Woolf says a woman needs "a room of her own" to be a writer.

At that moment those words lit up like a Christmas tree in my head. "A room of one's own" could be a metaphor for our journal, a place where we could come and privately write about our secrets, our life struggles, and even our traumas. On those pages we could break the silence of isolation. On those pages we could pick up the broken pieces of our stories and reassemble them. Our journals could be a place of healing — *a room of our own.*

After I drained the blood from the grenade-shaped surgical tube in my bathroom sink, I secured it inside a strange vest contraption I had been given. And then I returned to the questions spilling out of me. Could our personal writing help us heal from illness? How about trauma? What about loss? How could I answer these questions?

And suddenly, like the glint of a shell on the sand, I saw an image. An image of disheveled pages. Of discarded journals. I became a bit giddy as I realized the possibility that my old journals would hold answers to these questions. By sifting through these pages, I could gain insights into the value of my writing. How many journals did I have? How many had I hidden in junk-stuffed drawers, under mattresses, and in those no-one-else-knows-about spots? Soon I was laughing, for I was engaged in the hunt. A genuine treasure hunt.

Initially the search was easy. I found #6 and then #7 hidden on a closet shelf by my bed. These were newer journals purchased from bookstores and selected because I loved a certain quote or artwork on the cover. Above that shelf behind old out-of-date videos were older journals. A blue leather one my dad had given me for a childhood birthday, and old spiral notebooks from school days. Now I was up to #12. And finding old journals was like finding dear, old friends.

By the end of the week, I had found, tucked around the house, twenty-seven journals or bits of journals — for some were no more than a collection of odd scribbles. As I began to skim through them, looking for themes and insights, testing my memory against the writing I did at the time and wishing I had written more, been more authentic, had more courage on the page, and yet delighting in the archives that I had captured, I began my search for an answer to the question, Does our personal writing matter? Does it change us and possibly heal us?

Later that same week, as I was thumbing through my rediscovered journal booty, my surgeon called. Dr. Liu now believed my left breast appeared to have calcium deposits, like sugar sprinkles spread through it. Since these small lumps now appeared to be precancerous, she sounded worried.

"It will be okay," I said. A week later, when I was released to drive again, I went out and bought a hot-pink nightgown and a new childlike Buddha for my garden. The possibility of a double mastectomy no longer frightened me.

Our Past: A Journal Path to Who We Are

After unearthing twenty-seven journals from dusty shelves and long-forgotten hiding places, I began reading them. I thought I would skim through them, a glass of red wine in hand, in two to three hours. Wrong. A week later I was still caught up in the thick of them. I learned how I opened up as a thinker. How I loved to read and explore books. I learned how some authors captivated me, while others tied me in knots. How writer Christina Baldwin taught me the value of keeping a journal for life. How I became a writer. How ideas intrigued me. How becoming a mother changed and fascinated me. And I was only halfway through my reading journey!

When Steve and I ate dinner each evening, he would ask for the update on my journal reading. I never disappointed him, sharing many long-forgotten family moments. The time when Zach, at age three, scaled several stacking tables and toppled a TV to the ground, and was unhurt. Or the time Matt invited us to a school jazz concert and we had no idea he would be the star performer. One evening Steve noted, "Your journals sound like a novel — but we know all the characters!" I was thankful he liked the cast.

From my journals I came to understand more about who I was. In the back of my mind was an independent girl who at age twelve furtively inched *The Feminist Mystique* off her mom's nightstand and read it. This young version of me leaned in, believing she could handle it all. She wanted it all. She wanted meaningful work. She wanted to have children. She had to write. Doing-it-all was in the deepest part of her being.

As I read, I developed a powerful sense of the character I was. I was able to see myself through a new lens — from a distance and in a way I had never seen me before. I enjoyed people and books and learning. I loved discovery and ideas, scientific or artistic, logical and emotional. I embraced a simple philosophy: *I was still learning.* I liked that about me, but there was much I didn't like, too.

As I peered into my journals, I could see *who I was*, but I could also follow the threads of personal stories that showed *who I had been*, and I wanted to cut out a few of these painful sections. On the flip side, and far more intriguing, I could see *who I was capable of becoming.* The clarity of this self-reflection, and I don't mean self-absorption, was life changing.

Our Past: The Journal Path to Who We Were

When we go back and review our journal writing, it is easy to see patterns. As I read my old journals, I could see that I had learned by writing with abandon; and by working through difficult stories, I had completed some chapters in my life. But, and this bothered me, I blew a fuse in some chapters and was frozen in a bad experience. *Stuck.* At one point I was ruminating about a difficult job situation. On those pages I was able to see this cycle as an unhealthy repeating pattern. Over and over I recycled the same questions: Was I going to drive a long distance to be a part of a new high school with dynamic teachers who practiced community service together, or was I going to stay at an older school enmeshed in backstabbing trials because a new, first-ever woman principal had been hired and made sweeping changes? I wanted to support this new principal. I wanted to be close to my babies. And I wanted to feel I had charted my own course, not followed my peers. At the same time, I didn't want to be sucked under by the negativity that had surged into my workplace. Staying at the old school proved to be a psychological struggle that I had not foreseen. And I began to slip into a depression.

I had wanted it all, and now I had it. The meaningful work. An article-writing gig. And two beautiful boys. But I didn't know it would feel like a Sisyphean task, like pushing a twenty-ton rock up a hill each day. And I was watching the man I loved struggle with an equally colossal challenge as he worked to start a small engineering company where he could build innovative machines. He, too, loved to tackle the impossible. This was why I loved him.

And there was our beautiful four-year-old son dancing across those pages. Matthew. He was excited about preschool, and when we both came home in the afternoons, he would put on my old Frye boots and a Superman cape. I would chase him around our house. When I caught him, I would bear-hug him, and I can still hear him shrieking with delight.

At the start of that summer, I had given birth to our second son, Zach. Maybe my depression had to do with my abrupt end to breast-feeding the baby when I returned to teaching that fall. Maybe it had to do with being a sleep-deprived mom teaching five classes of highly energized seniors. Or perhaps it hit me that my closest colleagues had all vacated my old school for a new school on the other side of town.

Perhaps the boy was the tipping point.

One day he showed up in my AP English class, long after the semester had begun. He was an outcast from another class. The next day the teacher who threw him out of her class popped into my room to explain. "The kid is an arrogant bastard. Thinks he knows more than I do!"

I don't know if this boy was smarter than that other AP English teacher, but I suspect he was smarter than me. The boy was brilliant. He had spent his seventeen years on this planet cloistered in gifted programs, where he had made a tight-knit group of friends. With their approval he had learned to write poetry to express himself. And to read. And to play guitar. Often when gifted students are trapped in tightly rule-bound classrooms, they struggle. This boy clearly did — and this is probably how he found himself in the only empty seat in my classroom.

Somehow the environment, maybe the questioning and constant discussion, liberated him. A sensitive teen, he connected with the inner turmoil of Hamlet as we read the play. Later, when we read James Joyce's *A Portrait of an Artist as a Young Man*, about a young writer struggling with his creativity, the boy lit up. Like Joyce, this student was battling with his family's religion. He wanted to grow up enough — inside — to be a writer. To put his own ideas out there for others. Joyce's constraints were ones he understood. He wrote essays about them. He wrote poems about them. He helped me to teach the ideas in this novel to his classmates. Toward the end of our year together, he wrote me a poem.

> I become the waves that caress her shores
> When logic, like music, opens her pores
> She is the sanctuary of delivered minds
> She is the razor blade for all constricting binds

As I read through my old journals, this poem fell out. When I read it now, of course, I understand it even more fully than when the boy first gave it to me. I teared up this time, but I doubt that I did all those years ago. I know I was touched by this kindness, but I was exhausted, too. I was working hard to get tiny Zach to sleep through the night, I was grading papers until the wee hours, and I was spending my lunch hour with my students prepping for their AP exams.

In my sorry state, feeling stressed and strangely alone, the boy had paused to find beauty in what I did as a teacher. A teenager nearly half my age was honoring me. Honoring what I did as a teacher. Giving me what he could give me. Words. It *was* beautiful. And my journal held this moment for me — a badly needed moment of confirmation.

Near the end of the year this idealistic, sensitive boy surprised me again, this time with a love poem. And it broke my heart. For I loved him, but not in the way he wanted. I loved the chance to talk about literature with him and his peers. I loved that he wanted his words to be art. I loved the beauty inside him — the openness, the honesty, and the attempt to face off with the tragic gap courageously by expressing his true feelings, even if he didn't yet know that our feelings evolve. The poet knew I would rebuff him — and I did.

The truth is, hurting this kid felt like having splinters forced under my fingernails. He was just trying to grow up. Shortly after I received the love note, the school year ended and the poet graduated. I asked him to keep writing, and he did. He mailed me a suicide note, and having to follow up with him drained me of the last ounces of emotional energy I had.

The poet did not commit suicide, but at the end of that year, I went home and tumbled into bed drained, exhausted. And I wept. I needed colleagues and confidants, and I didn't have any. My lunch-hour AP group had helped fill my need to talk about ideas and literature, but they could not be my peers. I could not have them falling in love with me, and I fully blamed myself for failing to see what was happening to this student.

Now my students were gone. My closest peers were engaged in a new school. And my husband was in the throes of starting his new business. For weeks that summer I felt depleted. Completely.

I had trouble rising from my bed, and I had little boys to raise. I see it in my journal. The writing is fragmented. I sometimes spit out disjointed, somewhat incoherent poetry.

> During the day I sort clothes for Goodwill bags
> Hand-wash dishes with spaghetti sauce stained across them
> Then I slice onions to make a pot of soup
> Like a warrior I fight back the sting of tears
> For a moment I contemplate turning on a soap opera —
> Thankful I don't even know their names or channels
> All this — to avoid the pain ripping through my soul.
> But when he comes home and gently touches my arm
> And asks how I am
> I shudder inside
> Then a wave of thunderous tears erupts
> Like a volcano — I am unsettled.

Concerned about my I-feel-like-I-am-six-feet-under exhaustion, I saw Benjamin, a counselor whose services were free on our HMO insurance. "Postpartum depression," he said on one of the afternoons when he didn't nod off during our session. I suspect he was tired of hearing the-mom-who-thinks-she-can-do-it-all-but-cannot-do-it-all saga. He recommended that I take Zoloft and that I stop worrying about others and focus on *me*. Neither strategy seemed to work. Zoloft made me feel like a floating zombie. I would look at my face in the mirror and think, "Where have I gone?" At that point I didn't understand that some drugs work for you and others do not. I went off the drug. When I tried to focus on me, my personal growth did an unwarranted U-turn. I sounded like I had moved to Planet Self-Centered. During this period I whined once again about whether I should move to the new high school, where I had been offered a job. I hated this "me" voice as it ruminated for pages. It was a merry-go-round of lists and self-centered jibber-jabber.

But even this phase in our personal writing is important, for our whining prepares us for change. Of course it can be dangerous territory if we become stuck, but simply by putting our story down and reading it, and repeating it, neurologically we begin to free it up and rework it.

Our Future: The Journal Path to Who We Can Become

Abruptly that journal stopped. What happened to the exhausted young mother? Was she okay? It was clear that after a few weeks of "journal silence," I had abandoned these pages and purchased a new notebook in hopes of being able to move on. Although I was frustrated to see my pattern of being stuck in the earlier journal, I was pleased to find that the entries in the next journal showed I had used my writing to take hold of myself. There was no more sad song. No more rumination. I had ended it and moved on by making a late but clear decision to move to the new school. In the new journal I was excited about planning new lessons. Excited about Zach, who was taking his first steps, much like a joyful drunk man. Excited about Matthew and his Lego inventions. Thrilled to have made a new teaching friend who loved books as much as I did.

Who could I become? A few entries showed that I was toying with a new me, even the *writer* me. I wanted this identity to be a stronger part of my future. In one entry, "Reaching for the Stars," I had played with the writing and polished it. I was enjoying the kids. I read this section aloud to my husband at dinner one night.

Reaching for the Stars

"Wait!" I shout. "You missed the laundry basket." But the door slams on top of my words, and I watch from the window as a sandy-haired boy races to catch up to his school chums. "Matt," I sigh dejectedly, picking up the pile of He-Man sheets discarded by his door.

"Ah-hah!" I spot another sock that his famous left-hand hook shot has failed to deposit in the wicker basket. It lies wedged between stuffed creatures: big and tiny, soft and chewed. As I tug at the sock, two of Matt's favorite stuffed animals tumble to the floor. One, Old Dog, has degenerated into shredded rags. The other, Wrinkles, rolls his head back and looks dead. I laugh.

But my laughter turns into a squeal when my heel lands on the plastic sword of He-Woman Teela. Beneath me stands a collection of He-Men, posed for battle. My son's voice echoes in my imagination: "Skeletor must fall. Good must win!"

Another misplaced sock draws me to Matt's cluttered desk. As I pull it free, I knock over a half-built space vehicle. It crashes to the carpet into another pile of mini Legos, dozens of them. In the afternoons Matt sits here for hours building airplanes, machines, the rocket ships of tomorrow. Last Halloween he dressed as an astronaut, and he rarely stops talking about the space flights he hopes to take someday. Above his Lego inventions hangs his prized poster of the Space Shuttle Challenger. He knows it is gone. Blown to bits. He cried the day of the accident.

Hung above the shuttle is a picture Matt scrawled of a strange caterpillar with huge wings, and it seems to be flying over clouds. He insisted we hang it here. When I asked him why, he explained. "Mom, that bug is climbing up and up — reaching for the stars. I don't want anything to stop him."

In the midst of the clutter of sheets, filthy socks, and half-built space ships, I pause. At that moment I realize how much I love the child who lives in this room. Knowing my son, I have complete faith in his — in our — future. He's a five-year-old who wants to reach the stars.

I believe he will.

Steve agreed with me. This passage showed that I had changed. I had a found a new a metaphor for the joy that comes of raising kids, and this metaphor was not simply for my children and their future — it was for me, too. I had found *myself* reaching up and believing in a brighter tomorrow. All these years later, as I redis-covered this experience, I was reminded of Alice Walker's words about her journal writing. She wrote that suddenly "there's a kind of spiritual alchemy that happens and you turn that bad feeling into something that becomes a golden light." For a time I, too, had touched the light.

In the pages that followed in that journal, I had sketched out plans for a sabbatical to study and write and take better care of my family as well as me. Now I could clearly see how this journal had helped me chart important changes. Expressive writing allowed me to write and rewrite my understanding of who I was as well as — and this was the best part — *who I could be.*

By keeping journals through the years, I learned how to ex-plore my life — and this has made all the difference.

Journal writing gives us insights into who we are,
who we were, and who we can become.

Writing Prompts and Suggestions

If you have old journals or diaries, or even an autobiography or memoir you have written, you may want to dig them out for these writing explorations. If you don't have them, you may want to pull out old photo albums or flip through photos stored on your computer or cell phone. If all you have is memories, they work quite well, too. Make a list of time periods in your life — youth, high school, your first job, perhaps a fulfilling job, maybe a time when you accomplished something, when you married or became a parent or a grandparent.

You can begin this exploration by just choosing a photo, or you can use a memory that is captured in your mind. Remember, the Personal Writing Guidelines can be found on pages 18–19.

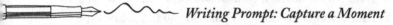 *Writing Prompt: Capture a Moment*

Choose an intriguing photo (or substitute a memory) that captures you or someone you know well. When did this moment happen? What happened right before this event? What feeling does this memory evoke? Write the story of this experience. What do you learn about you or another individual from this photo/memory?

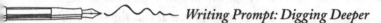 *Writing Prompt: Digging Deeper*

From time to time it helps to reflect on your life and learn from it. If you have your old writing, poems, diaries, or journals, you may want to invest time in exploring your words from different periods of your life. You could do this by reading your journals or old writings or searching through your old photos. Think about these questions as you explore:

- What time periods were especially fulfilling?
- What time periods were especially challenging?
- How would you describe yourself as a character when you look back on these experiences? What were you like? What can you learn from yourself?

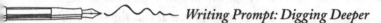 *Writing Prompt: Your Past — Who Were You?*

After spending time with your old writing, photos, or memories, choose a time period from your past. It could be five years ago, ten years ago, or longer. Write about who you were at this age. What was important to you? What can you learn from this past you? (If you want, repeat this exercise, using other periods of your life or other memories.)

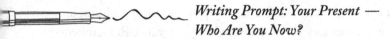

Writing Prompt: Your Present —
Who Are You Now?

How would you describe yourself in one page or less? Or how would a good friend describe you to someone she wants you to meet? What do you enjoy doing? What do you believe is important? What do you like about you? Is there a story you like to tell about yourself? What does this story say about you?

Writing Prompt: Your Future —
Who Are You Becoming?

Experiment with your future. Imagine a day five years from now. What you would like to see? What would you hope to be doing? What do you believe will be important to you at this time? Try to visualize and to describe a positive day in your future.

CHAPTER FIVE

Writing Down the Self

*In the journal I don't just express myself more openly
than I could to any person; I create myself.*
— Susan Sontag

O ne summer night when I was a kid, my dad took our family
to a drive-in theater to see *Gone with the Wind*. The classic
film opens on the eve of the Civil War, and it centers on Scarlett
O'Hara, a charming belle of a large Southern cotton plantation.
The handsome Tarleton twins are competing for Scarlett's attention, but she is in love with Ashley, and she has just learned he
plans to marry his cousin. Heartrending struggles follow. The war
erupts. Scarlett hastily and foolishly marries. And the dashing
Rhett Butler weaves in and out of the story.

While unusual in Indianapolis, midway through the film the
fog rolled in, and we could no longer see the screen. Amid horn
honking from frustrated viewers, the theater manager announced
the film would be stopped and our money would be refunded. I
did not want to leave the drive-in that evening. I was completely
caught up in the trials of Scarlett O'Hara. Fortunately, my mom
found a copy of the book for me to read, and my dad agreed to
return to the theater a few days later to see the end of the movie.

Inspired by the character of Scarlett, I began writing my first novel — my follow-up to Scarlett's story. This was a few decades ago. I was nine.

As do most writers I know, from a young age I harbored a deep-seated belief that I would become a writer. I believed I had a story deep within me and that it needed to be found and told. But when I headed off to college, I did not take my journal. I had the faulty idea that diaries and journals were adolescent mementos that should be boxed up after graduation and left behind with boy-band music, posters of favorite movies, and high school yearbooks. But that didn't work out so well.

When I discarded my personal writing and headed off to college, I hit a bad funk. My first English teacher tortured me with B after B on my essays. The homework was heavy, and my brain could not cozy up to calculus. Eating comforted me, so I put on fifteen pounds. My roommate hated me. She was caught up in love and peace. I was at war — with myself, uncertain about God, faith, and meaning. And I had no outlet for all the questions stacking up inside me.

While I didn't have my journal, at least I began to acquire a small paperback library. I discovered *Siddhartha* in the bookstore and devoured it. I related to the struggle, the life journey. Then a friend gave me a well-worn copy of *Man's Search for Meaning*. I believe it changed my life as much as any book I have read. It told the story of Viktor Frankl, a well-known psychiatrist who was deported, at the height of his career, to a German concentration camp during World War II. Beneath his coat he hid his only copy of an unpublished manuscript that held a record of his ideas. But in one instant this manuscript, his life's work, was taken from him and destroyed. He could have given up, as many of the prisoners chose to do, but Frankl decided to find meaning in this event. He learned — and taught me — that we can't escape tragedy and hardship, but we can control *how we think about it*, we can find meaning in it, and we can move forward. These two books were a college life raft for me.

Although I was no longer writing, the words of other writers steadied me. I was so enthralled with the power of words, I became a reading tutor for young kids at one of the inner-city churches. One afternoon after watching live-wire, nine-year-old Rodney unwrap the meaning in a story we read together — *unwrap it as if I had given him the best gift ever* — I hiked over to campus counseling. I knew what I had to do.

I changed my major to education because I wanted to share the power of writers like Harper Lee, Steinbeck, Faulkner, and Morrison. We all deserve to have a few books under our belts as we tackle the challenges we encounter.

When I was a senior at Purdue, I had one of those life-changing teachers. James Barth asked me to write lessons for the education department. "I like what you do with words," he said. He offered me my first writing job. About the same time a high school friend sent me a copy of an essay I had written our senior year. She told me she had kept it because she knew I should be a writer. I was so moved by this act, I thanked her and then I went out and bought a new journal and began to inch my way back into a writing pattern — a unique way of approaching my personal writing. It took years to establish it. And this is what I learned.

Find *Your* Writing Pattern

To reap the benefits of writing, it works best to find your individual pattern of writing and lock into it. How can we do this? We begin by exploring questions such as: What will we write? When can we write? Where will we write? What will help us to revel in and reveal ourselves in our words?

We can journal in our own way. Or we can avoid a journal. But before you opt out, consider what my students taught me about this practice. There are endless ways to journal. I use my journal to find my voice. I do this by freewriting or simply letting my words come as they will, but sometimes I jot poems, doodle, make clusters around words, or create lists. But my writing students proved to be far more creative.

Sara journaled in poems that rhymed and didn't rhyme, that made sense and were nonsensical. As long as she could capture her thoughts in poetry, she was content. Samantha, a friend's daughter, shared with me pages that held amazing collages that she had threaded throughout her journal. Students often used art as a way to communicate in classroom journals, doodling or drawing cartoons that held their stories, their meaning, their struggles. My former student, Esao, used to turn in more sketches than words in his journal. Derek often included M.C. Escher–type designs with his writing. And the power of musical notes and pop lyrics always danced through Erin's journal. If a particular art or science is a part of who we are, we can bring it to our writing. Einstein was said to sketch out his evolving theories in his notebooks. In other words, our journals are not locked into words.

Choose a Journal

Do you like to write on a computer? An old yellow-lined notepad? Do you like to post on a website? One of my former students, Ally, who collects old typewriters, felt typing was the only way to write her inside thoughts. She admitted it was messy, and sometimes when she hit the shift lock the carriage would fly off, a serious time sink! But Ally loved the feeling and the history of her old Underwood typewriter — for she was pounding away on the same keys her grandmother had used long ago.

True confession: I like *writing* on a computer but I like *journaling* in whatever notebook holds my current fancy. Good news. In reviewing the research on journaling, I found that it does not matter which way you choose to write. Whatever feels comfortable is what you should do. Cheap notepads, tablets, classy journals, computers, napkins, I-paid-for-it websites: all of these work.

Another true confession: I get a kick out of buying new journals. Each one is a new life chapter for me. So buying them is an event. A ritual. When I finish with a journal — and that has less to do with the last page and more to do with finishing a chapter of my life — I put the old journal in one of my hiding spots and head out to my local bookstore to thumb through the new choices. Then I choose a journal that fits "the now" of my life. Shortly after being diagnosed with breast cancer, I headed to the bookstore and found that bright-red journal. It seemed to shout to me, "*Red alert! Cancer is your current challenge. Now sit down. Write. Get through this!*"

When I finished with my cancer treatment, even though the pages were not all filled in that journal, I came to the end of it. I wanted to close the cancer chapter of my life. To celebrate the end of my treatment and my cancer-free diagnosis, my husband and I took a mini vacation to Portland, Oregon. On the first day I rode the streetcar up to Powell's Books. In their huge journal section, I found a blue journal. I admit to being attracted to the serene color, but when I pulled it down, I saw that its cover had imprints of words from Antoine de Saint-Exupéry's *Wind, Sand, and Stars*. My heart started to pound. I loved Saint-Exupéry's works, both to read and to teach. I wanted a journal that would help me relaunch my life on this new and unexpected path. Post-cancer. The magic of Saint-Exupéry seemed essential. I bought the journal and found a bench in the adjoining coffee shop, where I christened my purchase.

Do journals need to be fancy? No. I have kept journals in old left-over-from-college notebooks; I have used my computer, my note cards, and bits of hotel brochures when I had nothing else in my suitcase. Years ago, in New York City, a friend dragged me to a Picasso retrospective. There, much to my amazement, were snippets of paper and napkins where Picasso had sketched out his future. I have never forgotten those artistic scraps and how they helped define the man. *Bits of paper* can chart our course.

Find a Writing Place

The place where you write is as important as the journal. It is rumored that Shakespeare wrote in the pubs of London. Zoe Kazan, author and movie star, hunkered down at a Brooklyn coffee shop while writing the script for her first film, *Ruby Sparks*. Bestselling author Nora Roberts writes in her study overlooking the peaceful greenery of her garden in rural Maryland. "This is my place and I recognized it immediately when there was nothing here," said Roberts. "This is where I want to be." J.K. Rowling wrote her first notes for the Harry Potter series on a napkin while on a delayed train. She often worked on the first Potter book in Edinburgh cafés.

Find a place where you can connect with your ideas and feelings. If you need coffee or tea, music or TV in the background, find a spot that meets your needs. I usually start the day in a booth at my favorite local café, where they brew my favorite passionfruit iced tea. By the time the lunch crowd starts to trickle in, I head out for my walk and end up researching at home on the kitchen bar — which looks into my badly tended but tranquil rose garden.

I try to meditate to clear the cobwebs from my brain before I start writing. Usually. Sometimes I forget. Doing yoga before writing in my journal provides a sense of serene abandon. Work to find what enhances your writing process. I want to believe that tea and dark chocolates work, but I am pretty sure they don't. I do both anyway.

Do You Need Privacy?

If you plan to keep a private journal, most experts on the process recommend that you need a safe place to keep this writing. Initially in my cancer journey, I was too stricken by trauma to write, but when I found my words, I did not want them to go viral. I did not post about my cancer on Facebook for months. And this is where the privacy of my journal proved wonderful. It allowed me to juggle my emotions, as well as my inner thoughts, in a safe space. And I hid it as I have all my past journals, even though I never felt they contained any gritty, grimy "shades of gray" stories. But I wanted to own my stories and give them to the world only when I was ready. And from working with vets and cancer patients, I have learned that many of them harbor stories that need to be held close to the heart. Not for publication — at least until they are ready.

During his writing experiments, Pennebaker allowed participants to tear the pages out of their journals and destroy them. If you need privacy for your writing, find a way to lock it up or shred it. This is your call — but you need to protect yourself. One psychiatrist assured me that child custody battles have been waged over personal writings read in courtrooms. That said, personal writing offers us invaluable insights and benefits. Do it. Don't overdo it — and *be careful* with it.

Blogging: Do You Need an Audience?

Today a popular form of journaling has become the blog, with more than three hundred million blog accounts reported recently. Many writers admit they need an audience. Author Amy Silverman, managing editor of the *Phoenix New Times*, created a blog because she hoped to manage the unexpected, the birth of her daughter Sophie, who has Down syndrome. When we met at a Tempe café, I asked her if she kept a journal after Sophie's birth. She said no. "I have never been able to journal. I would just look at a blank page, and I would feel way too self-aware. I can only write for an audience."

I would argue that her blog *is* a form of expressive journaling. Silverman's blog, *Girl in a Party Hat*, has allowed her not only to write about her struggle to understand her daughter but to share it and receive support. "We need to tell our stories, and we need to be heard. People are so hungry for stories and connections,"

Amy adds. She found those connections in the relationships she has made through the blog. And her blog also supported her efforts to write her first book, *My Heart Can't Even Believe It: A Story of Science, Love, and Down Syndrome.*

Fire Your Inner Critic

For expressive writing to help, you have to let go of criticism, including your own. Recently at a writing workshop, an instructor turned to me unexpectedly and asked me to read a piece I had just jotted off in response to a prompt she had assigned. I was caught off guard. At that moment my imagination formed a huge, blue Aladdin-like genie that seemed to leap out of my head and look down at me, laughing wickedly. Then he leaned over and in the voice of Robin Williams whispered, "You can't read because *you can't write.*"

But I read anyway. While I don't remember what I read, I remember the positive response from the other writers in my group. Ironically, I had been certain "I had nothing to say." You have to work hard to turn off your *I-can't-write* voice, and you must beware, for we all have one.

And Fire Your Inner Editor

The goal of personal writing is to explore, and you have to be liberated from the rules that grind down thinking and creativity. Declare yourself free to use punctuation. Or not. To get your verb tenses correct. Or not. You are free to spell correctly. Or not. You are free to be silly. In 2009 David Sedaris told the *New Yorker,* "I've been keeping a diary for thirty-three years and write in it every morning. Most of it's just whining, but every so often there'll be something I can use later: a joke, a description, a quote. It's an invaluable aid when it comes to winning arguments. 'That's not what you said on February 3, 1996,' I'll say to someone."

Set Up Your Journal

The way you organize your journal is up to you, of course. Through the years I have developed a pattern that works for me. Feel free to borrow whatever you think will fit your style.

- Inside the cover of each journal, I write my name, date, and contact information, along with a request that if the journal is lost to "please return it."
- I date each entry. It helps when I do reviews of my work to know when I wrote a specific entry. I didn't always do this, and when I recently reread my journals it was a huge pain to reconfigure a few of the dates.
- I label or title most entries. Usually when I start to write, I know what I want to write about, or a label comes as I write. If you use your journal work later, this will save time.

Mapping Your Interior

In her classic work on creativity, *The Artist's Way*, author Julia Cameron stresses the importance of writing three stream-of-consciousness journal pages each and every day. She shows no mercy when it comes to this requirement, since she believes this writing allows people to get rid of the nonsense that distances them from creativity. That makes sense. Cameron said, "Morning pages map our own interior. . . . Using them, the light of insight is coupled with the power for expansive change. It is very difficult to complain about a situation morning after morning, without being moved to constructive action. The pages lead us out of despair and into undreamed-of solutions." And I have watched as this method has guided many writers forward.

But I won't lie. I don't do this. I write almost every day. But there are many days when I head directly to my writing project, not my journal writing. There may be weeks — possibly months — when I don't crack open my journal. But usually I tackle journal pages about two days a week for twenty minutes — sometimes more and sometimes less. If I catch an idea that zooms like a lightning bolt, I travel it. I even sit back and revel in it. But, if I am facing a difficult time, as when I was diagnosed with cancer, I turn to my journal more often and write openly about what I am facing and what I need to do. Even then I avoid writing every day because I don't want to become trapped in self-pity or navel gazing. I like my journaling to be centered on self-reflection, not self-absorption. This practice took a while to establish, but it works for me, and that is what matters.

Think about it. How does your writing practice work? Recently I had a student who is a husband, a father of nine kids, and a full-time employee at an IT company. Josh claimed he could manage all of it, as long as he had his "evening hour." From 9 to 10 PM each night, he went to his "study," a corner in the back of the kitchen, and no one bothered him. For that hour he was a writer pursuing his craft. His computer was his writing instrument for his journal, his notes, and his stories. His output was downright amazing.

Author Cheryl Strayed has a completely different practice. "I am a binge writer," she joked when we talked. "I don't write just a couple of hours a day. I go away for a few days and find the cheapest hotel, and for forty-eight hours I just write. I get more work done that way than any other way. Different brains work differently. I go into a trance and can work for fourteen to fifteen hours, barely sleep, and then go back to it."

The point is, you get to decide how writing can fit in your life. What is *your* pattern and *your* practice? Where can you successfully write? When can you write? More is better. The more writing you do, the more you reap the benefits. But when you write *even rarely*, it enhances your life. Pennebaker noted that writing fifteen minutes or more during four sessions provides health benefits. Even if you can squirrel away only a few minutes, it matters. And if you *won't* write — telling your stories matters too.

Writing Down the Self

Please know that it is never too early or too late to undertake personal writing. Journals have been kept in many unique forms by writers, musicians, leaders, folks from all career paths, such as Kurt Cobain, Winston Churchill, Fyodor Dostoyevsky, Bob Dylan, Albert Einstein, Ralph Waldo Emerson, Madeleine L'Engle, F. Scott Fitzgerald, Anne Frank, Che Guevara, Frida Kahlo, Søren Kierkegaard, Anne Lamott, Alanis Morissette, Anaïs Nin, Joyce Carol Oates, George Patton, Sylvia Plath, Ronald Reagan, David Sedaris, George Bernard Shaw, Susan Sontag, Henry David Thoreau, Harry Truman, Alice Walker, Andy Warhol, Oprah Winfrey — the list goes on. And your name could be on it.

Why do all these impressive people keep a journal? The reasons are as unique as each writer. While Anne Frank's diary helped her survive the challenges of hiding from the Nazis, it also served as a confidant. The humorist David Sedaris said he kept a diary to help him find clever ideas to enhance his joke telling. In *Reborn*, author Susan Sontag noted that her journal was far more than a confidant. "In the journal I don't just express myself more openly than I could to any person; I create myself."

Anyone Can Be a Writer

Since the 1970s, we have undergone a cultural explosion in writing. In 1974 author Christina Baldwin created a journal-writing class at the University of Minnesota community education program. In 1977 she published her discoveries from teaching this class in *One to One: Self-Understanding through Journal Writing*. At the time of publication, the Library of Congress had to create a new category for "diaries and journals, therapeutic uses thereof." All these years later, Christina still proclaims that keeping a journal is the most significant life decision she ever made. "It has led to and supported all my other life decisions," she says.

About a year after Baldwin's book brought journal writing to the forefront, Ira Progoff, a New York psychologist, published *At a Journal Workshop*, a detailed account of his Intensive Journal process. He had spent years using and refining techniques to help patients write to achieve psychological healing. At the same time, Tristine Rainer wrote *The New Diary*, a book that helped writers understand how a diary could be used for self-discovery.

During the eighties Pennebaker was starting his own revolution by helping to spawn a number of research studies proving that writing our stories can heal us both physically and mentally. Kathleen Adams, a psychotherapist in Colorado, began offering journal workshops, teaching tools for self-discovery and personal fulfillment. Her first book, the bestselling *Journal to the Self*, was published shortly after she founded the Center for Journal Therapy. Her tireless efforts have helped thread journal writing into our culture.

Young, miniskirted, and new to teaching, I was into it as well. I had my students at the high school writing journals, and they loved it. Their personal journals opened them up. Of course, this was pre-Facebook, pre–cell phones, and pre-texting your BFF. These kids needed someone to listen. A journal gave them a window into themselves. It changed them. And when they needed it to stay private, I would let them label their writing "private," and I would check it off but not read it. Yet when they needed someone to hear their call for help, I would be there when I read their words. In one journal Colleen told me quite openly that she just couldn't bring herself to eat anymore. Rob described how he was going to take a gun and blow his brains out if the students in a not-to-be-named class didn't stop taunting him for being gay. Even if he was gay. Or wasn't — he couldn't be sure. The path from my classroom to the counselor's office was well-worn. During these years I came to understand the power of journal writing to help us find and write our truth — and to save our lives.

And Write

Maybe you have a writing pattern and practice. Can you tweak it a bit? If you don't have one but would like to, explore your options. If you don't write, at least find a way to share your stories. You won't gain all the perks that come of writing, but it will certainly help.

Remember to bring to your writing what you must: poems, music notes, theories of relativity, art, or scribbles. Begin by setting aside some solitary time. And do it. Put the pen to the paper. Tap the keys on the keyboard. Be patient, and let the words or scribbles come. Who knows what magic will follow?

Writing down the self in a journal holds many benefits for us,
so find your unique pattern, discover your practice,
and just do it — write.

Writing Prompts and Suggestions

These ideas will help you explore the writer in you.

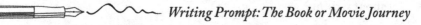 *Writing Prompt: The Book or Movie Journey*

Think back on all the books you've read and all the films you've watched. What books or movies have you loved? What ones have changed you? Is there a book or movie that had a profound impact on you? Describe your experience with one or more of these books or films. What did you learn? What did you value? If you have a passion for either books or films, you may want to consider keeping a reading journal or a movies journal where you explore your reading and viewing experiences.

 *Writing Prompt: Just Do It!*

What would help you *get your words out*? How could you experience writing in a way you would enjoy? Do you have a unique way of writing, your own pattern and practice? If not, explore these two important elements by thinking and writing about the questions that would help:

- Where do you share your private writings? In a journal? On a computer? Are you comfortable with this format? If not, what might work better?

- Do you need privacy for your writing? If so, what security measures could or should you take to protect your writing?

- Do you have a place where you like to write? If not, could you create or find such a space?

- Have you "fired" or found peace with your inner critic? Do you feel free to do the writing you need to do?

- Do editing, spelling, and grammar slow you down? Can you keep your internal editor quiet when you write?

- When do you write? Do you want a schedule or a more regular practice for your writing? Is it possible to establish a better plan for your writing?

- Are there rituals you would like to establish with your writing?

- What frustrates you about writing? What do you love about writing?

    If you struggle with writing, are you a storyteller? Can you share — and maybe tape — your stories?

CHAPTER SIX

Stages of Writing and Healing

There is no greater agony
than bearing an untold story inside of you.

— Maya Angelou

On school days my husband would wake me at five-thirty each morning by tickling my feet, and the next hour would be a flurry of cereal bowls, finding shoes and permission forms, stuffing homework into backpacks, hugging each other good-bye, and hoping to hit the eleven stoplights just right as I raced to the other side of town to the high school where I taught. As I unlocked the door to room 221, I always felt I had arrived at a learning sanctuary. A special space.

For room 221 was the place where I had found my voice, where I found meaning in helping students to craft words. To find *their* voices.

Through the years I had decorated my classroom as carefully as I decorated my home. My students and I sat with our desks in short rows forming a semicircle. Our eyes and minds often explored the stream of posters that blanketed every inch of wall space — the Beatles, Gandhi, Martin Luther King Jr., a sketch of Da Vinci's flying machine, Michelangelo's Sistine Chapel ceiling, paintings by Picasso and Dalí, Martha Graham spinning through the air, buildings like Fallingwater and the ship-like Guggenheim Museum in Bilbao. From time to time, posters for a favorite movie appeared, such as *Harry Potter* or *Life Is Beautiful*, pilfered by a student from a nearby theater. Well-known quotes were scrunched into tiny unfilled spaces. Even Nike's "Just Do It" and Apple's "Think Different" graced the walls.

Years ago a student left a farewell gift on my desk — a dot matrix–printed Emerson quote: "Nothing great was ever achieved without enthusiasm." I hung this unabashed hot-pink plug at the very top of the wall where I couldn't miss seeing it when the door swung open at the start of each teaching day.

What I remember most about that room is the sound of the voices — young, vibrant, alive. No melody or aria can match the lilting words of young people in the energetic pursuit of learning. I often guided lessons by posing difficult questions, but more than my questions, I embraced student discussion and *their* questions. Most of all, I loved the sound of their laughter. Student laughter came in waves and in wonderful ranges and cadences. It was precious music. It was learning.

But there was rarely laughter in the days after Lucas was killed.

Experiencing Our Pain and Grief

In teaching high school I experienced many moments of trauma. Early in my teaching career, I lost quiet Mike to a drug overdose. When her SUV was T-boned by a drunk driver, my student Jana was thrown from the vehicle and died of multiple injuries. Carl was paralyzed from the neck down when he flew off his dirt bike in the nearby desert. Ellie had to be hospitalized when she wilted to seventy pounds. And Justin was angered by the loss of his girlfriend. I never saw him again after the day he carried a loaded, concealed gun into my third period. Later, after threatening to kill others and himself, he was wrestled to the ground by a brave assistant principal.

After each of these events, my life would rip a bit at the seams. At the high school I had to juggle 130 to 150 students during five fifty-four-minute periods daily. And these students were not as street savvy as the kids I had worked with in the inner city. When I had tutored in college, I asked one barrel-sized second grader named Eddie about his dad. He narrowed his eyes and wrinkled his nose as if someone had farted. "He gone. Shot dead." This tough-minded little guy shrugged as if to say, *It happens.* He returned to our reading with no fanfare, but I was jolted.

The students in my high school classrooms were equally jolted after a traumatic event. Especially after Lucas's murder. There was silence and pain. We trudged forward like robots, and our talking and writing slipped in and out of gear.

Breaking the Silence

As I sit here at my kitchen bar thumbing through the pages of my old journals, I see so clearly how my writing helped me navigate the rough waters of such difficult classroom experiences. In studying my journals, I am struck by a pattern I was finding both in my writing and in the work of others. Initially after a trauma, in the flood of pain and grief, it is hard to write. Often there are no words. But eventually we need to find our voice and break our silence.

When Lucas died, I wanted to understand how someone could take a gun from a glove compartment, walk across a church parking lot, and shoot an energetic, lovable kid to death. How could this happen? Questions like this erupted from me like molten rock from a volcano. It took a few days before I could break my own silence and find a path to helping my students regain their voices.

About two weeks after Lucas's death, I asked my students if they were ready to write about this loss and how to manage it. They nodded somberly. Then I turned on *Pachelbel's Canon*, and my seniors wrote as if in a trance. I hurriedly scratched out attendance on bubble sheets, juggled my journal and my coffee cup, and attempted to scribble my own thoughts. The girls' eyes were signaling me with *how could this happen*, while the boys' eyes stared at the space in front of them — *it could have been me*. After the comforting strains of music and ten minutes of writing, we talked about the void in the room, the empty seat in the fourth row. We admitted how our hearts had been painfully pried open, and we talked about praying, and crying, and talking, and writing, and how all of it eased the pain but how we still hurt. There were sniffles, and a tissue box was passed. Somehow it helped. After this talk, there was a closeness in that classroom that drew us tighter and made it possible to live with the empty seat. Death happens. Even to young people.

We had broken the silence. We could now work on living with this tragic story. The next day daisies, a key ring, a book, and other gifts were left on Lucas's desk. In the weeks to come his desk became a treasured memorial space.

As I reread journal entries and dredged up other memories of the writing from my classes, I found myself awestruck by the pattern of writing that seemed to be surfacing. Certain stages kept cropping up over and over.

Inspired by this finding, I cleared out the cupboard beneath my kitchen bar and took a load of old pots and pans to Goodwill. I needed this space for books on writing and healing. Once again I was completely caught up in a new search. This time I was rummaging through my old books. Through the years I had read many of these works, highlighted ideas, and decorated them with Post-its. Sometimes I would reread parts of them or dig through them, searching — as I was doing now. On this quest I wanted to see if any well-known writers had used writing in the way I had — as a healing journey with similar stages.

I began the search in my closet-sized study. Here Isabel

Allende's first book, *The House of the Spirits*, seemed to jump off the bookshelf. With a bit of research I discovered that Allende had begun this book as a letter to her beloved grandfather as he was dying. She had promised to care for him, but she had been driven into exile for political reasons. When she could not keep her promise, Allende began to write to him instead. She wanted to quiet her anguish and to share his stories, her family stories. That letter became her first book.

While this story intrigued me, it was Allende's book *Paula* that affirmed my new theory. Allende had clearly embraced her writing as a journey to heal as she penned this work. About a decade after *The House of the Spirits* made her famous, Allende's only daughter, Paula, became ill and lapsed into a coma following an attack of porphyria, a rare inherited disorder. Allende flew to Madrid to be with her. For interminable hours she sat in the room of a Spanish hospital with her beloved daughter.

Overwhelmed with despair, Allende began once again to write a letter. She addressed this one to Paula and wrote, "My soul is choking with sand. Sadness is a sterile desert."

Allende started this letter because she wanted her daughter to understand her family's difficult history, but as she wrote her story, it ripped open long-forgotten wounds of her past. In the quiet of the hospital room, Allende broke her silence and began coming to terms with the traumatic episodes she had faced: the unexplained disappearance of her father after a sexual scandal and her own sexual molestation at the age of eight. By unraveling the pain of her past, Allende was able to reach a peace with who she was. Although she could not understand or accept that Paula was dying, the author could begin to make sense of her own story.

"I had a choice," wrote Allende. "Was I going to commit suicide?... Or was I going to write a book that would heal me?" She chose to write. Although her daughter died in her arms a year later, writing kept Allende from drowning in her grief. She wrote to survive. She wrote to heal. She wrote to find ways to overcome her loss — and she did.

While her words were originally intended for Paula, Allende's stories became a lifesaver *for her*. This is important. Our stories can be a gift we give ourselves. We do not have to share them or publish them. Our stories can be a gentle balm to ease our healing or an outlet for releasing the trauma inside us.

Accepting and Piecing Your Story Back Together

It makes sense to navigate difficult feelings by writing, but it makes even more sense to use our writing to piece together what has happened to us. We are the main characters as well as the author of our stories. When we face trauma, illness, or loss, we need to refit the pieces into our life. This may be a painstaking process, and it may require the help of a professional therapist, but our writing can help us clarify and work through a difficult period. After all, a good counselor attempts to talk us through our narratives and helps us make sense of our experience. But we can assist our healing by working our way forward with our personal writing as well. When Lucas died, I had no extra hours in the day to visit a counselor. My journal served as my therapist. Here is what I remember.

For me, Lucas's death was a story shattered like a piece of glass. He was a beautiful kid, not yet eighteen. Gone! I had to pick up the pieces and place them back into the puzzle of my existence. Each afternoon I raced across town to my sons' soccer games or home to cook dinner and convince my kids to eat their vegetables, practice the saxophone, and finish their math home-work. After ten or eleven I would haul out a stack of essays to grade. On evenings when I didn't fall asleep atop those papers, I would long to crawl into bed or to turn on TV or to pour a glass of red wine. Sometimes the red wine won out. But quite often I would forego the wine and dig down into my beat-up book bag, find my journal, and write.

And I am incredibly thankful that I made time to write. For it was in those moments that I was changed. On those pages — even the tear-streaked ones — I would find solace and discover how to manage the demon of worry and to face hard times, in this case the loss of a student. In my journal, on one of those late evenings, I rediscovered a bit of magic that Lucas had left for me and his friends.

Making Sense of Our Story

The week before Lucas died, his class had been reading Saint-Exupéry's *The Little Prince*. The story centers on a pilot who lands in the Sahara Desert. Having mechanical problems, he sets about repairing his plane when the odd, childlike Little Prince appears. Initially the Little Prince is quite put off by the pilot, who is completely wrapped up in his airplane repairs. But slowly the Little Prince uses his strange stories to befriend the pilot and teach him some important lessons about living. During one discussion about the book, I asked what important ideas had been unearthed as we read.

"The fox came up from his hole!" All eyes turned toward the voice coming from the fourth row. Lucas. "That fox teaches us about trust and friends. And that's okay...but the best part is the fox's gift. He gave the Little Prince a quote, a thought." Then Lucas paused, knowing his silence would give this quote the emphasis it needed. "*What is essential is invisible to the eye*," he said. "The quote is cool — and it was a *free* gift," Lucas joked. Then sitting sidesaddle at his desk, Lucas poised himself like Rodin's *Thinker*. He held our complete attention. "The invisible is the best stuff...goodness, truth, friendship, stuff like that...and how often do we stop and realize that?" There was a moment of silence as we pondered his words. Then Lucas turned and leaned forward on his desk, leaning into a future that should have been. That was my last vivid memory of him. And this image of Lucas would remain framed in my head. Forever. It would be wrapped

with a ribbon in my heart with a gift tag reading, "From Lucas —
I still want your car."

How ironic that our beloved Lucas had entered the realm of
the best stuff. *The invisible.* I often think of how important he
was — and remains — in our lives. While his death remains a
senseless event, my memories of him, scrawled in my journal on
one of those late nights, helped me to accept this tragic loss. They
would come to fill the hole in my heart that had been so abruptly
left there. Yes, my writing helped me to heal. It revised my connection to Lucas in a way that helped me manage my grief.

As I call up this memory, I remain thankful that I often found
the energy to reach to the bottom of the book bag and pull out
my journal. For it is on those pages that I sifted through emotions
both heart-wrenching and joyful that would help me understand
various chapters of my life. In my late-night scrawls I was able to
give meaning to my experiences.

Finding Meaning with a Resolution

I wrote about Lucas in my journal with the hope that I could
reach an understanding of his murder — or at least learn to accept it. In *Writing to Heal,* Pennebaker explains that it took researchers many years to realize the key to success in "writing and
healing" lay in participants using the writing experience to actually "construct a complete story." When the participants in his
studies wrote a story they had already told and did not change or
complete it, there were no great healing benefits. But if the writer
wrote about a traumatic event for the first time, to make sense of
it, then the writing had a profound healing impact.

When we transfer a difficult story from emotions into words,
we can work with it. Once a story is tangible, it is malleable. It is
ours. We can choose the meaning we give to it and how we will
rewrite our lives to help us live with it.

For days I have been combing through the piles of books that
I love. I indulge myself because I believe these books are opening

the door wider to a theory of how writing to heal works. Just as Maslow has a hierarchy of needs and Kübler-Ross has stages of grief, writing to heal has a ladder. While there is no definitive order in how we work toward healing, a clear pattern was surfacing, a pattern that framed how we could chart our way through difficulties. When a trauma or loss hits, we experience an emotional whirlwind, and few words come. Eventually — and it may take time — we open up. Initially our writing may be cathartic because we simply need to break our silence. Find our voice. Pour out our pain. As we accept our shattered story, we begin to piece it back into our lives. Once we reassemble the story, we can give it meaning and bring an end to our suffering.

I turned my attention to a book that my high school students always raved about — *The Lovely Bones* by Alice Sebold. Even the title tugged at my heart. Susie Salmon, the novel's narrator, speaking from the afterlife, opens her story with a shocking announcement: "I was fourteen when I was murdered on December 6, 1973." Susie shares the appalling account of being raped, brutally murdered, and dismembered by her sinister neighbor. The tale vividly portrays a violent death as well as the nightmarish struggles of Susie's family and friends as they wade through the grief, the healing, and the redemption that follow.

The story is authentic and powerful. "Sebold, how did you do this?" I asked the author as if she were sitting across from me at my kitchen bar.

After doing some research I discovered that Sebold herself had survived both a rape and a murder attempt. The author's real-life ordeal began on the last day of her freshman year at Syracuse University. She was walking back to her dorm when she was attacked and dragged into a tunnel. Once out of sight and with no possibility of help, she was beaten, bloodied, and raped. In spite of her wounds she staggered back to her dorm, where she was rushed to the hospital. When she gave her account of the rape, one cop offhandedly told her she was "lucky" to be alive because another girl had been "murdered and dismembered" in the same spot.

Hard years followed for Sebold. When she returned to Syracuse, she recognized her assailant and turned him in to the police. After a long and agonizing trial, the rapist went to prison. But Sebold continued to flounder. Her writing went nowhere, and she was caught up in dating the wrong men, drinking, and using drugs. Eventually she went into therapy and later enrolled in a writing program at the University of California, Irvine. At Irvine, with years of distance from her rape, the writer sat down at her desk one day and started work on what would become *The Lovely Bones*. As she wrote, it became apparent that before she could write this book, she needed to stop and write her personal story. "One of the things that was very important for me to do was to get all the facts of my own case down, so they had been written, they existed whole in a whole other book, and I could go back to Susie and she could lead me where she wanted to take me and tell me her story."

A meticulous writer, Sebold uncovered her old journal and studied the period of her rape. Then she looked up transcripts of her trial and returned to Syracuse, where she interviewed the former assistant district attorney who had helped to prosecute her rapist. The result was Sebold's memoir, a graphic portrayal of an all-too-common crime. The book was titled *Lucky*.

Rewriting and Re-Creating Ourselves

For expressive writing to help us heal and move toward positive change, we need *a complete story*. By writing her memoir, Sebold had finished her story and found a way to live with it. This piqued my interest. When we put our trauma into a completed chapter, does this give us the emotional energy to move forward — to transform or to pursue our creativity?

In reviewing my stack of books, I determined it did. Certainly Sebold models this process. The author returned to *The Lovely*

Bones and wrote a book of profound beauty, one that demonstrates her creative powers in full force. This author's experience mirrored the pattern I was seeing over and over in both my research and reading, a pattern I had seen for years in my teaching and writing.

And this pattern, a theory on how writing and healing works, was a part of my cancer story, too. At the start of this book you met me lying numb on the tile of my kitchen floor struggling with my diagnosis. I lay there engulfed in cold darkness — a woman in shock. A woman without a voice. In the ensuing days, as I absorbed this trauma, I talked with close friends and began to scribble about my feelings, my fears, and my frustrations. These journal notes show a cathartic release of emotions, peppered with odd little poems.

As my emotions began to thaw, my logic began to play with the pieces of what initially felt like my shattered life. By reading my journals, I could see that I was beginning to accept my cancer by making lists of things to do and ways to manage it. Now I could see how my mind had begun to redefine, reconfigure, rewrite, and even choose how I would live this new existence.

In the coming weeks I faced a failed lumpectomy. Then my doctors gave me some choices: Did I want more surgery, radiation, and possibly chemo, or would I prefer to lose one or both breasts? The decision-making process played out as I made carefully etched plans, recorded insights from my medical board, and explored the uplifting stories of fellow cancer patients. Women who shared their stories and even showed me their lovely reconstructed breasts. Women who would knit together as my new friends and inspire my transformation. I was changing. I had to.

My journal entries record an understanding of my dilemma. I knew what I had to do to complete this chapter in my life — and I wrote about the difficulty of my decision and the pain of losing my breasts. I described breasts that had thrilled to the touch of my husband's hands and had nurtured my sons as babies. Even in the throes of writing this, I realized how my words were — once again — helping me make sense of my life, helping me to set and reset my life's path.

And captured on the pages of that red cancer journal was also the story of my young son jumping into the swimming pool at the junior high on a hot summer day. Zach chose to face the challenge of swimming lessons with abandon. With acceptance. With joy. And now, once again, I embraced Zach's four-year-old wisdom. I, too, could accept my challenge and move forward.

On a dazzling spring day, after my second cancer surgery, I awoke to the earthy smell of daisies, mixed with the fragrance of roses and citrus in bloom. When I flipped open my shutters to peer into the garden, I was struck by the sunshine that seemed to flicker right through me. Perhaps I imagined it. Perhaps it was no more than a positive illusion. But it seemed I was changed at that moment. That I now knew who I would become. I sensed I had a new plan and that I could move forward, pen in hand, with my story — and with *our* stories — stories that I remembered or that I found on the pages of my journal. I began to search for them. I collected stories from classrooms, from books, from friends, and from fellow writers. And soon there were new stories pouring into my life as I interviewed and worked with both chemo patients and veterans. The story of the IED. The lump. The gunshots. The lost child. The tumor. The screeching sound of brakes. The undertow.

While I may never be a famous writer like Wiesel or Strayed, I have uncovered something that matters more for my well-being. I have learned the power of my words to pull me out of the troughs in my life. I have learned to distance myself and see myself objectively. Through writing and sharing life stories, I have learned how to reinterpret, rewrite, and re-create myself. My life has become one of story transformation — and this has made all the difference. If I can rewrite my life, I know you can do it, too.

There are five stages to writing and healing. These stages can lead to story transformation. Here they are:

1. *Experiencing pain and grief.* Grief is the process that helps us adjust to a major life change or a loss — a death, a lost love, an accident, an illness, a rape, or any other setback. There is no set order for what transpires, but initially we might want to ignore or deny what happened because this helps us endure the shock. Later we can experience various emotions such as anger, frustration, and sadness. Sometimes sadness can be so overwhelming, it turns into depression. Often we ruminate or keep replaying what happened in our brains. In the initial throes of a traumatic event, it appears best to embrace silence and avoid writing.

2. *Breaking the silence.* In this stage we are willing to share our shattered story with others, perhaps with a friend, a counselor, or in our writing. This process may center on simply pouring out painful emotions. Often the release of a painful story can prove quite significant if it has been buried deep inside for a long time. If we can find our voice and free up our broken story, we can begin to work with it.

3. *Accepting and piecing together a shattered story.* At this stage we reach acceptance of a painful experience. We acknowledge the event or circumstance, as well as the sadness and pain associated with it. With acceptance we begin to move our emotions into a logical framework. Writing can be profoundly helpful here. It allows us to begin making sense of what happened. We can explore various perspectives and gain some insights by distancing ourselves from the pain. Ruminations may continue during this stage.

4. *Finding meaning or making sense of a story.* In this stage of a setback, we are able to stand outside the experience

and see the complete picture. This objectivity allows for a breakthrough of understanding, a complete story, and a feeling of closure. We can reframe a painful experience once we can make sense of it, and writing is a powerful tool in this process. When we gain an understanding of difficult experiences — why they happen and how they will fit into our lives — often the pain and ruminations subside. The incident becomes integrated into our life stories as a finished chapter, allowing us to move forward.

5   *Rewriting our story and moving forward.* Without the emotional struggles caused by the traumatic incident, we can recover the energy needed to rewrite our stories and move ahead with our lives in fulfilling and creative ways. This often leads to personal *story transformation* through redefining or reinventing the ways we view ourselves. We often put our renewed energy toward creating something (designing a new room or writing a book) or becoming politically active (advocating for cancer funding or working for gun control). Frequently we focus on helping others face or avoid a similar trauma, while allowing us to create something good and meaningful from the pain we have endured.

Writing Prompts and Suggestions

If you need the Personal Writing Guidelines, you can find them on pages 18–19. If you have begun to establish your writing practice, get comfortable, select a prompt from the list below, and begin writing. Give it your best.

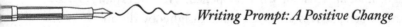 *Writing Prompt: A Positive Change*

Choose a person who has changed you in a positive way. You can also choose an experience that has changed your life. Describe this person or experience. Tell the story. Discuss how and why your attitude changed.

 *Writing Prompt: Finding an Ending*

Is there an experience inside your head that won't seem to go away? What is it? Why does it haunt you? Does this story need an ending? Explore your story.

 *Writing Prompt: A Letter*

If you are struggling, write a letter to a loved one. Decide what you need to tell her or him. Then simply put your pen to paper, and let your message and your stories come. Write for as long as you need to. Come back to this if you need to. When you reread this letter at a later time, decide if you should send it, destroy it, lock it away, or publish it.

PART THREE

FINDING MEANING THROUGH STORY

CHAPTER SEVEN

The Magical Mystery Tour
How Our Brains Create Story

What we think is what we become.
— **Often attributed to the Buddha**

Whenever Steve was home from college, he dropped by the local airport in Torrance, California, to visit with his mentor, an air force veteran and a United Airlines pilot named Chuck. In his teens Steve had traded in days at the sun-drenched beach to be at Zamperini Field, where a cadre of older pilots gathered to tinker with their aircraft. On some days Louis Zamperini showed up to be slapped on the back, for he was always heralded in Torrance as a great World War II hero. This local airport was where Steve discovered his passion: flying over the beaches crowded with sunbathers and surfers. He loved guiding a plane through the clouds — connecting with the air, the space, and catching sight of the pelicans flying along the coast.

On this Labor Day weekend the fog had lifted early and the forecast was for sunny and clear weather. The beaches were filling up quickly. Perfect flying weather. Chuck offered to take Steve for a flight in his experimental Wittman Tailwind. They climbed into Chuck's old plane and headed out first to Flabob and later to Chino Airports, where they enjoyed sipping iced tea from old peanut butter jars and swapping pilot stories with longtime buddies. They were about to add a new story to this pilot lore.

Late that afternoon the two headed home. Steve could smell the salt in the air as they flew toward the Pacific Ocean. Shortly before entering their approach into Torrance, and completely without warning, the propeller shot off the plane like a rocket. It traveled several hundred feet in front of the plane before it plummeted down and crashed onto a bridge below. Then the Tailwind's engine began to vibrate oddly.

Chuck handed the microphone to Steve. "Radio the Torrance tower. We are May Day," he explained in his calm airline-pilot voice. "The propeller is gone. We will have to do an emergency landing." While Steve radioed the message to the air traffic controller, Chuck turned the engine off and began to manage the plane controls as if he were flying a glider. It was all he could do — hold on and guide the stick forward. He found a parking lot at the Long Beach Naval Shipyard on Terminal Island, and although it was packed with jeeps and military vehicles, Chuck carefully guided the plane over the guard tower and toward the only clear roadway he could find. Shortly before they hit, Steve buried his head in his arms as Chuck had trained him to do. But there was no need. Chuck brought the injured plane to a careful stop on the short stretch of parking lot exactly three feet before they reached the fence surrounding the base. Three feet before they would have knocked through the fence and headed toward the ocean.

Within a minute of landing, a convoy of jeeps confronted them. Several marines who ran security in the area jumped out, and one wiry little sergeant began yelling at the pilots. "I waved you guys off!" He shook his fist right in their faces. "But you ignored me and went right ahead and landed!"

The deadpan-faced captain motioned the sergeant aside and cautiously approached Chuck. "Why did you land here?"

"I am sorry," Chuck said humbly. "But my propeller fell off, and I had to find a place where we could land." Strained silence. The captain walked over and examined the plane for a full two minutes before they heard his deep belly laughs. "There really is *no* propeller here!" Soon the marines were swarming around the plane. Then they turned to the pilots and heralded Chuck as a hero for his calm, next-to-impossible landing.

Steve has told the story of landing on Terminal Island often enough that to this day he can see the angry sergeant and hear him yelling. He remembers the smell of the ocean because they landed so perilously close to it. In his mind's eye he can see the captain inspect their plane and hear his sudden laughter. Steve has such a clear memory because his brain has this sensory-packed story ready for replay whenever needed, like a 3-D movie.

Once I asked him if the memory was traumatic. Steve cocked his head. "No," he answered. "It wasn't that traumatic. I just did what we had to do — hold on." This is how we have to face difficulties. Hold on and move forward. This message was wired into Steve's brain. It became a part of who he was and is — a pilot with a survival story. Although he likes this story, Steve is not a braggart. We had been married for several years before I heard this tale, but when I did, I marveled at the clarity of it. It defines him. We all have these *life-defining stories* stored in our memories. These vivid personal stories help us understand who we are.

Quickly this story entered the lore of local flying history at Zamperini Field and would eventually make its way out to the surrounding airports. Although Chuck avoided attention, he would be lauded as a local top gun for landing his Tailwind, minus a propeller, without a scratch. Was this a feat? Or was it luck? How did he avoid crashing? Recent discoveries can help us unlock the answer to these questions as well as help us understand how we can work on writing and rewriting our personal stories.

Writing and the Magic in Our Brains

Our minds are a miracle — filled with mysteries that can help us wade through traumatic events. How can we unravel some of the puzzles in our brains? Modern neuroscientists have done the heavy lifting for us. Understanding the brain and how it becomes a mind *or a self* will help us make better use of it by rewiring and rewriting what is inside it.

Our special brain cells, neurons, truly are mind-boggling. In *The Brain That Changes Itself,* psychiatrist and psychoanalyst Norman Doidge explains that these brain cells are unique from other cells because they have the ability to send signals across their long fibrous endings, known as axons, to neighboring dendrites. The microscopic space between two neurons is the synapse.

Now pause and take a gulp: the magic happens here.

When a neuron sends an electrical signal to an axon, this releases a chemical message into the synapse that jumps through the dendrite to a neighboring neuron. The more a message is sent from one neuron to another, the more they bond. We might think of it as neurons making friends. Out of this comes a common phrase that is used to explain how our brains work: *Neurons that fire together, wire together.* The more we use certain paths in our brains, the more established they become. These patterns become maps, and we are composed of these maps. These maps spell out who we think we are.

These maps are what saved Chuck and Steve. One key to the success of pilots is their expert training. Remember Chesley "Sully" Sullenberger? On January 15, 2009, after the jet he was piloting had sucked birds into both engines on takeoff, the engines shut down, and Sullenberger calmly flew his Airbus A320 into the frigid waters of the Hudson River. All 155 passengers, three flight attendants, and two pilots survived. Steve and Chuck's story is airport lore in Southern California; Sully's story is a cultural story that continues to model for us how to survive a disaster. Sully brought all of us through this nightmare.

Since learning to fly planes is complex, and losing a couple of planes in the learning process is both expensive and life threatening, flight simulators were created. A flight simulator gives pilots the opportunity to practice their skills before facing unexpected obstacles. In recent years, with improved technology, these devices have become capable of re-creating what seems like a completely real experience for pilots in training. Both Chuck and the now-famous Sully had spent countless hours in air force and commercial flight simulators practicing flying through all types of unexpected situations. It paid off. The neuron-to-axon connections that increased the chances of survival response and the skill to carry out the response were wired into the pilots' brains.

About ten years ago, when I asked Chuck how he pulled off that landing at Terminal Island, he shrugged as if it were no big deal. "Experience," he added. The neurons in Chuck's brain had been wired together into maps that knew exactly what to do. They saved Chuck's and Steve's lives. And since Steve is my husband, I am especially grateful.

Our Brains Create Our Unique Self

These brain maps give us more than automatic memory when needed. According to neuroscientist Antonio Damasio, our brain actually transforms into "a mind" when the activity of firing neurons becomes organized into patterns that are so well established they become dynamic maps. These active or dynamic maps become our way of translating our world by experiencing sensory images — sights, sounds, smells, touches, tastes, and even our pains and pleasures.

Our maps, filled with sensory details, hold our memories. If Steve recounted landing on Terminal Island tonight over dinner, the tale would sound completely authentic. While his memory maps have this story locked in his brain, they are dynamic, too. This means Steve could change the story a bit each time he tells it.

These dynamic brain maps contain the sensory input we need to be the individuals we are. We appear to have feelings as a result of certain neuron circuits firing and certain connections being made. Out of this activity comes a mind that feels, as well as one that thinks. In his book *Self Comes to Mind*, Damasio explains how we develop a sense of self. The first step in this process is the development of these dynamic feelings. Later a "core self" unfolds that is focused on our actions and relationships. The "self" reaches its highest point of development when we create an "autobiographical self." This part of us consciously acknowledges past experiences as well as future plans. The autobiographical self becomes aware of who we are on many levels, including social and spiritual.

At the time of the Terminal Island landing, Steve was nineteen. He had loved planes for as far back as he could remember, watching *Sky King* on TV and regularly building and flying model airplanes as a kid. When he tutored a high school friend in math and discovered her dad was an air force vet as well as a United Airlines pilot, he offered to drive her home. A lifelong friendship began with the dad, Chuck. When Steve left for college, he joined an aero club and began taking flying lessons. By the time of the Terminal Island miracle, Steve was studying to be an aeronautical engineer and a pilot. As a child he had heard John F. Kennedy's pledge to create a space program, and the idea became embedded in Steve's mind. His personal "self" was a symphony composed of several movements — a longing to fly, a longing to build airplanes, and a longing to chart a future with space travel and scientific exploration. Steve is not alone. We each have our own symphony.

A symphony? Indeed. Damasio, who sees the performance of self as a symphony, created this perfect metaphor to explain how all these pieces in the upper reaches of our consciousness come together and work together. All the musicians in our minds are needed, and their contributions, or "music," make it possible for us to function as a whole person. And our writing allows us to understand and rework the symphonic movements within us. These movements become our stories.

Wired on Stories

One of our brain's most astounding feats happens when the imagery and feelings in our minds are cobbled together by "a narrative brain device" — or as we prefer to say, *our stories*. Stories are the way we see ourselves. Steve chose to define himself as a young pilot, and he latched on to stories that would help him build this identity. He chose his stories — just as we choose ours.

Our brains run on stories. Think about it. How much time do we spend daydreaming, reading a novel, watching a sitcom, creating a portrait of ourselves on Facebook, or watching a movie? We even spin stories in our sleep. Story is how we connect and build community with others at the watercooler, in the lunchroom, at happy hour, at the gym, on the church patio, on the golf course, or at a yoga class.

A Story Needs an Ending

Our brains are captive to a good story — think Batman, Harry Potter, Romeo and Juliet. Stories lock into our brains. They connect us with friends and family. A few times a year my kitchen bar is book free. Mother's Day is one of those times. The kids drop by with flowers, and my parents join us for a kid-made brunch of cheesy eggs and sticky rolls that fill the house with the smell of cinnamon. We swap stories for hours. At one gathering we found ourselves locked in the web of a news story: What had happened to the missing Malaysia Airlines Flight 370 that disappeared on March 8, 2014? Captivated by the mystery of it, we swapped ideas most of the morning. My dad supported the sudden decompression theory, in which the occupants were knocked out and the plane flew on. My son raised the possibility of a hijacking, and my husband fueled this thinking by noting that one news team had found 634 possible runways in twenty-six countries where the flight might have secretly landed. My daughter-in-law, Jordyn, and I favored the possibly wacked-out pilot scenario. While our hearts ached for the families and friends of the individuals on that missing flight, the truth was we had no way of knowing at that time what happened to them, and we were driven to know.

For days after my family gathering, I was tweaking my ending to this story. I reminded myself that someone had turned off the communications and changed the course of the flight. This supported my "weirdo in the cockpit" thinking and helped give me a little peace. And this is how story works. We need resolutions or endings to our stories. An unfinished one keeps playing in our minds. At the time CNN kept replaying all the details of this disappearing plane when it was no longer news but simply a story with no ending. I had written my own ending because *I needed it*. That is how our brains work. We need to know "what happened" even when we don't know.

Not only do we come to know ourselves through our stories, but we come to know others through their stories. As scholar Joseph Campbell pointed out, all through history humans have been living out the same story format. Campbell is renowned for showing us how every culture treasured the universal hero pattern. The Bible is packed with heroes. There was Moses, who stood up to the Egyptians; Job, who modeled endless patience; and of course Jesus, who taught us to be kind and forgiving. There was Mary, who fled to another country to protect her newborn. We use story to teach our children about life. I sing the same songs to my young granddaughter as I did to my own kids. The "Itsy Bitsy Spider" lost his home, but he crawled up the water spout and started all over again. "Twinkle, Twinkle Little Star" reminds us of the beauty of wonder and learning.

We use stories to entertain ourselves, to learn, to solve our problems, and to help us find ourselves. We are the protagonists in our own stories. We act, and that creates a plot. Inevitably our actions — or the actions of others — cause a conflict. Conflicts create problems that must be resolved. Our brains search to resolve these issues — and this brings about a resolution or ending to a story. That is why I needed my own theory about Flight 370 — to find a respite from the conflict it created in me.

Brain Magic and Writing

For decades it was presumed that our brains were hardwired, or incapable of change. If someone had a stroke, it was believed he or she had "lost it," that certain functions controlled by the damaged area of the brain were knocked off grid. Norman Doidge debunks this myth. He explains, "The damaged brain can often reorganize itself so that when one part fails, another can often substitute; that if brain cells die, they can in time be replaced; that many 'circuits' and even basic reflexes that we think are hardwired are not." In sum, brain cells can repair, rewire, and remap — *we can change.*

Indeed, our writing can help us remap our brains or rewrite who we are. For years I watched this process unfolding in my classroom. Remember Ben? He took a long time to find his words, but he began to find them when he wrote a narrative about his uncle's death and shared it. When Lucas was murdered, my entire class began to write their way forward by creating a tribute journal for his family. And there was spiky-haired Amy, who bounded joyfully into room 221 each day, adorned in her clunky combat boots. She was a searcher who crafted lovely poems. These poems spoke the truth about her pain, pain I believed to be caused by her parents' divorce. Before she graduated she gave me her poems in a book as a gift. It is one of the best gifts I ever received, and I hope it helped her leave her suffering behind.

And the evidence moves far beyond my classroom. Remember the cupboard beneath my kitchen bar that I cleared out? More books kept finding their way onto these shelves. And as I dug through them, I found *Love Warrior: A Memoir* by Glennon Doyle Melton, a powerful story of personal change.

One day overwhelmed stay-at-home mom Doyle Melton noticed friends posting Facebook lists of "25 Things about Me." After putting her daughter down for a nap, she sat down at the computer and began to write her truth. Doyle Melton admitted that she was a recovering alcoholic and bulimic and that her marriage was struggling. Within an hour her in-box was filled with notes from friends as well as strangers who wrote to say, "Me, too. I'm struggling."

Doyle Melton felt that others were listening. She told her husband, "I'm going to be a truth teller. This is a key that can unlock people." And she began to write predawn each day, and within months she launched her blog, *Momastery*. Her willingness to talk about her struggles with parenting and her problems with marriage and sex earned her a following — of seven million readers.

During a therapy session with her husband, Glennon learned he had cheated on her throughout their marriage. Crushed, she separated from Craig. Then she realized that with three small children at home, she could not attend a support group to manage this crisis. Instead she sat down at her computer. *"Writing will have to be my meeting now. I will have to save myself this time,"* she wrote. She began by typing a list of what she needed to do. It was a hard journey, a journey that continues to this day. But in using her personal writing, Doyle Melton re-created herself as a woman — a better, stronger woman.

I see this same courage to remake oneself in *My Heart Can't Even Believe It*, written by Amy Silverman. Amy found herself knocked sideways in 2003 when her daughter Sophie was born with Down syndrome. The truth is I found it hard to open the pages of this book, for I knew it would be heart-wrenching. And it was. But it wasn't.

Silverman is a journalist who embarks on her writing as if she is going to learn *everything* she can. And she does. While her book enlightened me on Down syndrome and the struggle of living with a child who has it, the biggest lessons I learned were in how to parent and how to love. The real teacher is the charming Sophie, who helps her family grow in unexpected ways.

When we met at a café to talk, I asked Amy if writing her blog and book had changed her. "Yes! This is totally true," she assured me. In creating her blog and writing her book, Amy not only learned how to live with and help manage her daughter's disability, but she created around her a community of new friends who shared her plight. "They provided so many insights and support. The writing changed me, but *putting my words out there into the world* allowed that to happen." In her book she describes her change: "I morphed from a spoiled, self-centered brat — one who used words like *retard* and switched lines at Safeway when I saw a bagger with special needs." I know Amy, and I want to attest she has become an incredible mom and a strong advocate for kids with special needs.

Our words can change us. Our writing can serve as our flight stick. It can guide us, stabilize us, and support us when we face bad weather and even when our engines sputter or flame out.

Our brains allow us to adapt and change — to write
and rewrite who we are.

Writing Prompts and Suggestions

These writing suggestions will allow you to open up and begin to explore some of your difficult yet life-defining stories.

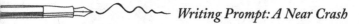 *Writing Prompt: A Near Crash*

What near crash have you faced? What unexpected event or diagnosis or loss has disrupted your beautiful afternoon? Were you able to hold on to your flight stick? How did this experience work out? Explore.

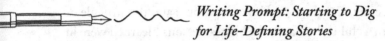

*Writing Prompt: Starting to Dig
for Life-Defining Stories*

Do any stories come to mind as important life experiences? Explore one of these stories. Did it help define you? Why or why not?

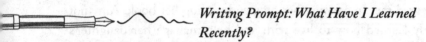

*Writing Prompt: What Have I Learned
Recently?*

Choose something you have learned recently. What did you learn? How did you learn it? What surprised you about learning it? Explain.

CHAPTER EIGHT

Stories

Our Lives Hang on Narrative Threads

*My story is myself: and I am my story. This is all you will
know of me, it is all I will know of you. This is all
that will survive of us: the stories of who we are.*
— Christina Baldwin

Many summers ago, when I was a kid, we loaded up our
station wagon, and my dad drove like a maniac for fourteen hours from our home in Indianapolis to get to the beach in
Ocean City, Maryland. There we rented a small beach bungalow
and spent the week with my dad's family. One night after a grand
day of splashing in the waves and collecting shells, gorging on
hot dogs dripping with mustard, and playing Monopoly with my
cousins, we sat on the beach looking up at the dark night sky with
its billions of stars. I remember that moment for one reason. I was
sitting beside my dad, eating a chocolate ice cream cone, and I
asked him, "How did all those stars get up there?"

And I remember my dad saying, "We don't *really* know."

"How did I get *here*? On Earth?"

"That's an equally puzzling question," my dad said and
laughed.

I am not even sure how old I was. Maybe ten? But I recall
that moment in my life because it startled me. I was unsettled. A

cork had been popped, and the questions began pouring out of me. I needed answers, and I thought my dad knew everything. But he didn't.

Years later, on his television series, *Cosmos*, Carl Sagan made a valiant attempt to answer the questions I had asked my dad. Sagan began his series by overlaying the last fifteen billion years of history on a one-year calendar. In this overview of time, we get a clear picture of how limited our human role has been. Earth does not condense from interstellar matter until September of that year. Plants do not colonize until December 20. Men and women show up on the last day — around 10:30 PM. Human history — which is our collective story — proves to be brief in the scheme of it all.

After watching the first episode of *Cosmos*, I called my dad. I had to tell him we are but specks in this huge and spinning universe. He was, after all, right. No one completely understands it all. And at age ten I was right, too. It is unsettling. *Downright scary*.

Living with unanswered questions becomes an existential quandary because — as I learned on the beach long ago — we want to understand. We want answers to all life's difficult questions: Where did we come from? What is our purpose? Who should we love? What is good, and what is evil? What happens when we die?

As our brains have evolved, we have become seekers of knowledge. We want to understand why we live and how to live. Our lives are an ongoing quest for knowledge and wisdom. We turn to parents, to teachers, and to our religions to help ground ourselves in the midst of the unknown. And we have found a profound way to share and to record our answers. The way, of course, is *through stories*.

As Antonio Damasio says in *Self Comes to Mind*, "The problem of how to make all of this wisdom understandable, transmissible, persuasive, enforceable — in a word, of how to make it stick — was faced and a solution found. Storytelling was the solution — storytelling is something brains do, naturally and implicitly. Implicit storytelling has created our selves, and it should be no surprise that it pervades the entire fabric of human societies and cultures." We are composed of more than carbon and oxygen. *We are composed of our stories.*

Storytelling Animals

All our lives are centered on story. Author Jonathan Gottschall calls us "storytelling animals." If we stopped to consider the time we give to story each day, I suspect we would find we agree with him. We are immersed in story. With the help of tech-savvy media, our stories have become ever-present, ever-complicated. We watch TV, including reality TV shows. We play video games based on story. We create our stories or watch the stories of others on YouTube videos, Hulu, Twitter, and Facebook. On blogs we readily share our inner experiences.

Remember Walter Mitty, the Thurber character who lived in his daydreams? Maybe his life is closer to our reality than we know. Think of our interaction with stories each day. We daydream about getting a bagel and coffee at our favorite spot before our feet even hit the floor in the morning. While working we recall a fight we had with our spouse or friend and wonder how to resolve it. When in a meeting or classroom, we might remember that it is taco day in the cafeteria, and soon we are playing out the entire scenario. We have about two thousand daydreams a day, and each one lasts only fourteen seconds. In other words, we spend about a third of our time scripting our fantasies. Even our sleep can be interrupted by our attempts to create stories that will solve our problems. Last night during a dinner out, our friend Ed told us that at 2:00 AM he awoke and was mentally in the midst of an argument he recently had with his boss. "I kept replaying our talk, and I was ending it in different ways." At that moment I realized that I had been awakened early that same morning by my husband, and I was in the midst of a dream where I was in my bed, buried by a landslide of papers for this book. I was trying to dig my way out. Even our dreams are captured in story form — complete with characters and conflicts.

Our Brains Speak in Story

As mythologist Joseph Campbell pointed out, when we examine folklore and myths from ancient cultures, it becomes clear that human beings have used story to understand themselves since the beginning of time. Campbell liked to teach that we could find universal story patterns across cultures. In his book *The Hero with a Thousand Faces*, he established the existence of the "universal hero pattern." *Star Wars* creator George Lucas and dozens of other writers have studied and used Campbell's pattern in their films. The reason is that this pattern rings true for all of us. We map it over and over in our minds from the time we are children playing at being Princess Elsa or Spiderman.

At a workshop at the Omega Institute, author Cheryl Strayed explained that her memoir followed this well-known pattern. "In writing *Wild* I realized I was writing the old hero journey. There are about ten mythic stories that we love — and we keep telling them over and over. Our individual story is what makes them unique.... My story was centered on the loss of my mother. At the core of my writing are these questions: How can we live with loss? How can we live with the unbearable? How can we accept our suffering?" After the death of her mother, Strayed began to unravel. In her memoir, *Wild: from Lost to Found on the Pacific Crest Trail*, the author's challenging hike can be easily aligned with the stages of the classic hero journey.

I bet we can recognize the structure. It begins with a hero or main character who we connect with because in some way he or she is like us. Strayed is an "everyman" — or in her case, an "everywoman," because she is genuinely someone with whom we can identify in her books as well as in person. She is completely open about the setbacks she has faced — her drug use as well as her mom's death.

In the hero's journey the heroic character is called to do something. In Strayed's case she had an intuition that she needed to hike the Pacific Crest Trail. Campbell explains that though the heroic character may initially resist the challenge, she or he eventually undertakes it. While planning her trip, Strayed wavered, uncertain if she could pull off the hike. Slowly she saved money and began to spend time at REI talking to experienced hikers and making needed purchases. Often there is a mentor, teacher, or friend to help a hero undergo the tests, challenges, and ordeals that must be faced. When she began her trek, Strayed was initially overwhelmed by the difficulties of the weather, the weight of her backpack, and her fears about the animals on the trail. But she met Doug and other hikers who supported her. Their encouragement gave her a profound sense of community that drove her forward, against difficult odds, to complete her goal.

In the end, Campbell explains, the protagonist overcomes the obstacles and is rewarded. The reward is not always material. It may be inner growth and wisdom, but the important piece here is that the character becomes "heroic." As casual as Cheryl was in talking about completing her hike, pulling her life back together, and moving forward to become a writer, it was easy to view her as a hero. But even more impressive when I talked with her was how down-to-earth she had remained amid the flurry around her book and the resulting movie. She gave the sense that if she can do it, then so can we. "You must be willing to take your own journey," she explained. "You must find the stories within you."

Throughout human evolution, story, with its universal pattern, has been mapped in our brains over and over. We find it in novels, Broadway plays, songs, poems, in artworks, in blogs, on Facebook pages, and even in TED Talks; we see the pattern and the traditional elements that help us make sense of story. We find *characters* who struggled with difficulties or *conflicts* in various *settings*. The *plot* centers on actions taken to overcome the conflict, and when these actions reach a peak, or *climax*, usually the trouble unwinds or reaches a *resolution*. What we learn, or the kernel of meaning, is called the *theme*. These elements of stories do not thrive just in literature. They thrive in our heads. They help us create our stories and share them with others. Just as Strayed's trek up the Pacific Crest Trail has come to define her, the personal stories we choose come to define us. But we don't have to be bestselling writers. We don't have to walk a thousand miles. We only have to find our own story, write or rewrite it when it falls apart, and move forward to meet our own calling. And in doing this, we discover our personal myth — our unique story.

The Stories We Choose Define Us

In reviewing my journals I realized the power of story as well as the power of writing my story. I had come to my personal writing to face the shattered moments in my life. To survive them. I discovered all the broken moments of my past — my dance with depression, my struggle with a disabled student, the death of my brother, my cancer, followed by my son's cancer — and as I finish writing I have just faced the death of my dear dad. These were difficult stories and not easy to reframe or rewrite. But I did it. On these pages I struggled with these events in all their glorious and traumatizing detail. Here my brain maps were rewired. Reworked. Reframed. Here I found the courage to swim up and out of the trough of life, where we often find ourselves stuck. Reworking my hard stories gave me the life I know. A much better life.

Imagine that we are on the beach at night, as I was with my dad all those years ago. If it is clear outside, lie down on the ground and look up at the stars. And wonder. Where did we come from?

"Twinkle twinkle little star...how I wonder what you are."

This is my two-year-old granddaughter's favorite song, and for good reason. It calls to mind questions that can't be answered. She is still dazzled by the wonder of the stars. She has not paused to ask her dad where she came from yet. But she will. And her dad will have stories to help her face the unknown. Our brains have latched on to stories to help us answer the questions of living that must be answered.

And later I will slip a journal into my granddaughter's hands. And I will encourage her to make sense of her stories — of her life — in words.

Stories Answer Our Questions

One summer morning when I was eleven or twelve, my younger brother and I were supposed to be cleaning the kitchen while Mom weeded the garden. As Charley washed the dishes, he started telling a string of jokes — *blonde jokes*, which I hated because I was blonde. As I scrubbed the counter, I eyed an open carton of eggs. "If you don't stop with the jokes, I am going to egg you!" I announced.

"Be my guest," my brother said, certain I would never toss eggs at him. "Two blondes fell down a hole." He continued to torture me. "The first one said, 'It's dark, isn't it?' The other replied, 'I don't know; I can't see.'" He froze when he saw the egg spiraling through the air in his direction.

For my part, it was a wimpy toss. Stunned, Charley caught it and returned it to the carton. Just then I threw a fastball egg. He caught it, too, but in his grab he crushed it. Egg oozed from his hand. I hardly noticed, for at this point I had visions of Wilt Chamberlain in my head. I had taken a hook shot and an egg flew toward Charley, who ducked. It smashed into the wall behind him. Feeling the sweet taste of victory, I shot another. Bull's-eye. I hit him smack in the heart. That did it. Charley snatched the carton of eggs, and he launched his first pitch in my direction.

I sidestepped it. We heard the splat on the wall in the same moment we heard the back door bang open. Mom appeared.

We froze. She wiped her hair from her sweaty brow and eyed us critically. "Hmm." She could see smashed egg on the wall, the eggy mess on my brother, and the incriminating eggs in his hands. "You have one job," she said calmly but sternly as she looked from Charley to me. That is all she had to say. We got it. She had told us millions of times, with a Ping-Pong paddle in hand, that our job as her children was *to be good.* The final image I have of this incident is of Charley and me scrubbing the dishes, the counter, the walls, and the kitchen floor as if world peace depended on it. We *never* tossed eggs again — or anything else, for that matter.

My midwestern parents had made the rules about being good clear to my brothers and me. Every Sunday we were up early to sit in the sixth or seventh row at the Southport Methodist Church, where dozens of Bible stories reinforced my mom's credo. After church was Sunday school, where we read and discussed the stories of Moses and the Ten Commandments, Jesus and the Good Samaritan, and dozens of other tales — over and over. And after that came the best part. We raced downstairs, often slipping on the linoleum floor of the fellowship hall, where we could smell the Folgers coffee brewing. There we lined up and dropped dimes in the basket and retrieved our prize, a doughnut. (I preferred the sticky glazed ones.)

These church stories stuck and answered many important questions for me. I was not consciously aware of how powerful they were until years later, during one particular moment. It was third period, right before lunch. I know because I remember my stomach growling.

I had assigned my students to read the only Bible story in our literature text. Suddenly, like the shock that might come of touching a doorknob, I understood this parable in a profoundly new way. In it Jesus describes the dilemma of a father with two sons. The older son is obedient and hardworking; the younger son, not so much. The younger son asks his father in advance for his share of the inheritance. When he receives it, the foolish son travels far away, parties, and squanders it all. When the money is gone, he ends up feeding pigs. One day, in desperation, he swallows his pride, returns home, and admits to his dad he has been a fool.

The father is thrilled and throws a party for the son. When the older son learns of the celebration, he is angry. "How could you do this?" he asks his father.

The father answers, "All my things are yours. But it is right to celebrate for your brother was lost...and now he is found."

After we read this story, my high school seniors debated the meaning. They questioned and struggled with it.

"Why in the world would a father make a big deal over the son who was a jerk?" Alex asked, scratching the back of his head.

"Yeah," added Julie. "It is confusing. Are they celebrating the kid's failure?" I thought about it. As a youngster, I had struggled with this story and also found it perplexing. But now I was a parent — and I got it. I bit my lip, waiting for the students to unravel the magic of the prodigal son.

Finally, soft-spoken Wendy leaned forward to speak. "But the love of this parent is unconditional. He is happy to see his son come home to be a part of his family. Who is to say? Perhaps the foolish son will learn from this and change."

At the time I was raising two boys. While one of my sons questioned and butted heads with his teachers, with his father, and with me, the other son seemed to observe and learn how to navigate the world without such conflicts. While one son was challenging to raise, the other was effortless. Yet the wellspring of love that I felt for both of our sons was endless.

A couple thousand years ago, an itinerant, brilliant storyteller shared the story of the prodigal son on a mountainside. The story was retold, handed down, written down. Then Sunday school teachers shared it repeatedly with me when I was young.

And when I taught it myself, I found the story to be a part of who I was. A life story. With this tale embedded implicitly in my brain maps, I had automatically understood something important about parenting. One can have two incredibly different children, and it is possible to be filled with unending love and wonder for both. No matter what.

Story Characters Create Personal Character

We are all composed of these guiding stories. We are also made up of personal stories that come from our families and our experiences. My egg-tossing story is a personal tale that shows I was experimenting in how to stand up for me. In these stories we become our own main character, or protagonist. The important questions for us are: What kind of character are you or will you become? How can you be good? Should you be good? What are *your* answers?

There are stories and characters that we connect with as children. They change us and help us define and understand who we are. Looking back, I realized I collected stories and characters from more than just my parents, my church, and my school. I often learned from the characters in the books I read, fiction and nonfiction. I learned to be inquisitive from the dozens of Nancy Drew mysteries; to care about others, even the strange ones, from Scout and Atticus Finch in *To Kill a Mockingbird*; to try to be a strong and independent woman from Harriett Tubman, Anne Frank, Helen Keller, Maya Angelou, and Rosa Parks; to understand the significance and beauty in service from the stories of Dr. Tom Dooley and Eleanor Roosevelt; to control my own thoughts regardless of the circumstances from the concentration camp experiences of Elie Wiesel and Viktor Frankl; to follow my bliss from the books of Joseph Campbell; and to have a dream from Martin Luther King Jr. Their thoughts were translated into my own story, my own way of viewing the world.

We continually add new heroic characters to our lexicon —

Nelson Mandela, Malala Yousafzai, Pope Francis, Oprah, and even the fictional Harry Potter are some more recent choices. Their behavior impacts our behavior. The characters we integrate into our lives matter. They affect who we become. And writing about them solidifies who we are and who we are slated to become.

Stories Teach Us to Solve Problems

While we learn *who to be* from characters, we learn *how to be* from the conflicts in stories. "I don't go looking for trouble," says Harry Potter. "Trouble usually finds me." Harry Potter, one of the most endearing characters of recent time, reminds us that his story, like all stories, revolves around trouble.

We tend to be most intrigued by the obstacles or problems in a story, especially ones with conflicts that we can connect to our personal struggles. Janet Burroway, author of *Imaginative Writing: The Elements of Craft*, points out that to understand literature we usually study a story's conflict, crisis, and resolution. Burroway writes, "This model acknowledges that, in literature, only trouble is interesting. *Only* trouble is interesting."

In *How the Mind Works*, Steven Pinker explains that our minds use stories from literature because they allow us to watch fictitious characters pursuing their goals in the face of obstacles. Pinker claims that as we observe them, we mentally take notes on what works and what doesn't as these characters struggle. Our stories are by nature problem-solving tools, and we are problem-solving beings.

Harry Potter's ongoing saga includes endless conflicts. In looking through the Potter peephole, we find his parents have been murdered and that Harry has been forced to live in a cupboard under the stairs, cruelly mistreated by his relatives. When Harry discovers he is a wizard and is allowed to attend Hogwarts School of Witchcraft and Wizardry, *his* hero journey begins. In his first year at Hogwarts, Harry and Ron Weasley attack a troll and prevent it from killing fellow student Hermione Granger. Out of this trouble a powerful friendship is born. But friends can't protect Harry from the challenges that beset him. In addition to the normal teenage struggles, Harry has to face being constantly stalked by the evil Lord Voldemort, who killed his parents and nearly killed Harry as a baby. While Potter is not a willing hero, he meets the call by facing these ongoing travails — be it doing battle with Lord Voldemort to protect the Sorcerer's Stone, or entering the Chamber of Secrets to rescue Ron's sister, or facing an epic battle of good and evil that results in both pain and loss. Through it all, Harry teaches us how to face our struggles. He displays courage and resilience. *And* he shows us how to hold on and move on.

While the Harry Potter books started as children's stories, they have become universally accepted as mainstream hero literature. Other children's stories are equally replete with full-blown conflicts. Disney's children's movies, from *Cinderella* to *Frozen*, contain profound human dilemmas. The heroines must be tested and must rise above their challenges. Against the wishes of the wicked stepmother, Cinderella makes it to the ball and into the heart of the prince. The lovely Queen Elsa in *Frozen* cannot stop freezing what she touches. But with unending support from her sister, Anna, Elsa proves to be resilient and learns how to live with her handicap — which eventually comes to be her gift.

Think about the nursery rhymes that have been handed down from generation to generation. Many of these little songs were attempts at helping children face death, violence, and even war. "Ring around the Rosie" centers on the plagues from the Middle Ages. Children were singing about how "they all fall down" because people were dying all around them. In both "Jack and Jill" and "Humpty Dumpty," the main characters crack their heads open, showing us how easy it is to get knocked down in this world. A more modern version of Humpty Dumpty, which I found in my granddaughter's pile of books, frames a Humpty

Dumpty that bravely puts his pieces back together and climbs back up on his wall. Like the "Itsy Bitsy Spider," this Humpty teaches us to move forward and solve our own problems.

Modern writers continue the tradition of weaving tales into our psyche. In his novel *The Kite Runner*, Khaled Hosseini captured the heart-twisting story of friendship between a wealthy Afghani boy and the son of his father's servant, a tale told against the devastating backdrop of the past thirty years in Afghanistan. The novel explores the pain of betrayal in friendship as well as the hope for redemption that can carry us forward. Equally staggering is the real-life story author Laura Hillenbrand gives us in *Unbroken*. Although in boyhood Louis Zamperini had been a delinquent, his life takes dramatic turns that grip the reader. With the start of World War II, Zamperini became an airman, and after a doomed flight that leaves him stranded in the ocean, he is forced on a harrowing journey to survive.

In *The Storytelling Animal*, Jonathan Gottschall outlines how our minds make use of story. First, stories focus on a variety of predicaments and struggles that we face in living, struggles that cycle around love, sex, power, death — unending challenges. Gottschall writes, "I think that problem structure reveals a major function of storytelling. It suggests that the human mind was shaped *for* story, so that it could be shaped *by* story." Story teaches us how to be ethical or good, but equally important, our stories help us learn how to face the myriad of problems that beset us. Stories teach us, when we are about to crash-land, to hold on tight. We can survive.

The important thread for us as writers links back to the hero's journey. It is not an easy job to undertake the challenges given to us. We are not all asked to take a thousand-mile trek up the Pacific Crest Trail. We are not all expected to save a school from an evil wizard. But we are all called to take *our journey*. Regardless of the level of risk or the calling, it is going to be hard. We will sometimes be sucked into the undercurrent. Cheryl Strayed was sucked under. So was Harry Potter. But we can follow their lead. We can wade through it. And writing is one of the best tools we have as we undertake our journey.

The Flight-Simulator Theory

Remember the heroism of Chuck Pyeatt and Chesley Sullenberger? Both landed planes without a hitch in the most difficult of situations. Both trained for literally hundreds of hours on flight simulators in the air force and later with their commercial carriers. Flight-simulator training was easy to measure by simply looking at the proficiency of the pilots after their training.

The work of psychologist Keith Oatley shows us that stories work the same way — as training instruments to help us navigate our problems. Oatley argues that we use our own experience to figure out what others are doing or thinking, and that literature works in the same way. Characters we encounter in stories offer us insights into how other people survive hardships. A few months ago, when I read a book on Lincoln and learned the power of writing letters in the heat of an argument — in his case with a general — and not sending them, I internalized Lincoln's behavior. Recently when my parents were robbed by a caregiver, I wrote an email to the responsible home-care agency that would make the earth shake. In rereading my correspondence, even I was surprised. Fortunately, I did not send it.

Oatley's metaphor, that our stories are "the flight simulators of human social life," is perfect. When we hear or read stories, we travel through the experiences in the same way that a pilot travels through a flight on a simulator. We watch characters face difficult situations and overcome them. We feel what they are feeling. Just as pilots internalize their "pretend" travels, we internalize our journeys through stories.

When I first taught *Hamlet* as a young teacher, I was nervous. It was a tough piece to read. How could I teach it? And then the story unexpectedly ripped into my brain maps. Powerfully.

When I read Hamlet's internal dialogue, and discovered his ethical struggles, I realized I often spent too much time thinking and rethinking ethical dilemmas. I was often indecisive — or a bit of a Hamlet.

This realization was shoved into my face as I reread old journals from my early teaching years. Painful, wishy-washy sloshing around. Sometimes I was trapped in the what-to-do more than doing. But through the years I can see in my journals that I learned to rewrite how I thought.

A few years ago I had a troubled boss, and when I was applying for another job, she opened my correspondence, broke into a confidential survey I did on her, and repeatedly called me into her office to harangue me. I loved my work, my peers, and the program I was building, but I knew what the right decision would be. When I left, my husband noted, "You are not the Hamlet you used to be." And he was right, for my journal was the proving ground where I can see this change.

When my son Matt was a teen, he was a live wire of hormones who questioned all adults. In navigating my life with an adolescent, I relied on my explicit memory, or what I consciously knew from studying and working with teenagers, but my mind was also deeply encoded with stories and the implicit or unconscious learning garnered from them. Tales such as the prodigal son grounded me as a parent. Indeed, the flight-simulator theory shows us that with realistic practice we can be better prepared to handle our challenges. Our stories become our teachers.

Becoming Storycatchers

"Every person is born into life as a blank page — and every person leaves life as a full book," says Christina Baldwin. In *Storycatcher* Baldwin traces her personal tales to show us how to make sense of our lives through story. We need stories to answer our questions, to show us how to face our difficulties, and to help us find who we are and where we are headed. The stories we hold inside create our being, our self, and by working to become storycatchers, we ground and enrich our lives.

> *Our stories embody our answers on how to live,*
> *how to become the character we want to become,*
> *and how to solve the problems we encounter.*

Writing Prompts and Suggestions

These prompts will help you to connect with stories, characters, and human characteristics that influence your life.

Writing Prompt: Character Search

Choose a character you connected with from learning or reading — as a child, as a teen, or as an adult. How did you discover this character? What did you have in common with this character? What did you admire about her? What experiences of this individual allowed you to feel a connection to him? Explain.

Writing Prompt: Story Search

Make a list of the stories you remember from your childhood. Write a quick summary of a story you loved. Then explore it. Why did you connect with this nursery rhyme, fable, folktale, book, or movie? What intrigued you about it? What did you learn from it?

Writing Prompt: The Hero Search

Describe a person or character you believe is heroic. This person can be someone you know or wish you knew. This character can be real or fictional. Describe the individual's heroic story. What qualities make him or her heroic in your eyes?

What qualities make someone heroic? What qualities do you have that you hope will contribute to your own hero story? Explore this.

CHAPTER NINE

Finding Our
Life-Defining Stories

If you don't know the trees you may be lost in the forest,
but if you don't know the stories you may be lost in life.
— Siberian elder

"Adam, are you ready?" I called. We had agreed to stop for doughnuts before we made the mad dash to the high school that morning. A foreign exchange student from South Africa, Adam had lived with us for a semester now. He came to us through a local service club when his original sponsor, Mrs. Thomas, wanted Adam reassigned after only two weeks, claiming he was *simply odd.* This was a phrase Adam had heard her use in phone calls as she arranged for his move, a phrase that cut deeply.

Adam was a student in my writing class, a polite, intelligent young man, so when a counselor stopped me in the lunchroom to ask if I could sponsor him, I said, "Sure." When I checked with Steve that evening, he was totally onboard. Our son Zach had just headed off to college, and we agreed it was eerily quiet in the house. Another young voice would be nice.

When I asked Adam about what had happened the next day, he looked as if I had smacked him hard in the face. "I was

113

evicted," he said and then awkwardly tried to choke out a laugh, but the hurt emanated from him like heat radiating off a tar road.

In the third week of his senior year, Adam moved into our home, along with two beat-up suitcases and his clarinet. That afternoon as he unpacked, he scrubbed down Zach's old desk with the Wet Ones he toted everywhere. Then he set up his books neatly, organized by subjects. After dinner that night he pulled out his clarinet and meticulously shined it. When he finished, he asked if he could play it. In the coming months he played his clarinet endlessly, and we never tired of it. He had a gift.

Often Adam would ask Steve how Wi-Fi worked or grill him about the latest computer gadgets. Together they found parts in the garage and hooked up Zach's old computer. Adam had never had access to Google before, and he was hooked.

Since Adam was in my class, I knew before the move that he was a bit awkward and clearly had a few eccentricities — a fear of germs and a hatred of alarm clocks. But he was also witty, polite, and fascinated by all things American. Especially deep-fried dough immersed in sugar. The doughnut.

Four months into his stay with us, we had an agreement. When he didn't have morning band practice, we would try to leave early to indulge in the ooey-gooey American confections Adam so loved. He was already discussing the possibility of opening a doughnut shop when he returned to Cape Town.

As I waited for him, I rummaged through the bathroom drawer and found my set of school keys. I tossed them in my purse and grabbed my comb, running it through my hair one last time. First day back after semester break. First-day jitters.

"Adam!" I called again. Suddenly he appeared in my bathroom mirror. Seventeen. Barely awake. Vulnerable. Adam stood bedraggled in a rumpled white undershirt and *Simpsons*-character flannels. He ran his hand through his thick tufts of shaggy blond hair. He was not ready for the doughnut run, and his troubled cocoa-colored eyes cut a path through my brain.

He almost never asked for my attention. But at this moment he tilted his head to the right — a habit that signaled I needed to be in the moment. With him. All time stopped.

"Ms. M., I spent the night on Google, and I have something I need to tell you." I did not move. I did not breathe. "I know what is wrong with me now — and I am more than *simply odd*." For all the months he had lived in our home, Adam had been unable to stop ruminating about his expulsion from the Thomases' house. "I have obsessive compulsive disorder." While the words seemed stuck or glued in his throat, once he said them, he released a long, deep sigh as if his secret was out. "OCD. My brain gets stuck. I think it is…*broken*."

And I still can see his face, with the sad dipped line of his mouth, and I can feel the power of his admission as it sliced into my gut. Adam had a disorder.

By now Adam had seeped into our lives. While he was not my son, he had become like a son. Steve and I cared about him. And by now I understood there was a phantom chasing him. As his substitute mom, I could *feel* it but not pin it down. He was troubled. He had struggled with conversations that would play over and over in his mind — like the words he had heard Mrs. Thomas utter on the phone before he was reassigned to live with us.

Often, after we realized that he had OCD, Adam would sit at the kitchen bar doing homework while I made dinner, and we would chat about his struggle with a brain that moved in unstoppable cycles. Washing hands. Fighting germs. Doing math. Practicing music. Through the years he had done his best to house this phantom in silence, afraid to share it. But it would slip out. His mom knew about it. An elementary school teacher had asked him, *Why do you wash your hands all the time?* During middle school his English teacher wanted to know, *Why do you ask so many questions?* And the cop who brought him to our home in a police car one school night that past autumn wanted to know,

*Why is he marching around like he's doing some kind of routine? Over
and over?*

When the world slept, Adam could not. His phantom kept
him awake, recycling music, math, ideas. He would finger the
notes to the school band routines over and over. He knew them
cold. When he couldn't sleep one night, he slipped out the bedroom window, only a few yards from the street in our cul-de-sac.
Since it was late, he decided to walk around the block practicing
the high school band's entire Hollywood Blockbuster routine for
that fall. To avoid waking up the world, he fingered the routine
with an imaginary clarinet. He often practiced this way. Silently.
Over and over. When Steve and I did our own Google quest,
we learned that this is how OCD, obsessive compulsive disorder,
works. You do things over and over — until forced to stop. And
he was forced to stop that night when the neighborhood cop saw
him marching endlessly around the block and hauled him to our
front door at 2 AM.

We all have defining stories that help us understand who we
are. They are turning points, key events that change us. "The Boy
Before the Mirror" is one such story — for Adam, for his family, and certainly for me. Adam's neurological disorder had to be
faced. He had come to America with the hope that he would be
free of it. But he was not. Instead, with his newfound ability to
research via Google, he discovered a name as well as an explanation for what troubled him. After he told me, we contacted
his parents. Caring and supportive, they encouraged us to move
ahead with counseling and any needed professional help. And we
did. The long journey to help Adam navigate the challenges of
his disability had begun.

Know Yourself

I watched Adam's journey with growing respect for a young man
with the courage to examine himself, to accept his limitations
with clear eyes, and to do all he could to work through them. As

a mother of two boys, I empathized with his parents, who had to come to peace with the fact that their son had a disorder and that such disabilities were quite common; in fact, they silently surround us. Would I have been able to embrace such an understanding of my sons? My experience with Adam was enlightening, humbling, and rewarding.

After Adam accepted the fact that he had OCD, he told me his favorite classroom discussion in our English class had centered on the quotes of Socrates. "And the best thing he ever said," Adam explained as we chatted at the kitchen bar, "was *know yourself.*" Adam was already moving forward with his newfound self-knowledge.

With threads of these conversations echoing in the recesses of my brain, and long before I faced my cancer, I made an appointment with my physician. At that time genetic testing for cancer was new, and I wanted to see if I carried the BRCA1 and BRCA2 genetic mutation. My aunt had died of breast cancer when she was young, and my mom had recently experienced her second bout with the disease; twenty years after she lost her first breast, she lost her remaining one. It looked like I might be genetically predisposed to this disease.

"You don't want this testing," my then doctor insisted. "What are you going to do? If you have this gene mutation, are you going to sit around and worry?" I didn't argue with her, but I was unsettled by her response. I wanted the information.

A few years later, the first thing my breast cancer surgeon asked was, "Why haven't you had genetic testing for the BRCA1 and BRCA2 mutations?" By now most of us know we are far more likely (55 to 65 percent) to develop breast cancer if we have it.

Dr. Liu sent me immediately to be tested, and I learned that I did not have the mutation. That evening I was able to call my kids and report this finding with great joy. My first granddaughter had been born recently, and I was thrilled I could not have passed this mutation to her.

It turns out that information and knowledge *are good for us.* Folk singer Woody Guthrie died of complications from Huntington's disease when he was only fifty-five. The symptoms for this disease usually show up in people who are in their thirties or forties. It causes nerve degeneration in the brain and ends life in middle age. Guthrie had a 50 percent chance of getting it because his mother had it. But he had no way of knowing. No knowledge.

Today if one of our parents had Huntington's disease, we could take a test that could tell us if we had inherited the gene that triggers this terrible disease. Would it help to know? It would. Research solidly supports this.

In one well-known study of young adults who had a 50 percent risk of getting Huntington's disease, the information was beneficial to their happiness. Participants, who willingly took the genetic test, completed measures of psychological well-being before they knew the results, immediately after they received the results, and again six months later and one year later. Initially participants who discovered that they would get the disease were devastated. Those who received the good news showed far less stress and depression. But as time progressed something surprising was discovered: at both the six-month and one-year points, those who knew they would face early deaths were no more depressed than the disease-free participants. In time those with the bad prognosis had adjusted and their measures of well-being showed they were just as happy as their more fortunate peers.

Even more impressive are the findings from a third group. Individuals who refused to take the test or did not receive conclusive test results demonstrated significantly lower well-being after one year. In sum, those who had been assured they would get the disease and die early were better adjusted and happier than those who did not know whether they had the gene. Follow-up studies have confirmed this finding. The old phrase is *knowledge is power.* In this case, knowledge is well-being, even happiness.

When we have information that helps us to understand ourselves, we can adapt and work with it. We can make changes and realign our personal narratives. By knowing ourselves, we can re-write and re-create our stories in ways that allow us to lead better lives.

Our Lives Hang on Our Narratives

Our lives hang on a narrative thread. Life stories, especially defining moments, give us important self-knowledge. They are critical if we want greater understanding in our search for well-being. As we mature we create our identity by selecting these experiences to map out who we are. Our world is shaped by the stories we tell ourselves — what we believe about our lives and what we hold to be true about our world.

"The Boy Before the Mirror" was a narrative that would change Adam as well as me. Together we talked with the school psychologist and arranged for counseling. Adam began going regularly to a psychotherapist, and I was invited to the initial visits to get a handle on how to help Adam.

Now as I peer back through time at this experience, it becomes clear to me that *we choose the stories that define us.* We choose the stories that matter to us. If an event is troubling, we can realize it is a story that needs work. We can unravel it and knit it back together. Adam began the work of discovering that his ability to focus intently on music and math was not simply a disability. It could lead him to a fulfilling future — and it has done exactly that.

Finding the Stories We Need to Tell

We are tellers of tales that can lead us to self-understanding. Our stories can perplex and confuse us, but if we are willing to find them, know them, and work with them, they can lead us to our hopes, our truth, and what holds meaning for us. But how do we find these life-defining stories? There are many paths to our narratives, among them friends, counseling, and of course, our writing.

Friends often help us find our way through the rugged terrain of story. Becca certainly helped Adam. As a fellow classmate, Becca started driving Adam home after school that fall. She often lingered for dinner and homework. Becca had a low, warm laugh that danced in the air and always punctuated Adam's wit. As the year rolled on, I would hear them talking quietly at the kitchen bar. When Adam began seeing a psychotherapist, he revealed pieces of his stories to Becca, and she would listen, as any good friend would. She cared and remained nonjudgmental. At my local independent bookstore, I had found a used copy of a book called *Brain Lock: Free Yourself from Obsessive Compulsive Behavior*. After I read it, I gave it to Adam, but he ignored it until Becca picked it up from the kitchen bar one night. In the coming weeks they read sections from the book, marked it up, and talked about it. Adam was consciously reworking his understanding of his OCD and how to manage it.

As Adam began talking regularly with a psychotherapist, I was delighted with the outcome. Adam walked a little straighter now, and I never heard him mention the Thomas house travesty again. While he continued to practice his music obsessively, there were no more late-night music sessions. On the rare mornings when we made it to the doughnut shop, Adam joked more and seemed rested. I believe he was busy rewriting his understanding of who he was in ways that would allow him to sleep at night and to grow in self-understanding.

Initially I was caught off guard by my experience with Adam. While I had embraced the idea of sponsoring a foreign exchange student, I had failed to understand that Adam was in the throes of a teenage identity crisis. At first I felt troubled and confused about how to parent him, but in our talks and with the support of our school psychologist and my journal, I found my way. I am incredibly thankful that Mrs. Thomas released Adam and that he came into our home, where he became a heart-warming, life-changing experience for our family. His story is a life chapter that I can relive when I reread the pages of my old journals. Amid those scribbles I discovered how to help Adam move ahead and how to remain engaged as a wife, a mother, a curious person, and a full-time teacher with late-night essays to grade.

From the blue-green plumed journal that held my notes about this period, I discovered how writing or sharing our stories allows us to define and understand who we are. And, if we let them, these stories can redefine us. We can reframe and recast our lives — not with lies, not with deceptions, but with the truth of who we are and of who we are choosing to become. I have done this. And I watched with wonder as Adam did it, too.

Our life-defining stories matter.
We need to find them and tell them — or write them.

Writing Prompts and Suggestions

Let's begin by exploring various pathways to writing about our lives. Get comfortable, and plan to spend at least twenty minutes engaged in any one of these activities. Choose the activity that fits you. If any single pathway leads to a wave of writing, ride the experience and let the stories unfold. If you hit a roadblock and the words dry up, move to a different prompt. Your goal is to find and begin the process of telling some significant life stories or to explore your personal life-defining experiences.

Okay. Get comfortable. Sift through your experiences. Dig deep. What stories have made you the person you are? What moments should be fully woven into the narrative that is you? What stories will define who you are and who you can become?

Writing Prompt:
Finding Our Life Chapters

When I reviewed my journals, my life unfolded in chapters that could easily be summarized. With or without a journal, you can begin the process of finding your defining stories by making a simple list of the main chapters of your life. Here is the beginning of my list:

- Childhood in Indiana
- Living in England
- Southport High School and friendships
- Purdue — new ideas, new friends
- Discovering community service — tutoring, teaching

The chapters do not have to be chronological. They can be listed thematically, as feelings, values, or even a mix of these. After you make a list, you may want to *briefly* summarize each period. As you do this, look for the events that were significant turning points in your life. What moments changed you?

In *The Stories We Live By: Personal Myths and the Making of the Self*, scholar Dan P. McAdams suggests identifying chapters but focusing on *specific events in detail*. He suggests that you tap into:

- peak experiences
- low points
- turning points
- significant memories

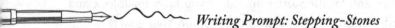

Writing Prompt: Stepping-Stones

Stepping-stones is one of the best-known activities for helping you to find your stories. It was developed by the late Ira Progoff, a psychotherapist who devised the Intensive Journal Method. While helping others search for an understanding of their experiences, Progoff suggested they "spontaneously reflect" on the course of their life and list the significant moments. "The Stepping-stones," he explained, "are the significant points of movement along the road of an individual's life." These markers can help you see the big picture of who you are. They allow you to reconnect with events that define you.

The process is easy. You make a list of seven or eight life experiences — or more, but no more than twelve. Place them in chronological order and read them aloud. Then explore each event in writing. Do any themes or threads keep reappearing to teach you something about yourself? You may need time to digest your markers. If so, come back to the list later and find one or more of the experiences that you need to explore in depth. Write about this event or time period in as much specific detail as you can: What happened? What do you remember? Who is a part of this story? What did you experience? What did you learn? Pour it all out to see what you can find.

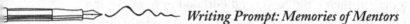 *Writing Prompt: Memories of Mentors*

Another way of finding our defining stories is by rummaging through memories of significant people in our lives. Who are the teachers, friends, relatives, or mentors who changed you? Make a list, and see what memories surface for you.

I wrote down James Fulcher, my high school humanities teacher. Out of curiosity I went back and thumbed through the journal I kept in his classroom. While his lectures dominate my notes, what I remember most are the open-ended questions that he raised and asked us to write about: *Why do we create? What is happiness? Does being ethical lead to being happy? Why do we fight wars when they devastate lives and cultures?*

Explore the significant individuals who have mattered in your life. What did you learn from each of them? How did they change or influence you?

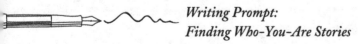 *Writing Prompt:*
Finding Who-You-Are Stories

The goal here is to tap into your stories. While you don't need to do all these activities, you do need to find the ones that will help you shine a light on who you are. Defining experiences can grant you a renewed understanding of yourself. They can help reframe who you are and help you grow.

Create your own ways of finding these stories. Recently, when my first grandchild was born, my sons and their wives were digging through the family albums. They wanted to know, *Who does the baby look like?* Before long we were crowded around the kitchen bar telling old and treasured family stories.

- *Photo search.* The photos in albums, on phones, and in the cloud can resurrect dozens of meaningful experiences. Dig through them. Write about the stories that surface.

- *Map search.* Do you want your story-tapping brain to take over? In working with students who claim to be stuck or unable to remember their past, I often ask them to draw a map of their childhood neighborhood or to map out a place they love and visit often. These maps rarely disappoint, for they transport you back into your experiences.

- *Create your own search with songs, games, blogs, trips...* Do you center your life on music and song? You may want to dig through the songs that have held special meaning for you. Many moments in our lives can be dated and recalled by the music we heard at a concert or hummed for days in our head. What games have you played? When? Do you play games endlessly on your phone or Xbox? Do you have memories of playing Monopoly with your cousins or marbles with a childhood friend? Maps, trip itineraries, Facebook pages, old CDs or albums, artworks, cell phone or family photos, journals or a blog you keep — all are a treasure trove of memories.

CHAPTER TEN

Making Sense of Self with Stories

Writing a story or a novel is one way of discovering sequence in experience, of stumbling upon cause and effect in the happenings of a writer's own life.

— Eudora Welty

At age fifteen Liam had dropped out of school and withdrawn from his friends. When his mother, Penny, came across his journal, she was already seriously concerned about him. In it he wrote about how senseless life seemed. He had already taken steps toward suicide.

Distraught over her discovery, Penny called Michael White, the founder of narrative therapy. She explained that she and Liam had lived with an abusive husband and father for years. Recently Penny had taken her son and fled this nightmare. She hoped the change would help Liam, but so far it had not.

White arranged a session for the two of them on the pretext that Penny needed help and that Liam could help her. Liam agreed to come to counseling — but only for the sake of his mom. In their first session, White posed a number of open-ended questions. As White asked Penny about Liam, several amazing stories emerged. Once when his father was beating his mother, eight-year-old Liam threw a rock through the front window of their home. Surprised, his father stopped beating Penny and turned his wrath on his son. Even at a young age Liam had shown courage. Another story emerged from Penny's memory: at age six Liam had taken extra food to school for two kids without moms and for one child who was teased mercilessly. Then Penny recalled that recently Liam had talked with his teenage cousin, Vanessa. He told her about his abusive dad because he was afraid that she, too, was experiencing abuse. She was, but until this point she had been unable to admit it. Shortly after their talk, child protective services were called in to help Vanessa.

Making Sense of Self

Slowly White and Penny were able to help Liam reconnect with a few significant life stories that defined him as fair, brave, and courageous, and as someone who was consistently willing to reach out and help others. Liam's new understanding of himself — his ability to reframe his life story — made a huge difference. He began to find meaning. To live again. Before his next session with Michael, he had reconnected with his friend Daniel, reaching out to yet another friend who needed help.

We all have unique ways of coming to understand ourselves. When I headed off to college, I tried attending a church, but going to church did not sync with me as it had back home. My sense of self was bouncing around with unsettled stories. My brain cells could not cozy up to math equations. When my rat died in our psychology lab, I wondered if I was cut out for psychological research. Finally, I went to a call-out for tutors and ended up working with nine-year-old Rodney in the basement of an inner-city Presbyterian church. Teaching math and reading to this live-wire youngster grounded me again. I discovered the church of social service — and my story began to unfold in ways that made me love life again. I soon changed majors.

To create a personal myth, we have to be able to thread our narratives together in ways that make sense to us. We become uncomfortable when our personal stories seem out of whack or meaningless. When Liam could not make sense of his story, it needed to be realigned. When he rediscovered the good pieces of his life story, he found reasons to continue living. I discovered the same thing in the basement of the old church while at Purdue. Rat lab and calculus were not a part of my story. Ball-of-energy Rodney was.

Our stories have to ring true. Our personal myths cannot be woven of self-deception or delusion. They need to be constructed of the pieces that make the most sense to us. We need to discard the pieces that don't fit. To find our unique purpose and live with meaning, we have to create a narrative that embodies our personal story — and no one else's.

Untold Stories

In working with cancer patients, veterans, students, and writers, I have rediscovered one of Pennebaker's findings: that breaking the silence about our broken stories helps us to heal. These are, indeed, the stories we need to accept and tell. Once Adam was able to acknowledge what troubled him, he stretched and changed in positive ways, as did Liam. But sometimes discovering our stories is not easy. Often our painful stories are buried deep within us and remain there until something triggers a realization.

Shortly before my bout with cancer, I met Grace. One day in the workout room at school, I foolishly attempted a one-hundred-pound leg lift. It was no surprise that afterward my knee began to buckle as I walked. I tried to ignore it, but eventually I was assigned to work with Grace, an outstanding physical therapist. Her slender body, toned from yoga and early-morning jogs, made it clear she took her health seriously.

Equally wonderful, she valued the health of her patients. Grace taught me the discipline of working out individual muscles. Four weeks stretched to eight, and after I had my double mastectomy, I returned to do more rehab with her. She helped me learn to exercise and work my arm muscles back into shape.

All the while we chatted, me about my cancer, my son's cancer, and caring for older parents, and she about her two sons. When she told me about her struggle with her autistic son, I bought her a blue serenity journal. I was just starting to birth the idea for a book about writing and healing, and I hoped to introduce her to the power of writing to survive parenthood.

But Grace had already learned how to write her way through difficulty. "*I am drowning!*" she had penned in a gold journal she loaned to me a few weeks later as a way to tell me more about herself. "This is the place where I learned to stop burying my stories inside," she said to me the day she handed me the journal. "Instead I wrote them down in here." Inside the well-worn pages, I discovered her account of a barbed-wire year. Here Grace faced the institutional quagmire that often surrounds getting a child tested and placed in special education. This was a challenge she faced on her own because her husband had retreated into his default coping mechanism, alcoholism.

Autistic son. Alcoholic husband. That would be enough to deal with, but that is not what made me set down her journal and call her the day I read it. On these pages Grace had recounted how her father, a physician, had been diagnosed with terminal cancer. As Grace contemplated his upcoming death, she began to acknowledge the awkwardness of her relationship with him. In the midst of her conflicted thoughts, she wrote about an odd dream. In it she was young and she faced a man in a coffin who held a burning sword to her.

"When I wrote about that, I knew," she explained to me. As a child she had been molested by her father multiple times, and the memory of it had been buried in the deepest crevices of her brain. Suddenly it came pouring out.

"Did you unravel your own molestation on these pages?" I asked.

"Yes," Grace answered. "My dad was dying, and I kept thinking about him and then it was there — in my dream and in my journal. A memory I had tried to forget. But there it was, and I needed to deal with it. It was an untold story." As she explained to me later, she has faced this trauma in her writing and through therapy. Grace broke her silence in her journal, and this allowed her to accept what had happened and begin to heal. And she has moved forward quite admirably.

Wired to Make Meaning

Our brains hold the magic that allows us to find our stories and to make and remake our meaning. When split-brain research began in the 1960s, the findings expanded horizons on how our storytelling minds work. Hoping to prevent serious seizures in patients, researchers began a series of experiments in which they severed the corpus callosum, the nervy band of fibers that carries communications between the right and left sides of our brains. This procedure not only helped prevent these seizures but also gave neuroscientists new insights into how the two areas of our brains work. Although brains can be mapped differently, the findings showed generally that our left brain handles our logic and reasoning and manages heavy cognitive work and speaking. The right brain, is more creative — focusing on the visual, on imagery, and on motor skills. A pioneer in this field of split-brain research, Michael Gazzaniga helped us unravel how storytelling works.

Along with his collaborators, Gazzaniga was able to identify an area in the left brain that he named "the interpreter." In this part of the brain, certain neural circuits are tasked with finding order and meaning in the flood of seemingly disconnected information that is filtered into it. Here our neurons take the incoming sensory input and wire bits together to create what become our stories. This is where the magic happens, and it might be dubbed our personal "storyteller."

In dozens of brain experiments, Gazzaniga and his colleagues explored how this worked. In one classic study they flashed different pictures to the two hemispheres of a split-brain patient named PS. They showed a chicken claw to the left hemisphere of PS's brain and a snowy scene to the right hemisphere. Then they asked him to point to cards that matched each picture. (It gets a bit complicated because the right side of the brain reads input for the left eye, while the left side of the brain reads it for the right eye.)

Here is what happened. PS's right hand chose the picture of the chicken. When asked why, he explained that he chose the chicken because he had seen a chicken leg. PS accurately connected the picture seen by his right eye (processed through his left brain) with the picture he selected, *and* he could easily explain why he had made this choice.

But, and this is where it becomes interesting, the same task was not as easy for PS's right hemisphere. While he saw a snowy scene, and he correctly matched a snow shovel with this picture, he could not explain it accurately. Although his right hemisphere had processed the accurate image, it lacked the verbal ability to explain this choice. This is where our storytelling brain steps in. PS's left brain had to fill in the gap, and it did this with complete confidence, even though it had to make up the answer. In other words, it assimilated the information it had and then fabricated the answer. The response PS made was, "The shovel is needed to clean the chicken coop."

Even though the left brain had *no answer*, it came up with an explanation — it found a story that fit the scenario. The fascinating-beyond-words conclusion here is that wired for story, our brains automatically do their job. They find a story that helps us find meaning and make sense of what is happening to us. Our left brain is wired to avoid the unknown or the scary uncertainty of living. It acts as *an interpreter* even when it does not have an accurate answer.

Gazzaniga and his colleagues completed a number of studies that consistently revealed the same outcome. When our left brain has accurate information, it tells true stories. When it does not know the specifics of a story, it can use the information it has and fabricate an ending — *and believe it*. In sum, our storytelling brain has to make sense of what is happening. We are wired to make sense of events — to create a story — even when we don't have all the pieces. Gottschall explains, "The storytelling mind is a crucial evolutionary adaptation. It allows us to experience our lives as coherent, orderly, and meaningful. It is what makes life more than a blooming, buzzing confusion." Our stories allow us to make sense of our lives — even if we have to create pieces of our story to find our meaning.

Our Brains Embrace Our Fictions

No wonder we love fiction, stories that are completely made up. Support for how this storytelling feature of our brains works is everywhere. Think about the conspiracy theories we create. Let's return to my kitchen bar and that Mother's Day when my family busied themselves with creating the ending of the story of the missing airliner. No one knew what had happened. There was *no way* to know. But each member of my family spun a possible story to help them cope with this tragedy.

When our minds struggle with a traumatic event, alternate stories surface to help us explain the unknown. Conspiracy theories mushroom because — as we have seen — our brains are wired to make sense of what happens. When we are upset that a president has been shot and can't believe that a lone gunman could get away with murder, we create stories to help us cope. Regardless of what the Warren Commission discovered, conspiracy theories still abound to help us make sense of President Kennedy's assassination.

Although members of Al-Qaeda have claimed full responsibility for the terrorist attacks on the World Trade Center on

September 11, 2001, one can still find conspiracy theorists who believe the U.S. or Israeli governments were involved.

In 2013, sixteen years after Princess Diana's death, Scotland Yard reopened the investigation of her death because questions continue to be raised: Was the British Special Forces involved? Both the French and British governments have ruled that Diana's death in 1997 happened as a result of an accident. The car was driven by a drunk driver. But we still hate to think of the lovely princess facing such a pointless death. Many stories that don't make sense to us have creative fictions, or conspiracies, swirling around them. Think of all the wacky denials of climate change and the Holocaust. Celebrities are particularly vulnerable to having fictions created about them — think Elvis, Marilyn, and Michael Jackson. Even our novels propagate cultural stories. Since Dan Brown's *Da Vinci Code*, Jesus and Mary Magdalene remain embroiled in our imaginations in new ways. Were they married? Were there children?

Nonfiction books, especially personal memoirs, are often faulted for slipping into fiction, and given how our minds work, this is no surprise. Our stories are often more "truthy" than true. It is tempting to step over the line, moving from our memory to our fiction. A literary scandal erupted when Oprah Winfrey endorsed a book written by James Frey, *A Million Little Pieces*. In it Frey claimed to be an addict, an alcoholic, and a criminal who had turned himself around. He was touted as an inspiration to others. When he appeared on Winfrey's show, Frey even traveled to a clinic in Minnesota "and gave an on-camera pep talk" to a viewer who entered rehab after discovering Frey's story.

After Frey's appearance on Winfrey's show, his book became a runaway bestseller. Then after a six-week investigation by reporters at the *Smoking Gun*, the author's story began to unravel. In detailed reviews of police reports, court records, and interviews with law-enforcement officers, it was revealed that Frey had "wholly fabricated or wildly embellished details" of his criminal career and jail terms. In one shocking ploy, Frey, although he was never there, created a role for himself in a real-life accident that cost the lives of two high school students. Clearly he had gone too far in embellishing his work, and his "true story" was discredited.

Given our left brain's propensity to make sense of what we know and what we write, we need to accept that our stories are based on our search for truth but that our story-wired brain is going to fill in the missing pieces. And since the updated, filled-in gaps make sense, we come to believe them. It is a part of our humanness. It is how we come to make sense of our life stories — and understand ourselves.

But as I sit here writing a nonfiction book, I am working hard to share valid research. Actual findings. Real stories. Frey failed us. For the truth is *not made up*. If we want to help others learn, we have a responsibility to share our findings ethically and honestly. Although all writers have an inner storyteller, nonfiction writers have an obligation to try to avoid the distortion that can seep into a story. As a writer I am a curious mind, probing for the truth. Can truth set us free? I believe it can.

In our journals, in our poems — in all our expressive writing — we have more creative freedom to say what we want. To imagine. But even then, it is crucial that we understand how our brain works, and that our inner storyteller is always at play. We can use this inner storyteller in positive ways. For example, we can re-imagine new ways of understanding our life stories, and we can re-create new ways to live with our troubled stories. While we need to avoid erroneous fabrications, our inner storyteller can help us rewrite and reframe our traumatic experiences. And this is what we will learn to do.

Searching for Our Myth, Our True Story

While our minds tweak and change our stories, I believe most of our stories are an authentic attempt to reach understanding and find our truth. About a decade ago my student David was certainly caught up in this search when he turned in his "This I Believe" essay to the assignment box perched on the bookcase by the door of room 221.

When I asked him if he would read his essay to our humanities class later that week, he readily agreed. Since he was skinny and short — a wisp of a kid — I was thankful he chose to stand up and read it from the classroom podium. His paper crinkled as he unfolded it, and then he looked out at us, gray eyes scanning his audience and blinking as if the fluorescent lights were blinding him.

"This I believe," he began and paused, allowing his eyes to settle on a classmate. "I was born gay. This was not a personal decision."

He was not afraid. His voice rang strong and clear like that of a television newscaster, and his eyes maintained contact with his peers. When I noticed that he never looked down, I realized David had memorized his essay. With this realization a shiver ran up my spine. Although I didn't fully understand it, I could sense something unfolding in the room. In his speech he chronicled how he had been bullied, insulted, spat at in the halls, and punched out behind the lunchroom trash cans — not once, but many times. When he was in junior high, he was not even allowed in the boys' locker room because he was *different*.

"I did not choose to be born gay. But I was," he explained. "This is not the choice I would have made." His words were filled with pain and passion, with hopes and dreams. And when he finished there was a silence as if his thoughts were still encased in air bubbles that had not yet popped.

In a few moments, as was our custom, students asked questions: How did you know you were gay? How did your parents take it? What is it like to live in a culture that often rejects gays and gay marriage? What can we do? Why doesn't this school have a Gay-Straight Alliance to help?

Later David told me that his "This I Believe" essay was his coming out, his public admission that he was gay. "When I turned it in," he explained, "I wanted to have the courage to read it. I am glad I did." For years he had hidden who he was and struggled to come to grips with it. Often his peers had rejected and tormented him, but as he matured he understood that he could not change who he was: a young gay man. And in this essay he was rewriting his story to acknowledge his truth and help others accept it.

His openness has helped. Later a few of these high school students banded together and asked me to serve as their sponsor. We formed the first Gay-Straight Alliance in our community. My students wanted to create a safe and accepting environment for David and for all students, and they made important strides in this direction.

Our Hero Myths

We all have conflicts and unresolved issues that need our attention. Liam did. Grace did. David did. Sometimes these are shattered stories. Often they are untold stories. When we have had enough time and space to absorb the pain that comes from trauma, writing about it can help us with the challenge of reworking this experience back into our lives. It can help us take cancer, or abuse, or loss, or whatever befalls us and find a way to understand and recast it. If we can reach this point with a difficult experience, we can rise from the depths of the trough where we have been stuck.

As I look across the kitchen bar at my cluttered mass of papers and stacks of books, and as I continue to interview those who are writing and struggling, I have a newfound awareness that our untold traumas are the stories we need to tell. For if we can find the courage to tell them and the resilience to live with them, we may find more than our way out of them. By navigating through the setbacks that will inevitably litter our lives, we can become stronger, better human beings. And isn't this ultimately our hero journey?

We all face ongoing challenges in a world that has been defined by politics, economics, terrorism, and social media. Life is fraught with difficulties both large and small. If our goal is to find our way through those snags and stresses, then we are called to undertake our personal hero journey. And in the process, we will hopefully become the kind of person we want to be — wiser, more compassionate, and more connected to others, our communities, and our planet.

Our sons, Matt and Zach, are grown. Adam lives in South Africa. Steve still works too many hours, and often I sit here at the kitchen bar thinking. Alone — but not lonely — for I sit here using words to find myself and make sense of who I am. My cancer took me to the threshold of my mortality. The dilemmas of juggling older parents — and recently losing one — continue to confound and confuse me.

One year after I was diagnosed with cancer, Matt called to tell me he had advanced testicular cancer. "Surgery is tomorrow — it all happened quickly," he explained. "Chemo will start as soon as I am well enough." I sat there numb. "Mom, we are trying to save my sperm, but it may be too late." When I clicked off my cell, I was stunned. And while I understand this is a story I will need to tell, I still am not able to find a voice for it — not yet. I will note here that my son has joined me in the ranks of cancer survivors, but at the time, facing his illness was terrifying.

With my words I ground myself and find my way. While the journey is often arduous, it is more often filled with joy, for it is in the pages of my journal that I realize how thankful I am for the chance to live my life past my cancer and to have older parents to juggle and to have a son who lives in a time when chemo and surgery can — *and did* — save his life. Life is beautiful, and my words have allowed me to find and revel in that beauty.

Finding Our Heroic Stories

According to Dan P. McAdams, author of *The Stories We Live By*, our life stories help us create our own myths to define who we are, and ideally, to discover our inner hero. Recently, to celebrate my granddaughter's third birthday, I visited Disneyland with her in California. There Macy was on a mission to find the character Elsa of *Frozen* fame. Elsa is a royal princess who discovers she has a handicap: she turns everything she touches into ice. Eventually she learns to turn her disability around and manage it. Elsa proves strong and resilient. Heroic. Although Macy did not find Princess Elsa in the park that day, she was not upset. "Elsa is busy," Macy explained. "She is a superhero — and that is hard work."

Macy shows early signs of wanting her own hero story. Shortly after our visit to Disneyland, she drew me several pictures for my refrigerator. Each picture had a story. One had a ladder with ten tiny figures climbing down it and one large-headed, smiling girl keeping the ladder steady. "That's me," Macy explained. "Those people need to get down — and I am holding their ladder. I am their hero."

As I was reminded with Macy, we begin piecing our stories together, even our potential hero myth, at a young age. By the time we reach the teen years, we may be struggling, as Liam was. When he reconnected with life stories that allowed him to see his better self — and his heroic potential — he moved forward. As we knit our stories together, we are able to create a personal myth that can give our lives meaning. We can choose to embrace our best stories — even our best fictions. McAdams says, "In order to live well, with unity and purpose, we compose a heroic narrative of the self that illustrates essential truths about ourselves."

Our brains are wired to find our stories
— untold stories, broken stories,
and stories with missing pieces.
These are the stories we need to tell.

Writing Prompts and Suggestions

Again, you will be exploring various pathways to writing about your life. Plan to spend twenty minutes or more engaged in any one of these activities. Choose the activity that fits you best. If any single prompt leads to a wave of writing, ride the experience and let the stories unfold. If you hit a roadblock and the words dry up, move to a different prompt. Your goal is to find and begin the process of telling some significant life stories.

Okay. Get comfortable. Sift through your experiences. Dig deep. What stories have made you the person you are? What moments should be fully woven into the narrative that is you? What stories do you need to tell?

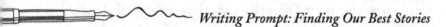 *Writing Prompt: Finding Our Best Stories*

With help from the late Michael White, Liam was able to re-align his understanding of who he was. Make a list of positive moments in your life. Have there been times when you helped someone else? Have you done something helpful for a friend or neighbor? Have you ever volunteered? Have you learned something new? Have you developed new skills? Earned a degree? Have you learned a new language? Written a story or poem or a book? Have you overcome a fear? Write about moments that show you in your best light. If you want, you can talk to someone who cares about you and ask him or her to help you find your best possible stories. Then write your stories.

Another option: you can turn this assignment around and make a list of something helpful you want to do or something new you want to learn. Then write about the process of trying to achieve this goal or this new learning.

When you complete this writing, leave it for at least a day. When you return to it, read and see if you can find themes that show the best you. What are they?

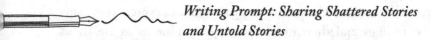

Writing Prompt: Sharing Shattered Stories and Untold Stories

The hardest pieces to collect in our minds are the broken ones. When a personal story shatters, we have to pick up the pieces, as Grace did. Is there a story you have not told? Is there an experience that you need to explore? You may simply want to jot down some notes about what happened. You may feel more comfortable making some drawings or writing a poem. If you are comfortable with writing, explore the details of what happened and the feelings you experienced. Try to write out the complete story. Come back to it later and review it. Is the story over, or do you need to explore it further? You may choose to continue your exploration in writing, you may want to talk it through with a close and trusted friend, or you may want to see a counselor to make sure you have worked through the experience.

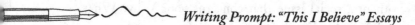

Writing Prompt: "This I Believe" Essays

Originally "This I Believe" was a popular radio series hosted by Edward R. Murrow in the 1950s. Today "This I Believe" has evolved into an international organization, engaging people from all over the world and all walks of life in writing and sharing essays describing their values and beliefs. National Public Radio has archived more than 125,000 of these essays, and you can hear them on public radio, on webcasts, and at thisibelieve.org.

By writing one of these essays, you have a chance to express and clarify ideas that matter to you. You can choose to begin writing for ten minutes on any one of the questions listed here. If one idea takes off, develop it into a full-fledged essay that you might want to send to an op-ed page of a newspaper or submit to a blog or appropriate magazine. You can also develop your own questions or ideas for this writing. What topic is important to you? Mental illness? Gun control? Climate change?

Write about what matters to you. Work to express your honest feelings and thoughts. Support your thinking as clearly as you can.

Here are some starter questions to work with:

- What is most important to you?
- What do you believe?
- What have you learned?
- What do you value?
- Is creativity important to you? Are you driven to create? Discuss.
- How important is family? How is the nuclear family changing in our culture?
- What makes you happy? Is happiness different from fulfillment?
- What change would you like to see in your community or culture?
- Is there a social issue that concerns you? Why? What needs to happen?

PART FOUR

REWRITING OUR SHATTERED STORIES

CHAPTER ELEVEN

Writing to Heal

If a story is in you, it has got to come out.
— William Faulkner

Her hair was on fire. "Mom!" I screamed, pointing at her head. She had been cleaning the stove in the camper when her brunette bob brushed against the gas lantern and lit up before me. She took the dishtowel in her hands and swiftly wrapped her head. I was eleven, and we were on a long VW bus camping trip — my dad's brainchild that my mother tolerated. After deftly smothering the flames of her hair, Mom calmly pulled out a clean dishtowel and continued to scrub the stove as if nothing was amiss. I sat there stunned.

Mom was a staunch survivor. Her father, my granddad with the glass eye, lost his lumber company when she entered her teens. Grandma Rose supported the family with her gift for sewing and gardening. My mother, the oldest of five, helped raise her siblings. While she loved school and had been a stellar student, high school became a depressing experience for her once the family descended into poverty. And college, which she had dreamed of, was out of the question. After high school, she worked nights at the newspaper until she could get a day job.

My dad, a Purdue engineering student at the time, came to Richmond, Indiana, with a fraternity brother to celebrate Thanksgiving because he was short of cash for the train back to Pittsburgh. While in Richmond he was introduced to Mom. "She was the smartest woman I ever met," my dad told me later. There was a hushed silence before he added, "She was never uppity. Just so gentle and beautiful — and there was this *light* in her blue eyes." He began hitchhiking to Richmond regularly.

When Dad graduated, they married and my mother followed my dad to Southbend, where my brother Les was born, and then to Hartford, where I was born, and then back to Southbend, where Charley was born, and eventually onward to Indianapolis, where we grew up in a suburb south of the city. While Dad pursued an intense engineering career, my mom learned to grow the neighborhood's most admired roses, and she was bound and determined to raise equally admired children. The roses were prickly and demanding, requiring hours of pulling weeds, spraying, trimming, and assuring they were protected from the first frost. The children were less prickly — but certainly more demanding.

Her guidance was often subtle, her messages to me spelled out in gentle side comments: I would be good, I would be able to take care of myself, I would go to college, and I would know there is value in being a woman. A strong woman — for she modeled this.

While she discouraged me from thinking I would grow up to be a homemaker, she seemed to enjoy being one. She never turned on the soap operas that many women seemed to feast on. Instead, Mom preferred beating the rugs clean, hanging the laundry outside to dry, sewing our clothes, and scrubbing the kitchen floors by hand. Often in the afternoons she baked chocolate chip cookies, which we could smell as we ran up the street after the school bus let us off. When she had extra minutes, she weeded her garden or tackled newspapers and the books stacked on her nightstand. Her stash of books included *To Kill a Mockingbird* and *A Separate Peace* and *The Feminine Mystique*. I remember these titles because I would borrow these books without asking. I think it pleased her.

While soft-spoken, Betty Alice was one tough cookie. Moms in the old neighborhood were always stopping by to seek her insights and advice — and not just on roses. As I sit here, I realize that before there were divorce counselors, my mom was one. She was wise, independent, and a friend to all the neighborhood women and church ladies. I am pretty certain that both the phone and Facebook were created with her in mind.

When I faced my cancer, especially the turning point when I decided to lose both my breasts, she was there. And when I think back, I realize that she was always there — when I graduated, when I married, and when I had my sons. I could count on her.

And one morning I woke up and discovered that she was not going to meet me for a long-awaited lunch date. She couldn't get out of bed. At ninety-one she suffered from osteoporosis. Her spine was bending like a tree branch in a storm, and it hurt me to watch her toddle around as if nothing was amiss. But it was.

An MRI showed that several discs in her lower spine had eroded.

For years Mom had run her home with tight-ship efficiency: gardening and laundry in the morning; cleaning, shopping, and cooking in the afternoons. But after years of ignoring the pain in her back, suddenly she no longer could. She could hardly walk. A visit to her doctor confirmed she was "out of commission."

My dad volunteered to pick up the slack, but he had just recently taken a fall and was learning how to walk again while using a new walker. He tried to help with meals, but it became apparent that his cooking skills were limited to soups and Lean Cuisine. He even had trouble figuring out where the dishes went when he unloaded the dishwasher. I made extra trips to the grocery store and began delivering meals, but quite soon Dad stopped me in my tracks. "Mom is the best cook." His voice was kind, even gentle. "Please…only she knows what I like. We don't want you to be our caregiver."

When Dad expressed his deep-seated need for *her* cooking, Mom felt called to duty. Like Lazarus she rose up and started by making BLTs with the crispy bacon, just the way Dad loved it. But her excruciating pain returned, and this beautifully mom-orchestrated symphony stopped abruptly. Her doctor ordered her back to bed. We tried physical therapy. It made things worse. We arranged for epidural shots in her spine area. No immediate change. My mom was exasperated, I could sense it.

Early the next morning on my walk, I stopped in a bookstore, where I found Mom a garden journal. Later that day I told her about the research I was doing on writing and the Pennebaker writing method. I asked if she wanted to give writing to heal a try. She was either intrigued or frustrated with her situation, because she immediately agreed. For four days, using the writing process learned from Pennebaker, my mom wrote in her new journal. She hid this journal and made it clear she did not want others to see it.

Reviewing Our Writing for Insights

A week after writing in her journal, Mom talked with me about it. She admitted that she wrote about the inner turmoil resulting from her back problems. My dad, she explained to me, was often more of a hindrance than a help with housework. She resented that I was doing jobs she considered "her jobs," and worse, I was too gung ho on trying to hire home helpers for them. "At first, it felt like you were both working against me," she explained.

By writing about her dilemma, Mom began to get a handle on her new narrative. She felt she could look at her situation from a distance and see what was happening in her life and come to understand it. She had been an amazing wife, mother, and homemaker. She wanted to continue juggling all of it, but with her deteriorating discs, she began to accept that she had to change. She realized Dad was trying to be a pinch-hit home-maker and that I was trying to manage two households while recovering from my double mastectomy. These realizations made her want to join our team and find new ways to make life easier for all of us. And she did.

About a week later, when I visited their home, Dad proudly whispered, "I think your mom is back!" In reality, she was still not moving much, but her attitude had shot up like a spring kite in the breeze. And this made my dad sound like a joyful five-year-old himself. If writing gives us nothing more than a better attitude — and it gave this to my mom — then it is well worth our time.

Writing to Find Our Way

Weeks later when I asked her if she thought the writing had helped, Mom said, "I think several things helped." We had hired someone to help with house cleaning and a gardener to help trim the overgrown plants in her garden. The epidural shots began to kick in and lessen her pain. By Christmas she bragged that she could stand long enough to bake her famous sour cream coffee cake.

"I guess the writing helped me see everything differently. I realized how my back problems were impacting everyone, not just me," Mom explained. She had taken her story, scratched out what could not work, worked to understand the viewpoints of the characters, and then made some important revisions in how this story should play out. As she ages, she has continued to take steps forward and make important revisions in her story. Even with a back curved like a branch about to snap, my mom inches forward with grace.

My mom was finding her way. Unlike with a novel, we can-not read ahead as the chapters in our lives unfold. We don't know what we will face. We do know that bad stories happen to all of us. Risk, trauma, illness, and loss are a part of living. As last year was coming to an end, I sighed with relief. I was done with breast cancer. Within days, as I mentioned earlier, my son Matt called with the news that he had cancer. Later that same afternoon my friend Marcie texted me from the hospital to say she had fallen off a ladder while picking oranges and was nursing eight broken ribs, two broken vertebrae, and a punctured lung. On my way to visit her at the hospital, I hit a curb in the parking garage and cracked my car bumper. Life keeps unfolding around us.

We cannot change the reality of what happens to us. If your father molested you or your child was hit by a drunk driver, this event happened. We cannot deny what we experienced, but eventually we can stop a shattered story from running on replay in our brains. We can edit and even rewrite these painful episodes.

When we are able to make our experiences *language based*, or move them from our emotion-filled right brains into the words of our left brains, we can reach an understanding of what has happened. When we understand events, the interpreter in our brains can help us realign these pieces. When necessary, doing this can help us write new scripts that will allow us to move forward. Then our pain and confusion no longer serve as roadblocks.

Initially my students awakened me to this power of writing. In thumbing through an old journal, written when I was immersed in high school teaching, I found this note: *Writing helps so many of my students pull themselves from their downward spiral... It helps them right their course. "Write" their course?... Our words can rewrite us. Heal us. Our words can lead us down a path to renewal and increased personal fulfillment.*

Because of these upbeat experiences with students, I was taken aback when an administrator at my college made an offhanded comment to me. "What good is creative writing?" I had spent years watching all types of writing help students to clarify, change, and transform their lives. I was so thrown by this comment I could not respond. Late that night, after grading papers, I hit the Google search button. The *what-good-is-creative-writing* comment had prime-time play in my brain, and I needed to defuse my concern. Once I started the Google search, I rediscovered a name I had heard mentioned for years at writing conferences: James W. Pennebaker. Links to his studies and those of his former students were all over the web.

Pennebaker's Writing Process

As we saw in chapter 3, Pennebaker's bliss is research, and in his early work he stumbled onto the significance of writing. Originally he wanted to know if being open — sharing your stories — was healthy. He established that "being open" matters significantly for our health, but he used a four-day writing exercise to show this. As noted, Pennebaker's follow-up research — as well as more than two hundred studies — has established that expressive writing can help us heal physically, socially, and mentally.

Today Pennebaker's four-day writing process is considered a classic touchstone for writing to heal. Many therapists use it regularly with their clients. Let's explore it now. While this writing might cause some distress at first, the odds are strong that it will provide relief afterward and reward you with valuable insights. Remember, if the writing causes undue stress, put it aside. But if you are looking for a prompt that is backed up by scientific results, prepare to write!

Using Pennebaker's writing process can improve our physical health and transform our attitudes.

Writing Prompts and Suggestions

If you have a broken story that continues to bother you (an accident, a divorce, an illness, an experience with abuse, a painful loss), this activity may be the place for you to start.

Writing Prompt:
The Pennebaker Writing Process

Here are the steps:

- *Begin by choosing an emotional issue,* a difficult experience, or a trauma "that has profoundly affected your life." It may be difficult to think or talk about. While it may be from any period in your life, you might be experiencing it right now.

- *Find a comfortable and private place to write* where you will not be disturbed. If you are concerned about others seeing what you write, keep your writing in a safe place, or destroy it when you are done.

- *Tell your story without holding back.* Include both your thoughts and your feelings from the past, and then present them in as much detail as possible.

- *Write continuously for twenty or more minutes* without paying any attention to spelling, punctuation, or grammar. Just write.

- *Do this for four consecutive days.* During this time you can continue writing about the same experience and expand on it, or you may choose different topics.

- *If you write about the same topic on all four days, work to explore how this event has affected your life.* Did this event change you? How? Has it changed your work situation, your family, your relationships, or your beliefs?

- *Try to write a complete story or experience.* Length does not matter.

- *Review your work* after each session to see if you have shared your deepest thoughts and feelings. Monitor your feelings. Has the writing made you sad or happy? Was the experience valuable or meaningful?

 *Writing Prompt: Reflection*

Pennebaker suggests that you take a break before coming back to review the writing you did over those four days. When you return to your work, you will want to read it carefully and think about it. Were you able to express your genuine thoughts and feelings? Do you have a greater understanding of what happened? Did you find value and meaning in the writing? What have you learned? What insights have you gained?

Ideally, the writing will lead to new insights, and it is possible that you will not only learn from your writing, but you will gain a sense of relief from the experience.

CHAPTER TWELVE
Breaking the Silence

I am not what happened to me.
I am what I choose to become.
— Carl Gustav Jung

It was a Thursday, and I was jogging down the halls of the VA hospital. I slid into our crowded, cluttered box of a room and slipped onto a folding chair. "No," bellowed Kai, the loudest voice in the group. "That chair is for my backpack. *You know that!*" He stood, and I hugged his lumbering body. He comes to writing group every week. But he never writes.

Darren greeted me, his toothy grin demanding a hug equal to Kai's. Darren was knocked senseless by the straps of a jet fighter plane when it launched from his navy aircraft carrier a decade ago. He is forty or forty-four; it depends on the week you ask him. He remains in love with his high school sweetheart. She is the only girl he ever kissed, and in jumbled and confused words he rewrites this story every other week.

As the writing volunteer, I recently asked Darren to write his story from a different perspective. He did. He wrote about his new and passionate love for a married group member, Sienna. Sweet frizzy-haired Sienna smelled of strawberry lip gloss and always slipped into the group late, with a glassy stare that bounced around the room. Her writing cycled from poems to stories to lists that directly or metaphorically referred to the anesthesia used in a surgery that dulled her mental processes and denied her the legal right to raise her children. I have not seen Sienna much since Darren professed his undying love in three pages of rambling prose.

And there sat Tim, a Vietnam vet. Tim is a seeker who writes poems about the eyes that he sees at night, eyes that jolt him awake and cause him to shriek into the darkness. And the face of the boy to whom the eyes belonged. Tim shot the boy in a meadow in Vietnam forty years ago, but the memory revisits him often.

And then she entered. Barbara.

Her walk sounded like a slow drumbeat as she pushed forward, bringing with her the aroma of lemons. Her dark eyes met ours as she slammed her rumpled stack of poems onto the table. Then she dug into her oil barrel–sized purse for a tissue to blot her shiny skin. "I know I am late," she barked. She was always late. She scraped the metal chair backward and sighed heavily. "May I go first?" She was always slightly enraged. Rob, who managed our group, nodded, while the other vets shrugged as if they knew the routine. She would read first. She always read first.

"Emotional Autopsy," she said, announcing the name of her poem. Her voice softened unexpectedly. The lines holding dark and troubled meaning became barely audible as she read. The story cycled around rape. She stumbled over a word. Her lips quivered as she finished. I looked around the room. Twelve eyes. Tears in every one.

> When one resides just this side of sanity
> Sifting through details like a coroner
> Seeking cause of death,
> This becomes the mind's activity:

She carves the meat from the bone,
Separates the muscle from the fat.
The veins and the arteries tell a story
A story of life and death.

The bloodless cadaver is spread-eagled
Motionless on a metal table.
Staring through the viewing window,
Passersby glimpse the still corpse.
No thought is given to who she used to be.
The spirit of her watches
Hovering over her body
Until the flesh meets the fire.

Mending Our Broken Stories

Students taught me the power of writing, but working with veterans at the VA hospital helped me see the patterns in how we use writing to heal. Barbara, a beautiful mocha-skinned woman, had faced a trauma and lived with that trauma inside her for decades. She could not see or touch her own beauty — not until she became a writer. Watching her transformation, which I will discuss more later, gave me a new level of understanding of the power of writing to re-create us. She did the hard work to reground and rediscover herself with words. I simply watched her unfold like a tiger lily.

For many years I fell asleep at my desk late at night over pieces of student writing with my forehead crash-landed on a student essay. And it was an honor to devote myself to their work, for in these late-night moments, I could reach beneath the surface into the inner worlds of my students. Some were searching, and some were lost. But often they shared their deepest insights as they struggled to find themselves. And I have never read any book or watched any movie that captured a more moving quest. Their words were touching the universe as only young minds in flight can do.

After my bout with cancer and working for a boss who suffered from mental illness, I felt called to help underserved populations to write and sort through their pain and losses. Working with veterans suffering from PTSD, I was uncovering the same needs in them that I had discovered in my students, stories similar to *our* stories. Sienna, Darren, Kai, Tim, Barbara — and many other vets — wrote to find themselves, but they struggled to find their words because their stories were often shattered or stalled, like a needle skipping in the groove of an old vinyl record.

In wading through years of these shattered stories, I began to uncover ways to help others navigate these rough waters. Ways that could make a difference in our lives, such as breaking our silence, getting unstuck from negative and repeating thoughts, learning to embrace other perspectives, working to find meaning in setbacks, and learning to rewrite or re-create our understanding of who we can become.

Tapping into Ourselves and Breaking the Silence

This journey of mending a broken story begins with breaking our silence. And Barbara's writing taught me how this works. A couple of weeks after she read "Emotional Autopsy" at our veterans' writing group, I met Barbara in the cafeteria of the VA hospital. She was carrying her trademark huge purse, which she used to navigate her way through the crowded room. I wondered what was inside of it. *I wondered what was inside of her.*

We started meeting for lunch before our writing group so I could help her with her poems. "I don't know who I am," she explained to me over greasy cafeteria tacos. "I really don't. They gave me 70 percent disability so I don't have to work. But who am I now that I do nothing?" I wanted to give her an answer, but I had none.

She dove into the purse and pulled out a huge, tattered notebook with rule-lined papers sticking out. That notebook held the secrets to who she was. But I did not know this yet. On the front was a half-completed sketch of a horse. Her talisman. He eventually surfaced in her poems.

In the writing group we had been taking an assigned word and writing about it: *fear, pain, resilience*. From her poems based on this assignment as well as our lunch meetings, I had come to understand a bit about Barbara. She described herself as a *slab of meat* — raw, cut open, discarded. Raped.

She had asked me to write her story because she thought it should be told. But I was conflicted. I wanted to; I didn't want to. Every time we ate lunch, I asked her questions. But she deftly skirted around them and spoke of her art, her experiences with equine therapy, and her late-night poetry writing.

All I knew from these lunch meetings was that in Panama in 1985, she had been raped by a fellow serviceman. The story within her was tightly wound and surfaced in undulating waves of rage. But that afternoon a small portal opened. Barbara admitted that a few years ago, when she was a counselor, she began helping a thirteen-year-old girl recover from her rape at the hands of a sixteen-year-old neighbor. As Barbara listened and worked to help the young girl navigate her trauma, Barbara began to relive the horror of her own rape. "I was falling apart," she explained. "One day after work I drove to Lowe's and just sat there in the parking lot and cried. I knew then I couldn't be a counselor any longer."

"Was this pain the result of your own rape?" I asked her. But she had climbed back inside and remained silent. By now I understood that she had probably not told anyone. Long ago she had sealed her rape inside the vault of Barbara, where she must have believed it would be safe. She could keep her air force job. The rapist could keep his. But the poison within her had begun to bubble out. Painfully.

Eventually Barbara left her counseling job and came to Phoenix to seek help at the VA hospital, but that process did not always go smoothly. One time in writing group, Barbara admitted to "losing it" with her psychiatrist. Apparently Dr. Ross was a small, intense woman who prescribed drugs to help Barbara fight her depression. At their last meeting Barbara was struggling with a story that she needed to tell. She asked Dr. Ross if she could talk and was shocked when the doctor curtly responded, "Barbara, I am here to check your drugs. I am not a counselor!"

In that moment an earthquake went shooting through the neural pathways in Barbara's brain, a brain that was filled with twenty-plus years of rape pain. Once again she felt discarded. Ignored. She pulled forward in her chair and looked across the desk at the neatly coifed doctor. "You are supposed to be here to help me, but you won't even talk to me. You aren't doing your job." Her voice was enraged.

Dr. Ross was alarmed, even incensed. Later Barbara would realize that although the doctor acted tough, she was afraid of Barbara. The doctor immediately summoned security. Barbara shook her head in disgust as she shared the ending of this experience. "Security came and they escorted me out of her office. Like I was a criminal. I was interviewed. My file was red-flagged. Dr. Ross thought I was going to hurt her, which was crazy. Was I going to punch my psychiatrist?" Barbara asked. "No way. I only needed to talk to her — and she was afraid *of me.*" Barbara looked down, shaking her head sadly.

Barbara's history, her struggle, filled me with compassion. Although I was frustrated with her inability to tell the story she had locked inside, I kept meeting her for lunch with the hope that she would eventually weave her way through her trauma and be free of it.

After our talk the two of us turned to Barbara's latest poem, which she read aloud to me. I asked her about a word. She changed it. I wondered what would happen if we flipped a couple of sentences. She tried it. I fell all over her metaphor — she saw herself as a discarded rotten avocado. Then I asked her to read the poem again. But this reading was light-years away from the last one. Her voice was stronger. Her energy permeated each word.

Wasted Potential

Withered, dark, misshaped fruit litters the landscape —
Sun ripened, unfit for human consumption.
Yellow-green flesh threaded with black,
Decayed succulent meat, lying in waste.
Shrunken grainy skin smothers the seed within.
Blackened in death's hollow pursuit,
Returning to Mother Nature's womb.
Remembered only by the unwilling sexton,
Unfulfilled potential buried beneath the avocado tree.

"What about the title?" I asked.

"Don't mess with my titles." Her voice raised several decibels. I shrugged. She laughed. Then we noticed the time on the metal clock above our heads.

She stuffed her poem back into her hapless pile of papers in the horse-sketched notebook and gathered up the purse she would use to charge out the doors and forward to our writing group. But on our way out the doors, she turned to me unexpectedly. "I don't usually like my writing," she explained, *"but I see something here...I am connecting to something."*

"Barbara," I said, touching her arm, "maybe you are a poet."

"That is the craziest thing I ever heard." She laughed so hard she snorted.

But she *was* tapping into something. With her freewriting — her poems — she was tapping into Barbara.

Freewriting to Break the Silence

In my veterans' writing group, many life stories spun amok. But words flowed from their freewriting assignments. And in releasing their feelings, these vets gave words to their traumas.

Freewriting is writing without constraint. This form is like dancing with words — you do not edit, you do not censor, you do not revise, you simply keep your pen attached to paper (or your fingers connected to your keyboard) and write whatever comes to you. It can be — and often is — the spewing of words onto paper. When I worked with students and now as I worked with vets, I found freewriting allowed for a genuine psychological release. It helped students who had nothing to say, find something to say. Now it was helping the vets get their stuck stories out and onto paper.

Why did this help? Writing that lets words come and dance with you can be a powerful form of self-revelation. Freewriting keeps your left-brain critic at bay. Instead, your right brain pours forth feelings and emotional experiences — even bad ones like Barbara's rape. While Barbara could not tell me her story, eventually it surfaced, in poem after poem. She was, at last, getting unstuck.

Psychotherapists and counselors have labored for years to help clients liberate their internal struggles in talk therapy. If you don't need or don't have access to professional counseling, writing still holds the same possibilities for you. The process helps us take steps forward on our own. Writing allows us to get the painful experiences out and find a framework in which to understand and live with them. But getting it out — or breaking the silence — is the first step.

Author Cheryl Strayed said, "I don't write for catharsis, but in sharing my stories in my writing I have achieved the greatest catharsis in my life." While catharsis is only the beginning stage of healing, it is significant because it opens up and helps release our pain.

"There is no portal I will avoid going down," explained Strayed. "When I wrote about killing my mother's horse it was the hardest thing I ever experienced. I was terribly sad. But I did this writing because it was important. You have to risk going to a place that is difficult. You have to be willing to go there. And it will be hard. But there is no danger in examining your life." With this release we can begin to work toward surviving and eventually transcending sorrow. *We can bypass self-pity — and go straight to self-revelation.*

Barbara did not keep a formal journal, just random notes. As part of her process, she would jot down a metaphor, and eventually words and phrases would come to her. Later she would rework these lines into a poem. After a few weeks, I began to understand that this form of freewriting was how Barbara's untold story was surfacing.

Remember, freewriting can take any form you choose — words, lists, poems. View this writing as a free-form canvas, a Picasso or a Pollock. Or view it as a jazz composition played by Coltrane or sung by Bessie Smith. Or spin your words as freely as Martha Graham danced. But write without constraints.

> *Freewriting can allow us to break our silence and find our voice.*

Writing Prompts and Suggestions

Centered on the process of freewriting, these prompts encourage you to let go and allow your words to come.

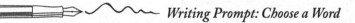 *Writing Prompt: Choose a Word*

Often a word pulls thoughts and memories from us. Find a comfortable spot. Use your journal, notepad, or computer and begin to write. Don't think about it — just put words, whatever comes, on paper. Here are some possible starter words: *Fear. Anger. Pain. Loss. Hope. Resilience. Love. Peace. Friendship. Connection.*

If you start with one word and find another, go with it. Set a timer, and write for at least ten minutes. If you want to go longer, do. If you get stuck, write, "I am stuck. I am stuck...." until your brain kicks in with another thought.

Review your work later to discover what is inside you. Then make a list of the words you want to explore. And if you are ready, begin again.

 *Writing Prompt: Find a Poem*

You may want to write in response to a poem. Poems hold powerful insights, and often they open us up to places we need to go. Find a poem. Read it. Choose a line or a few lines you love, and begin to write.

I often begin with two lines from Ellen Bass's poem, "The Thing Is," and use these lines as a prompt:

> to love life, to love it even
> when you have no stomach for it

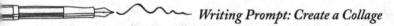 *Writing Prompt: Create a Collage*

Create a collage using pictures from personal cards, photos, clippings from magazines, and words. Create it randomly, or choose a theme.

CHAPTER THIRTEEN

Getting Unstuck

*If you're constantly ruminating about what you just did
— or what you should have done — or what you would have
done if you only had the chance, you will miss your life.*

— Sam Harris

L et's return to the Thursday afternoon when I met Barbara
Lee for lunch at the VA hospital. After we reviewed her
poem "Wasted Potential," we hustled down the long halls to
join our veterans' writing group. Our gathering started as usual.
Darren told a joke and warned us he was going to read something
he had read before, Kai complained that he had not been able to
finish his poem, and Barbara volunteered to read first.

Perhaps because she had practiced, Barbara's reading sounded
more like singing than reading. We were all glued to her Aretha-
like voice. Her poem — or song — was lovely. After she finished,
there was the usual silence. Then our group leader, Rob, coughed
and cleared his throat. "Wow," he said.

I asked Barbara to read it again. But this time as she read, I
jotted down the images she had crafted to describe herself: "dark
misshaped fruit," "yellow-green flesh threaded with black," and
"shrunken grainy skin that smothers the seed within."

When I read these words aloud to the group, Kai looked

surprised. He turned to Barbara and gently asked, "Really? Do you see yourself as a *rotten avocado?*"

"Yes," she answered in a tone that was equally hushed.

And then Tim, who almost never spoke in group, looked up and stared straight ahead as if he could see something invisible beyond us. "I think — I think you are writing about your sexual abuse *again.*"

Barbara's eyes flickered and she arched her back, sitting up straight. "Yes. I seem to be stuck on it." Then she looked at me, giving me her wry smile.

"On what?" I asked softly.

"On my rape." She sucked in a huge gulp of air. "On my rape," she repeated and sank back into her seat, relieved.

Barbara, like so many of us, had become trapped for years in her own horror story. Her brain had recycled the story of her abuse over and over and drained incalculable energy from her. Slowly, in our writing group, she had broken her silence and begun to rework the power this event held over her. In the coming weeks Barbara remained frustrated and sometimes even enraged by the mere memory of her rape. But as we talked, I realized she was using her writing to manage this anger and to try to find a way forward.

Earlier I touched on a time in my life when ocean waves seemed to be washing over me. I felt I was slipping under, drowning. I had just had my second child, and with the kids, the meals to make, the students to teach, the essays to grade, the workshops to lead, the laundry, the writing, the groceries, the bills to pay — the sum total was swallowing me. I was exhausted — physically and emotionally. When I reread this section of my journal, I was embarrassed at how stuck on the replay of *me* I was. I used my journal to dump out my frustrations. Same ones. Over and over.

Ironically, when Adam came to live with us, he became a wonderful teacher in helping me learn to cope with worry. His journey to manage his OCD began with visits to a doctor who introduced him to medication and a psychotherapist who coached him in new thinking patterns. But Adam did the hard work. He trained himself to recognize and understand his obsessive thoughts, and he learned to replace them with productive thinking and actions. I simply tried to learn from him and adopted his practice of being in the moment.

Earlier I mentioned *Brain Lock*, the book that Adam and Becca used to read from, a book that helped Adam get a handle on his OCD. In it neuroscientist Jeffrey M. Schwartz explains four steps for learning to overcome unwanted obsessive thoughts. These steps include learning to identify these repeating thoughts, learning to understand them for what they are, and learning to replace them with logical thinking and constructive behavior. The final step centers on working to make this a seamless process.

These four steps, like other forms of cognitive behavior therapy, train us to explore our patterns of thinking and to root out negative, unhealthy thoughts and actions. Scientific evidence has shown that we can consciously change our thinking as well as our behavior. As we know by now, our brain maps can be rewired. We can change. And by freeing ourselves from a story stuck in our brain grooves, we can embrace our present experiences. We can live in *the now*. Both Adam and I discovered that this was a much better way to live.

We Can Climb Out

An article by David Brooks, a columnist for the *New York Times*, confirmed my experience. He asked people over seventy to write to him and share what they had learned from life. He received a truckload of responses.

What did he learn from folks over seventy? One of the most important lessons was simply to *beware of rumination*. In his "The Life Reports II" column, Brooks reported that many of the older folks wrote long, detailed essays exploring bad life events. In their writings, as in their lives, these folks were driven to introspection.

"Through self-obsession," Brooks wrote, "they seemed to rein-force the very emotions, thoughts, and habits they were trying to escape." Sadly, these ruminators did not lead the most fulfilling lives. In fact, the happiest people were those who found a way to forget, forgive, or be thankful for their setbacks.

That spoke to the "me" I found in one of my old journals. At one point I had been that ruminator, and I am grateful I found my way out of that hole. Studies have shown that people who re-main fixated on their problems as well as the feelings surrounding those issues find themselves mentally frozen. Not a good place to be. This immobilization makes it impossible to solve problems and move forward. Rumination means that a bad story has not ended. Happier, more fulfilled people refused to remain stuck in their traumatic experiences. *They find their way out.*

Adam, who remains a dear friend, found his way out. When we spoke recently, he confirmed that living with OCD remains an ongoing challenge, but with help from both cognitive behav-ioral therapy and meditation, he has learned to minimize his ru-minations.

Thinking back, I see that as Adam changed, his whole *being* transformed. He was happier, funnier, and less awkward around others. With support from his family, professionals, and friends, he was able to grow exponentially in positive ways. He reframed his story. Turning his disorder into a gift, he used his intense focus to become a wizard in his studies of math, music, and eventually engineering. Today he is living proof that change is possible. He has a PhD, a fulfilling job, and a wonderful wife and new baby. His journey was — and remains — filled with challenges, but I marvel at how uplifting his experience has been for all of us who love him.

When we get stuck in our story, the first step is learning to pull back and look at our thinking or behavior. Some of our thoughts are illogical or destructive. Some of our interpretations need to be rewritten in our brains. We can do exactly that. We can rewrite our experience from a distance, and our writing can help us.

Along with his colleagues, Dr. Ethan Kross, a psychology professor at the University of Michigan, has studied how to deal with a traumatic event and overcome the tendency to ruminate about it. Kross found that when negative experiences were analyzed from a distance with the focus on reasons and not emotions, people gained important insights. While rumination can suck us down, *adaptive self-reflection* can lift us back up as we begin to reach an understanding of what happened. By pulling outside an event, we give ourselves a chance to observe a traumatic experience, make sense of it, and find a way to live with it. Both Barbara and Adam were able to step back and distance themselves from their difficult thought patterns, allowing them to rework those patterns in healthy ways.

> *Rumination can pull us down,*
> *but adaptive self-reflection can help us understand ourselves.*

Writing Prompts and Suggestions

Based on the work of Kross, this writing activity asks you to pull back and observe a difficult experience that is stuck on replay in your mind. You will work on seeing the event from a distance.

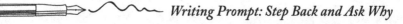 *Writing Prompt: Step Back and Ask Why*

Begin by closing your eyes. Now go back in time to the event. In your mind's eye, consciously move back or out of this scene. From a distance, watch the event as an observer who is simply trying to see what happened and why. You are observing yourself but as a character and from a distance. Take your time to play out this story.

Now write this incident as an objective observer, including all the details and emotions that you see unfolding. View the emotions, but remain distant and logical. *What happened? When did this happen? How did this character (you) feel? Why did this character (you) feel this way? Why did this happen?*

Later review your story. Try to make sense of what happened. Work to establish an understanding of *why it happened*. Remember, when we can logically understand a rumination, we can prevent it from running loose in our minds.

CHAPTER FOURTEEN

Embracing Other Perspectives

*You never really understand a person
until you consider things from his point of view.*

— Harper Lee

In one of my online creative writing classes, I had an army student who had recently returned from Iraq. Ethan kept writing the same story over and over again. It was exasperating to read of his ongoing fight with his boss, Major Richards. Each time he submitted his assignment, it was drenched in spit-fire anger and curses that rang in my ears. When we talked, Ethan explained his experience this way: "This is a true experience. My real boss was a *#*# a hundred times over."

"Ethan," I said, time and again, "this story has got to move forward. It is mired in Jack Nicholson anger flashes from *The Shining*. Although anger can be an important part of a story, it is rarely the emotion that can lead to healing. What happens beyond yelling? What is the real conflict here? What emotion is hiding underneath the anger? How could you end this narrative so that it ties all the pieces together and reveals the deeper meaning?"

Two weeks later I received a rewrite. In this version Ethan

bumps into his boss in the local bar. After a few drinks, and without any clear provocation, his boss begins yelling at Ethan, who responds by tossing a beer into the major's face. Conflict! Although this was progress, the piece still remained more of a rant against his boss than a story. When Ethan complained about his grade again, I said I would be willing to accept another rewrite. We talked about developing and resolving this unnamed conflict.

"But this is how I feel," Ethan explained over the phone. "My boss is a #*#!" And then it finally hit me. Ethan needed a change of perspective. I suggested that he rewrite this painful anecdote from his superior's viewpoint instead of his own. "Write it as if you were Major Richards." Although he balked, Ethan agreed to try.

Then he struggled. He kept requesting an extension. But finally he did submit his revision, and the change was surprising. The rant had been transformed into a meaningful narrative. When Ethan rewrote his short story from the viewpoint of Major Richards, he saw an army leader weighed down by his responsibilities in a war zone as well as a man with his own set of struggles: a daughter with a brain tumor and a wife who had threatened to leave him. He portrayed a frustrated man with nowhere to turn.

In the revision Major Richards still unleashes his wholly unjustified anger on Ethan early in the story, but later Ethan finds himself bumping into his boss outside the bar where the soldiers often ended the workday. Hesitantly, Ethan invites Major Richards to have a beer. Over drinks they talk, and this time Ethan listens. He does not throw his beer on his boss. Instead, they share a few stories and everything changes — for the better.

I don't know how things worked out in real life, but I do know that by changing perspectives in this narrative, the young sergeant was able to move outside his struggle and see it from another vantage point. By walking in the shoes of his superior, Ethan stopped ruminating about his own frustrations and began to see other ways of approaching his troubled relationship. His rumination gave way to reflection. The last phone conversation I had with Ethan was upbeat. It appeared he was moving forward, and at the very least, his story had.

Some new research points out that by changing our perspective in writing about a trauma, we gain significant benefits. Sometimes we explore our personal feelings and experiences. This writing is usually from a first-person or "I" voice. But when we give ourselves space from the emotional difficulty and see it from a third-person point of view, the "he or she" voice, we allow our logic to enter into our interpretation of the event. Ethan's re-written assignment mirrored this finding. Changing our perspectives allows us to shift from the mental trap of rumination — or ruination — to the empowerment of reflection.

Changing our perspective can empower our understanding of others — and ourselves!

Writing Prompts and Suggestions

Let's work to understand how others view your world.

Writing Prompt:
Write from a Different Viewpoint

Choose a difficult story from your life. But before you begin to write, explore it. Pull outside yourself. Be the person on the other side of this experience — perhaps your ex-husband, your child, or your boss. See the event from his or her side. Work to be understanding. Tell the story with insights into this character's feelings. See the details that would be captured in this character's mind. Write it, and then ask yourself: *How did I see this differently? What have I learned? What insights are important here?*

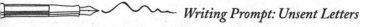 *Writing Prompt: Unsent Letters*

Write a letter to someone who has upset you (lied to you, hurt you, left you, betrayed you). In this letter help the other person understand your feelings. Then write a return letter from this person to you. Write from her viewpoint, trying to understand her side. Work to understand the event. Then try to leave it behind you.

Writing Prompt:
Writing as a Fictional Character

Sometimes we are not ready to write from the viewpoint of an assailant or abuser. When this happens we can benefit from turning to a fictional character. You might create a mentor, a teacher, a wise guide, someone who steps in to rescue you. Write your messy-difficult story, but allow this character, real or fictional, to tell your narrative and to guide you through it. Afterward, explore what you have learned from this character's experience. How has your understanding of the story changed? What insights have you gained?

CHAPTER FIFTEEN

Story Editing

Not until we are lost do we begin to understand ourselves.
— Henry David Thoreau

Five days after my cancer diagnosis, I received a call. Two friends were hosting a happy hour. Billie and Marybeth wanted to connect me with breast cancer survivors. I was a bit on edge, but I went.

That evening, while sipping wine and munching on veggies and pizza, three breast cancer survivors told me their stories, shared their ups and downs, and answered my questions, hundreds of them. In one heartrending moment two of them volunteered to show me their reconstructed breasts. "You can still look like a woman," one assured me. And she did.

Later, when one survivor remembered she had to pick up her daughter, hugs were shared and doors hurriedly swung open and shut. And as I drove home I realized that this event was a life-changing moment, for I had gained an understanding of what I faced. Indeed, breast cancer often serves as a model for how illness should be faced — with a community by your side. I am grateful for this experience, and I am even more thankful for my friends.

As we parted that evening, one woman had crushed a Post-it note into my hand and whispered, "Call Robin Obenchain. She is the best oncologist in the valley — she saved my life!" And the next morning I dug out the crumpled piece of paper from my jean pocket and punched the numbers into my cell. When I finally reached someone, I was told the doctor was booked for weeks in advance.

But two days later the same person with the mellow voice called me back. "Can you meet with Dr. Obenchain tomorrow at 7 AM? She wants to squeeze you in."

"Yes," I called into the phone. "Yes!"

I arrived so early the building was dark. In a few minutes lights popped on, and I was escorted into a room with bright yellow and orange walls. The walls were decorated with a ceramic sun clock and a metal artwork also inspired by the sun, with copper rays of sunlight shooting upward.

In a few minutes Dr. Obenchain seemed to float into the room. She rolled her chair over and cozied up to me as if we were longtime friends who simply needed to catch up. As we chatted, she pulled out a scrap piece of paper from her desk drawer and began drawing pictures of the calcifications she believed were hijacking my breast. She explained how sneaky they were. Together we talked about how to manage the disease. I asked questions, and eventually she began to ask questions as well. I told her I was a teacher and a writer and that I was thinking about exploring the connection between writing and healing.

"Writing and healing," she repeated thoughtfully. For the first time I realized she was either barely out of medical school or blessed with the forever-young look. And we were still chatting when her assistant thumped on the door to remind the doctor that her next patient had arrived. With a knee-jerk reaction, I jumped up and grabbed my book bag, certain I had violated an unspoken rule of courtesy by staying too long.

But Obenchain laughed and motioned me to sit back down. She leaned forward and asked if she could share an experience with me that might help. "I have a healing story that will only take a moment." She shoved her long blonde bangs out of her eyes. "When I was a second-year medical student, my mom discovered she had breast cancer." She frowned. "That really threw me for a loop, and for a time I was absolutely crushed. But she had a lumpectomy and she came through it — and I was inspired to become an oncologist." The doctor paused. She had started tapping her pen gently on the desk and seemed to be looking ahead into nowhere.

"A few years later I became a resident in a cancer ward in Nashville. I was excited to be in a new place, working in oncology, learning about various forms of cancer, and moving forward with my career. And then it all changed." She looked directly at me, still tapping her pen lightly. "It was strange. One day I was learning all about kidney cancer and thinking, 'Lordy, I would never want that disease. It is absolutely the worst!' The next day, *the very next day*, I had this excruciating pain." The tapping stopped momentarily. She paused, chuckled, and looked directly at me. "As is always the case, I was a doctor without a doctor. I ended up doing the only thing I could do. I went to the student health center. I had tests and scans — and guess what they found?" I swallowed hard. "I had *kidney cancer*." Her voice rose. Then she laughed and began tapping her pen again, but now it was rhythmic as if she held a drumstick. "This was my absolute worst nightmare," she recalled.

Then she described her treatment, which proved long, difficult, and painful. Later I would learn that even though she was a patient, she insisted on being available for her hospital patients. It is who she is. Fortunately, Obenchain's cancer was detected early, and this played a significant role in saving her life.

There was another knock at the door. "I'm coming," Obenchain called, but her eyes never wavered from mine. "My cancer was a rough time, but we both know the ending. I survived." She beamed. "And now I understand it," she explained. "I was able to experience this disease firsthand — the diagnosis, the fear, all the pain. Today, as a result, I understand what my patients are going through." The drumming of her pen stopped. "And I want you to know that cancer was *a gift* for me. It was absolutely a gift," she repeated. "Later, you will come to understand that cancer will be a gift for you, too." She paused and looked at me kindheartedly. "I am sure of it." And she tapped her pen on the desk one more time as if placing a period at the end of her story.

I sat there motionless, trying to make sense of her words, but before I could understand her message or even thank her, she had slipped out the door and forward to embrace another person caught in the clutches of this dreadful disease.

I rolled the words around in my head. *Cancer...a gift?* I was two weeks into cancer and busy juggling doctor's appointments, scans, and biopsies and preparing for surgery. At that moment cancer did not feel like a gift. And it would be a while before I would see it this way. But my oncologist had me thinking.

Interpreting Our Stories

As Christina Baldwin says in *Storycatcher*, "Words are how we think: stories are how we link." With lightning speed our brains grab bits of information from the thousands of pieces of sensory input bombarding us. The brain processes these sensory impressions and cobbles together a narrative of what's happening. It organizes input and makes meaning out of it by linking these sensory impressions. Each time we tell our story our brain reworks the words and smooths out the details of our memory. This allows us to create deeper meaning over time, and to make significant changes in the story we create of ourselves. In this process we often need to release attachment to first impressions and what we first accepted as the fact or even what we know as a truth.

As we link our narratives, we *are changing ourselves*. Baldwin explains, "The self-story *requires* editing. Editing is a constant process of updating who we think we are and how we speak about our histories and ourselves." And herein we find another piece of our human brain magic. Our brains allow us not only to create our personal story of self but to edit, interpret, and find meaning in what we are creating. Obenchain's story could have been one of despair or self-pity. But she chose to interpret her cancer in a positive light and, more important, she chose to act on this interpretation. When her mother experienced breast cancer, Obenchain decided to give her life to oncology. When the young doctor experienced kidney cancer and faced her own mortality, she chose to learn from the experience and the result was that she became a profoundly compassionate physician.

My meeting with this doctor changed me. I wanted to face my cancer as she had. I wanted to find the meaning in it. And I wanted to do something with my experience, as she had done. I doubted I could ever have the impact she was having, but if I had the chance to live past my cancer — unlike my Grandma Rose or my aunts — I wanted to find a way to honor the time I had been given. Eventually this thinking would lead to working with traumatized veterans and cancer patients. Eventually it would help me understand my cancer as a gift.

In his book *Redirect: The Surprising New Science of Psychological Change*, Timothy D. Wilson notes that three perspectives make us happy: finding meaning, living with a positive outlook, and living with a sense of purpose. I think he is on to something. Obenchain had found her meaning in becoming an oncologist. She was upbeat as she approached her daily life in the midst of cancer patients, many facing death. And she was living purposefully, working to heal those around her. But what if she had chosen to see this experience as devastating? What if she had dropped out of medical school?

The way we interpret our experiences is critical. We can choose unhealthy ways of viewing our traumas, and this can lead to negative outcomes, or we can direct our energies into editing our stories and giving meaning to our lives. If we can do this, and we can, the question becomes: How can we edit our stories? How can we edit our lives?

Story Editing

We can change our lives with a simple process. Wilson calls it "story editing," and he defines it as "techniques designed to redirect people's narratives about themselves and the social world in a way that leads to lasting changes in behavior." For example, if we receive a bad grade in a class, we can write the mental script of how we handle this, and we have choices in what script we write. We can blame the instructor and whine. We can tell ourselves we are dumb and do nothing. Or we can decide that we can do better by reading more, studying more, and attending outside work sessions. If we choose to accept responsibility and work harder, guess what happens? No surprise here — we do better. Our grades improve.

Wilson's work confirms my experience in classroom 221. Through the years I had watched my students not only editing their papers but *story editing* their lives. They would write and rewrite their narratives to make the story fit into their lives. Ben was trying to make his uncle's suicide bearable. The students in Lucas's class wrote alongside me to find a way to live with our painful loss. And David had written and rewritten his "This I Believe" statement to the point where he had it memorized. In his essay he acknowledged who he was and helped others make sense of the struggle of being gay in our culture. We can edit our lives by learning to edit our personal stories — and this can make all the difference in how we live.

We can edit our lives
by editing our own difficult life stories.

Writing Prompts and Suggestions

Let's explore how to edit a challenging personal story.

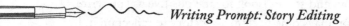 *Writing Prompt: Story Editing*

Choose a personal story or event. It may be one that troubles you or an experience you simply want to understand more fully. Perhaps you consciously want to face it or change your interpretation of this experience. Try working with these steps to edit this story:

- Begin by freely writing out the story.
- Then rethink it. Review your story by making notes that help you identify different ways of viewing it. (If you received a bad grade, are you going to see yourself as dumb or are you going to make constructive changes to help you improve? If you are in a bad relationship, can you move past blaming and faulting yourself to finding ways to cope and make changes?)
- List all the possible ways of reworking or editing this story. How can you make it a better story? Can you work to learn something new related to it? Can you volunteer to help others who have the same problem? Can you do or create something such as an artwork or poem or song to help you move forward?
- How can you choose to reframe or edit this story? Are there positive ways of working with this story? Place stars next to the specific ways you have listed that make good sense. This is critical, for it is here that you are making conscious choices in how you want to change.
- Rewrite your list working only with your starred items. They will be the center of your new interpretation.
- Now visualize how this will work. Give this process time,

and give yourself space and quiet. You can even leave this exercise and return to it later if you sense that would help.

- Now rewrite your edited story. You should write your final draft in the way that fits you uniquely. You can write this in your journal — or not. It can pour out of you as a freewriting exercise, as a poem, as a novel, as a script, as a memoir, and so on. Look for the positive as you write.

- Later you may come back to your story to reflect on it. In this review, ask yourself: Why did this happen, or why is it happening now? Have I edited this experience in the best way for me to move forward?

- If you feel successful at this challenging task, acknowledge it. And then work to accept and live your new story.

CHAPTER SIXTEEN

Rewriting and Transforming

*Your life does not get better by chance,
it gets better by change.*

— Jim Rohn

My mom has no breasts. She lost her right breast at the age of sixty and her left breast at eighty. Although we rarely talked about it — probably because it troubled us — cancer had woven its way into the cells of my grandmother and both my aunts. This disease ended all three of their lives. So when the radiologist announced to me that I, too, had cancer, I experienced shock — but not surprise.

Before that day I had taken my breasts for granted. Oh, there was the first time my high school boyfriend touched them. And later my children suckling from them and making them shoot sparks that tugged at my ovaries. But the best memories are of Steve, stroking them and making them light up like low-voltage wires that could only be grounded in the bedroom. And then there were the mammogram machines that flattened them like doughy pancakes.

After researching and talking to a series of doctors, I faced a hard decision. Did I want a lumpectomy with follow-up weeks of radiation to try to catch my disease? Or did I want to face a mastectomy and most likely rid myself of future cancer in one or both breasts?

I had a newfound relationship with my body, and I genuinely wanted to save my breasts. After six weeks of grappling with this issue, I opted for the lumpectomy. But I did not understand the truth yet. I did not have a lump. I had a cancerous area often referred to as sprinkles of calcifications. Thus I faced scans, an MRI, and biopsies. Nonetheless, I moved forward armed with the knowledge I had to make the best decision I could. I scheduled the lumpectomy for late February.

A day later my surgeon unexpectedly called and invited me to share my perplexing case with a board of six medical professionals. Four were doctors. By now it is probably clear that I am incurably curious. I believe in wanting to know. A week later I went.

On a lighted screen in a large gray conference room, the medical board's enthusiastic radiologist had posted scans of my breast, huge scans, in all kinds of poses. I searched the room for a red carpet — with all these scans it was clear my breast was a celebrity. No carpet. Instead there were handouts with endless data. Facing the medical professionals, my husband and I were seated at one end of the long tables placed in the shape of a square. After introductions the radiologist stood, and much like a college professor, he began his analysis of my left breast by pointing first at one scan and then another.

Afterward, for more than an hour, we all chatted comfortably about my odds of surviving breast cancer with a lumpectomy, a mastectomy, or a double mastectomy. These experts were intrigued by my family history and my dilemma. They asked penetrating questions. They fell all over my responses, rallied behind my efforts at research, and most important, supported my decision to have a lumpectomy.

Then there was a subtle shift in the conversation. One oncologist, Dr. Kato, mentioned the unknown — the mysterious calcium deposits that might be spread throughout my breast tissue. There were nods, but the doctors agreed that currently these deposits could only be seen in one area. But...and there was a long pause. The word *mysterious* surfaced several more times, probably because the doctors intuited that these spots were scattered across my breast. Silently hiding.

In the waning minutes of the meeting, I remained upbeat until I asked one last question. "If I were your wife or mom, what would you tell me to do?" Chairs creaked as bodies shifted. The frosted-haired oncology nurse gritted her teeth as if I had punched her in the gut. Dr. Kato pursed his lips tightly as if he were whistling Cat Steven's "Trouble" song. And my own surgeon placed her hand across her mouth. Others slumped in a deep meditation-like trance as if I had sucked all the air out of the room. To their credit, every professional in that room answered as honestly as he or she could. To their credit, it was clearly painful for them. Five of the six cancer specialists thought I should remove both breasts. Now.

How could this be? I had tried to be a good patient. I had written in my journal. I had read *Dr. Susan Love's Breast Book* from cover to cover. I had walked more than ten thousand steps daily. Meditated and prayed. Reached a careful, considered opinion. But now I sensed I had reached the wrong decision by choosing to have a simple lumpectomy. The doctors on my medical board suspected that I would eventually lose my breasts — that I *needed* to lose them.

Rewriting My Story

But I moved ahead with my decision. The morning after I met with the medical board, I awoke early, meditated, wrote several pages in my journal, and closed it with resolve. I was done. Done with lists. Done with reading books by cancer experts. Done with talking to oncologists. Done with calling Billie, my dear friend with a good ear. Intellectually I knew what I had to do. I had made a commitment to try to save my breasts, and I would follow through with it. But emotionally I felt a strange emptiness, like a balloon without air.

I called my mom. At ninety, she lived a few blocks from my home, and she was anxious to know my decision. This call started like all our conversations. The weather. The day. And then I said, "I have made my decision. I am going to try and save my breasts. I will have the lumpectomy..." Then I paused, for I was wavering over my choice. I thought of all the women who have repeat lumpectomies, making every effort to get clear margins and save their breasts. I wasn't even sure about *one* lumpectomy. "If we miss margins — even once — I am going to have a double mastectomy," I blurted.

Without pausing I began citing stats and sounding like the robot-like radiologist who had first informed me of my cancer, and suddenly, midsentence, in my mind's eye I saw the image of my Grandma Rose. Then I choked on the word *breasts* and began to sob. Not cry — sob. This must have gone on for some time, for the next thing I remember, I was still blubbering when my mom appeared on the scene, took my cell phone from my hands, clicked it off, and did something she had not needed to do for a couple of decades. She held me in her arms. She rocked me gently. And for a few minutes, I felt safe.

As the tears receded, I pulled back and dried my eyes. Then I realized I had been sobbing into the soft pads that had served as Mom's fake breasts for years. In that moment I understood that she had always been embarrassed by her fake breasts and the scars they hid. I doubted she had ever shown them to anyone. I reached out and touched the soft breast padding and asked, "May I see your scars?" She nodded, and without speaking, she unbuttoned her cotton blouse and unhooked her bra. And there they were. Long, jagged, red scars. *Beautiful* scars. Scars that had allowed her to keep her life, that allowed me to keep my mom. I studied them. With my finger I traced the lines gently where her breasts had been. Slowly. And then I hugged my mother with as much heart-gripping love as I had.

The Power of Reinterpreting Your Story

After my meeting with the medical board, I wrestled again with my decision, for I sensed women with my history and my condition usually ended up losing their breasts. But I marched ahead, determined to save mine by undergoing a lumpectomy. When Dr. Liu called after this surgery, she sounded upset. "There is so much more in there than we realized. We missed the margins."

"You are doing a phenomenal job," I insisted. Then I asked her to schedule me for a double mastectomy as soon as possible. For on the pages of my red journal, I had reached an understanding of why I had cancer, and with my words I had been able to edit and reinterpret this life story.

The reinterpreting of our story is critical. In a study that has become classic, Shelley E. Taylor, a distinguished psychologist from the University of California, Los Angeles, analyzed seventy-eight breast cancer patients and how they adjusted to their life-threatening disease. Taylor found that the cancer patients who had a "significantly better psychological adjustment" to cancer were those who could *find meaning*. These patients did this in two ways:

1. By creating a personal story that explained their cancer
2. By finding positive ways to restructure their lives

Even though most patients had no way of knowing why they got this disease, many believed their cancer was caused by a bad marriage, a bad job, by living in an unhealthy environment, by heredity, or even by a blow to the breast — one patient was convinced a Frisbee striking her had caused her cancer. Taylor and her colleagues came to call this "positive illusions." Even though these patients could not prove why they had cancer, they were able to find their own interpretation of it, and this allowed them to move forward to fight their disease. As we discovered earlier, our left brain can be a know-it-all. When we don't understand an experience, we create a personal explanation.

And my cancer worked the same way. When I flip through the red cancer journal of 2012, I see I floundered for a few weeks as I tried to understand why I had this disease. But I found my answer the day I touched my mother's long jagged scars. In that moment I sensed that cancer is somehow threaded through my genes. And the pained expressions on the faces of the doctors at my medical board confirmed this insight.

Since my genetic testing refuted my theory — there is no scientific support for my thinking — my understanding may be nothing more than a positive illusion. But maybe not. Aren't science and research ongoing? Isn't it possible that someday we will discover what causes cancer to thread a path through a family's genes? For now I am grateful that my left brain and the image of mother's scars have allowed me to rewrite my understanding of this experience. Like the cancer patients studied by Taylor, because of this understanding I am able to move ahead toward greater well-being.

Changed Story, Changed Life

When cancer patients in the same study restructured their lives by changing jobs, entering better relationships, eating better, or embarking on something important to them, they acquired a renewed sense of control over their lives, as well as improved self-esteem. Both these qualities guided these patients toward a positive cancer experience. In making these changes, they were editing their personal stories and improving the quality of their lives. Indeed, Taylor's interviews showed that most of these individuals felt their lives had improved significantly after cancer. It turns out that story transformation can lead us to personal transformation. And my experience reinforced this finding.

As I recovered from my double mastectomy, I began to birth

the idea for this book. I found my old journals and began to read them. Between episodes of *Downton Abbey*, I got online and began a long and rewarding process — researching the power of writing to heal us. As soon as I could drive, I started writing at a local café and stopping by the library when I needed to dig deeper. Soon I began interviewing chemo patients, veterans, and writers on their experiences with writing. I pared back teaching to one online class. I, too, had restructured my life to return to what I thought was important for me to do — write. And as I changed, so did my view of cancer. I came to view living with a new sense of wonder, and now I could genuinely view my cancer as a gift. Dr. Obenchain was right.

> *By reaching an understanding of our broken stories, we can find positive ways to interpret and restructure our lives.*

Writing Prompts and Suggestions

These writing activities allow us to work toward our changes, our unique story transformation.

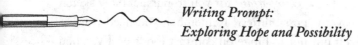

Writing Prompt:
Exploring Hope and Possibility

Choose to create a collage or a poem that explores your hopes and possibilities.

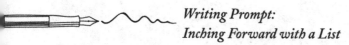

Writing Prompt:
Inching Forward with a List

When you have faced a crisis or a trauma, one technique that can help you inch forward is making a list of what you can do or need to do. Ask yourself how you can manage this event. Who can you talk to? What can you do to face this experience? Begin by jotting down any actions that might help. When you finish your list, prioritize these activities. Mark the important items with As and the semi-important items with Bs. The not-so-important actions can be labeled with Cs. Move ahead by working on your list of A activities. Cross each item off as you complete it. This will allow you to measure your progress and to find your path forward. Review and rewrite this list as needed.

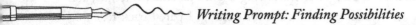 *Writing Prompt: Finding Possibilities*

Write a description of a current difficulty or challenge you face (a teenager in trouble, an illness in your family, the loss of a friend, or simply an out-of-control schedule). This is different from listing because you will begin by freewriting and work toward the creation of a doable plan. Start by sharing your concerns and feelings about what has happened. Then brainstorm and explore all the possible ways you could handle this challenge. Think outside the box. After you have explored all the things you need to do, work to add activities that will allow you to feel centered and balanced. Do you need time to visit with friends? Do you need to reconnect with an activity that you love and left behind in the craziness of your schedule? Do you want to paint? Take a trip? Hike? Practice yoga? Then go back and highlight or underline what seems doable and *important* for you to pursue. Now sketch out a plan — your "possibilities." Remember, you need time to balance yourself but not to binge on comfort foods or TV. Then create and try your new plan. Review it as needed.

PART FIVE

WRITING TO HEAL

CHAPTER SEVENTEEN
Writing to Heal
from Hardships and Trauma

*"Nothing that happens to us, even the most terrible shock,
is unusable, and everything has somehow to be built
into the fabric of the personality."*
— May Sarton

As I left my cancer behind, I began a series of interviews that would change my life. I had received a note from Matthew "Goldie" Goldston, who wrote to tell me he had kept a diary during his stint as a marine in Afghanistan. Shortly afterward, Goldie connected me to two former marines who served with him — Jeremy Lattimer and Todd Nicely. All three joined the service inspired by their idealism. "I was in high school when the twin towers fell," Jeremy explained over the phone. From the photos he had emailed, I envisioned him always looking like he had recently returned from a week on the beach, tanned and muscular. "I knew war was coming, and I wanted to be a part of serving our country."

"Yeah," acknowledged Goldie during our first interview at a diner near Luke Air Force Base. "I wanted to serve. The marines were known to be the biggest challenge, and I wanted a challenge. I wanted to make a difference — especially after 9-11."

Goldston, who had recently retired, continued to wear his

hair closely shorn, marine style. He loved the structure of the marines and the connection to a bigger purpose. "I especially loved the camaraderie. In my squad we were brothers. *Brothers*," he stressed. "I would die for those guys." Then suddenly he scratched his arm and twisted around in the booth, glancing nervously behind him. "Crazy," he explained. "I can't sit in any restaurant without checking behind me. War does that to you. You never know who is there, and you want your back covered." He turned toward me and sucked nervously on his straw. "It all started in Afghanistan — in Helmand Province — there were firefights every day. IEDs every day.

"Do you know what IEDs are?" he asked, eyeing me cautiously. "They're improvised explosive devices, homemade bombs created by the Taliban. They have flammable fuel in them and are loaded with rusty screws, dirt, all kinds of nasty things — and when you get blown up by one, you usually lose a leg or arm, and most likely you will get an infection. When that stuff gets into your system — well, you are probably going to die." Goldie, tall, thin, and stiff backed, twisted around in the booth again.

When he turned back to me, a dark shadow seemed to fall over his face. He lowered his voice. "That is when it got rough. Seeing people blown up. Most guys were affected by it. We lived in constant fear of stepping on one of those deadly devices. When I think back," explained Goldie, "this was definitely the start of my PTSD."

It would be a year before Sgt. Matthew Goldston would feel comfortable enough to share his tattered green war journal with me. I am grateful he did. From his pages:

This place is going to be rough. Few contacts. On patrol today we walked through the Marijuana Acre. Marijuana here is like grass in America. It's always going to be here.

It is the first week and we are on patrol and an IED goes off — followed by PRK machine gun fire. The number of Taliban is unknown. They are in a tree line on the other side of the canal. Gunfire is being exchanged here and sounds like people getting change from a cash register. At least no one was hurt today.

"When we first arrived there," Jeremy noted, "the altitude was brutal on us. It was blazing hot, too. We had a goal to push south in Afghanistan because there were no Americans in the south. We needed to go as far south as we could. That was our assignment, and at first it was exciting because we were blazing a new trail. There was a mixture of nervousness and excitement. We didn't even have maps." No matter. As the squad leader, Jeremy undertook this task with enthusiasm and a clear commitment.

"American businesses had built canals in this area to help Afghanis develop their agriculture. The number one crop was poppies," explained Jeremy, "and that needed to change. I read books on how to help the Helmand Valley improve agriculturally. The local folks controlled the rivers." He chuckled — a warm laugh. "As a result you were never sure what days you could actually cross the canals to get to the other side. Sometimes Al-Qaeda planted IEDs on the bridges, and we never knew where to look for them." Across Lattimer's left bicep was a large tattoo, and the imprint escapes me, but I kept thinking it should read, "*Committed to making a positive difference*." He was.

The platoon worked its way south. "On our very first day down there — and you need to know most of these guys were new to combat — we were caught in a bad firefight. All I could think of was *shit — it is different down here*." The daily firefights took a weighty toll on the mental health of these marines. "Every time you are in a firefight there is fear and an extreme adrenaline rush," Jeremy added pensively. "It causes terrible anxiety — especially as you put on your gear. When you go out to fight, you actually put your feelings on hold and just go through it. But beforehand the anxiety makes you sick to your stomach."

As their platoon pushed south in Afghanistan, carrying out their mission became increasingly risky. "We were down farther south all the time. Putting people through this — pushing us to this extreme was intense. Initially we had helicopters firing and supporting us and helping us to keep moving. And suddenly they stopped those air strikes. They were no longer covering our backs — the enemy was even shooting at us when we were sleeping at night." He paused. "It was unimaginable. When we had a rest, many guys would just lie down in a field, put on headphones, and try to escape through their music.

"Then we were ordered to build this little base of two squads in what was poppy territory," Jeremy explained. "They openly sell machine guns in the market place. It was risky even to be there. If anything happened, we now knew no one was coming for us — we were just out there. We found a stash of enemy weapons and ammunition, but we didn't have any support so we were trapped there for another three days just watching them build up their weapons. We believed they had hidden a bomb close to us. Finally we were able to radio back to the other squad to ask for help. And of course, Todd Nicely agreed to come."

> More gunfire. We have a patrol to Haredi Wall. Most firefights happen at the wall. I don't know what the outcome is going to be. What will happen? (From Sgt. Matthew Goldston's War Journal)

"Everybody loves Todd." Goldie's bushy eyebrows raised, and his straight-lipped smile faded as he continued. "That was the worst day ever. I believe my memory of that event really sent me over the edge when I came home." He paused, looking down into a plate with remnants of french fries, as if the whole hell-laced experience was happening all over again, right there in our booth. "We were on that patrol. Stuck. We needed support. We radioed back, and Corporal Todd Nicely volunteered. He came to help

— and he was always the first to go in. But this time, well, he stepped on a pressure plate, an IED." Goldie paused in reverent silence. "Everybody loves that guy — and having him blown up was too much for all of us." His eyes bore into mine, wanting to make sure I understood. "It was *too much*," he repeated.

Both Jeremy and Goldie were struck speechless at this point in their stories. Later in a phone conversation, Todd explained to me what happened to him:

> On March 26, 2010, when I was on a tour in Afghanistan, we got a call. I wasn't even supposed to go out. We had been out multiple times in the dark, checking the intel on the enemy. But Jeremy's squad was stuck out there alone — and they radioed in that they needed help finding some bomb. My squad volunteered to find it, and we did. On the way back we stopped to talk to the locals by the canal. In Afghanistan one of our main jobs was to communicate with the people, so I talked with them and assured them all was well. I liked doing that. After I talked to some of the elders, I turned to cross the canal, and since I was the squad leader, I always felt I should go first — so I took that first step and then BOOM...
>
> I heard it explode, and I thought, *I can't believe this sucker got me.* And then I felt the water and knew I had been blown into the air and landed in the canal — which was good because I might survive. I knew my legs were gone because that is what usually happens, but I remember looking out and seeing a bone sticking out of my arm. Oh — I looked away — I don't think I was ready to know about my hands.
>
> I wanted to scream and maybe I did once, but I didn't want to scare my guys so I kept telling myself not to scream because everything will be okay. I told myself over and over again that I had to get back to my family.

Over and over I said, *You can. You can. You can.* And that
is how I believe I made it. How I survived.

"When Todd was blown up, I was at the patrol base about a
half mile away," explained Goldie. "They called for me to get a
stretcher to him. I ran as fast as I could to help save my buddy,
and every step I took I was scared to death that I might land on
another IED. Those explosives were all over. And when I arrived
and saw him, I thought I would be sick. My God, he was not only
bandaged on both legs but also on both arms — you expect them
to lose their legs, but Todd had lost both hands, too." Goldie tried
to choke back his tears. I made no effort to hide mine.

"At that moment we all assumed Todd would die....But
the most amazing thing happened. Right before they loaded
him onto the helicopter, he signaled us by raising what was left
of his right arm and moving it up in the air, like a salute to us.
And then I had a sense he might live." Goldie's smile returned.
"Todd left us with hope. Hope that he would survive....And
he did."

Writing Your Way Out of Darkness

"How did I cope with it all? Quite a bit gets buried inside you.
And you don't talk about it," said Goldie. "But in Afghanistan I
did keep a diary. The guys can tell you. Some guys used music. I
used the writing.

"The writing helped." Suddenly Goldie's smile resurfaced.
"Yeah. It helped a lot. If you can simply write your story or your
thoughts and get it out of you, it helps relieve the stress and
anxiety."

"Touchdown!" a voice called. Goldie paused to check the
cheers coming from the bar across from our booth.

"This world still seems strange to me." He shrugged and
dipped a french fry into ketchup. "I wanted to talk with you
because I wanted others to know that when you are *out there*,

writing can help. I still struggle with PTSD...with all of it." He pointed over his shoulder. "I am still looking for the enemy. But I can tell you, when I was out there — in the middle of a war — the writing helped take the unseen monkey off my back."

> I see a lot of scared faces here. It's to be expected...It's hard here and so different, and I hate thinking of my daughter at home going Trick-or-Treating without me. (From Sgt. Matthew Goldston's War Journal)

News reports claim that eighteen to twenty-two veterans choose to end their lives each day. Many vets are unable to overcome their traumatic memories of war. They cannot see a future. Given what we know about the power of writing to heal, it may well be that Goldie's journal during his deployment kept him sane — and perhaps alive.

When Goldie wrote in his diary, when Robert used old letters to help him type up his war experiences, when Barbara Lee was writing her poems, and when I was struggling with my journal musings, something significant was happening to all of us. We were making sense of our stories.

In my own overwhelmed-with-life depression, the darkness did eventually turn to light. As I wrote day after day in my journal, the sadness lifted and I felt transformed. New again. For a while I felt I was seeing life through the wide eyes of a child. The sun felt warmer. The sky stretched beyond the horizon, and the colors were more brilliant than a Van Gogh painting of the fields in Arles. The words in my journal began to shimmer. With joy. With enthusiasm. I was no longer stuck, and I could move ahead with life, feeling both reconnected and *in the moment*.

Journal writing pioneer Christina Baldwin wrote, "It takes a period of disorder, I think, to teach us wonder, to inform the heart that we are not abandoned, that we may still find that we are being touched by the essence of something large and holy."

Writing and Transformation

Writing not only helps us make sense of living; it can help transform us. I had seen this in my classroom with Ben and David, and now I was watching it in my VA writing group. Week after week Barbara Lee had inched forward, writing powerful poems. Bravely she read them to the group. In them she framed the story of a rape that she had been unable to share with anyone for more than two decades. One day in writing group, I turned to her and said, "I see it now. I thought you were hiding your story from me, but it is all here — laid out in metaphors." She lifted her dark eyes and looked right through me. She was pleased.

But in the coming weeks, Barbara vanished. I called her, but no one answered. Like most of the vets, she faded in and out of the writing group. I was not sure she would return, and I feared I would never see her again. I missed her imagery. I missed her gifts-from-God metaphors. I missed her depth. I missed the layers of meaning in each of her poems. The woman had something happening with words. I loved that about her and, of course, it was only in her absence that I realized this.

In a few weeks, close to midnight, the phone by my bed rang. Was there the sound of drums pounding? Perhaps a cat mating? Or was it the sound of a young child wailing? I couldn't be sure. And then Barbara's voice bellowed over the racket, "I need for you to be at group tomorrow. It's important."

"Of course. Where...where are you?" I stammered into the receiver. But it clicked off, and I was left tormented: Where was Barbara? Were the sounds coming from a hospital emergency room? Could she be in a jail? Did she finally punch out that Napoleon-style psychiatrist? I did not go back to sleep.

The next day I arrived at the VA hospital early. When I entered, I nodded around the room at familiar faces — Tim. Kai. Rob. Darren beamed his toothy grin at me and immediately announced he had a joke to tell us. But it wasn't a joke. It was the same story he often shared about a kid on the bus who had on two mismatched shoes. "And this poor kid didn't even know it!" Darren's hands flapped like an airplane propeller as he repeated this punch line. It wasn't funny — but I laughed.

"Where's Barbara?" I asked, sucking in my disappointment in the same moment that the door to the room slammed open. Barbara. I wanted to jump up and squeeze her in my arms. But I did not move.

Within minutes she had extricated her latest poem from the depths of her monster-sized purse. And she began to read, slowly at first, as if the words were tumbling around in her mouth. I was in the moment, working hard to find her newest metaphor. But this poem was different from Barbara's other pieces. Her voice was softer. Quieter. Almost hard to hear. No rage. When she finished reading, the room was still and Darren looked at me as if to say, "What just happened?"

I was not sure I understood her poem, either. Perhaps we simply couldn't *hear her poem*. I asked her to read it a second time. Instead of giving me the usual stare that could freeze my insides for eternity, Barbara pushed her chair back and rose from her seat. She glanced around the room and gave us a wide-as-the-sun smile — which was something we had not seen before. Then she began to read again, in the same voice, but it was stronger and clearer and smooth as honey. And this time her words latched on to my brain cells. Barbara longed to be a seamstress draping, tucking, and pinning the fabric *of her being*. The message washed through me, and suddenly I envisioned Barbara writing it last night at her kitchen table with her little niece crying in the background and her mom washing up the late-dinner dishes. And now the whole of it — the scene and the poem — washed over my soul. In these words Barbara had come to understand something new about herself. Trumpets were blowing in my brain as she read:

The Measure of a Woman

I want to be a tailor, skillfully draping, tucking, and pinning
the fabric of my being
On the large-busted mannequin standing in the corner.
Organza, silk, cotton, and wool slip through my fingers.
Faded by time, darted and pleated,
contoured faithfully to the shape of my body.
The measure of a woman is not in the
curve of a breast or line of a thing.
The true measure of a woman is her ability to
take up space in the universe.
To stretch and reach for that which allows others
to be comfortable in her presence.
An abstract construct infuses the mannequin.
No longer content to be an IT.
I emerge from the shadows.

While Barbara had been unable to speak of her rape, it eventually began to erupt from her in rage and frustration. In her poems she was able to lay out her pain in powerful images. Now she was reaching an understanding of what had happened to her. Her words helped her reframe this event, feel the pain of it, and understand the "why" of it. Her words helped her "emerge from the shadows" of her trauma. To transform.

Months later I met her for breakfast at her favorite café in Phoenix. Surrounded by "hi y'all" waitresses with coffeepots in hand and by fresh flowers on the table, we both ordered the signature dish of southwest burritos. "I wanted you to know," Barbara explained as she poured salsa over her burrito, "my change was real. I am different now. My boyfriend recently asked, 'What happened to the old Barbara — the *angry* Barbara?'"

"What did you tell him?" I asked.

"Oh, we laughed. Neither one of us wants *that* Barbara back." Her sunshine smile appeared. "I am done with that nightmare. I understand it now, and I no longer think about it." She laughed. "All the writing — well, writing can change you."

I stood and reached across the booth to bear-hug this beautiful woman.

The next semester Barbara returned to college to study writing. She no longer attends the VA writing group, and I miss her metaphors. But she is still my friend. We continue to indulge in too much Mexican food, but she no longer laughs when I call her a poet. She is one.

If You Can't Write, Then Tell

While he no longer keeps a journal, Goldie Goldston and his friends are sharing their stories and working to heal from their war experiences. While in Phoenix Goldie volunteered with the Military Assistance Mission, sharing his struggle with PTSD with fellow veterans and encouraging them to seek help. After retirement he completed training and is working as a welder in Missouri. He confesses that his PTSD remains an ongoing struggle.

Upon his return to the states, Jeremy Lattimer received the Bronze Star for his actions in Afghanistan. He underwent treatment at Walter Reed National Military Medical Center for the TBIs (traumatic brain injuries) sustained during combat in Iraq and Afghanistan. He has returned to school to study history.

Todd Nicely remains an inspiration to many folks. He moved into a home especially equipped for a quadruple amputee. He has faced perhaps ten surgeries but recently admitted he no longer keeps track of the number. While his new life holds untold challenges, Todd continues to make amazing progress on many levels, including learning to walk on artificial legs.

All three of these impressive men have shared their powerful stories with others. And similar to writing our stories, sharing our stories holds the same promise of healing us — and connecting us. I am thankful that these heroic veterans taught me this. If you don't want to write, if you can't write, please tell your stories. This process, too, will change you. And the prompts at the end of these chapters can be used to guide your storytelling as well.

Keys for Writing through Trauma

Based on the stories told by these heroic veterans as well as from the countless other stories shared for this book, I have put together some key characteristics of writing to heal through trauma. This kind of writing does the following.

It Opens Us Up

Often creative writing students take online classes so that they can hide their identities. One student, Liza, admitted as much to me. She wrote a terrifying story about being beaten and tortured by a lover. When I finished reading it, I called her immediately. When we talked, she assured me I did not need to call 911. "This happened years ago, but I needed to get that story out of me," she explained. "This class seemed like a safe place — where no one would know me — and I could share this horrible experience."

Time and again researchers have reported that survivors of suicide, bullying, rape, sexual abuse, or other traumas feel it is unacceptable to talk about these experiences. We fear embarrassment or disapproval if we open up about these charged topics. Sadly, many of us bury these stories inside — and pay the price for it. Barbara hid the story of her rape for more than two decades. When I first interviewed Goldie, he assured me that talking about war was next to impossible. "It took me a long time to figure out that you need to get your story out. I still struggle with it."

If we keep our stories inside, compressed pain will cause our immune systems to struggle under the weight of the pressure. This increases our chances of both physical and psychological illness. A significant number of studies have demonstrated that people who opened up and "wrote about their deepest thoughts and feelings surrounding traumatic experiences" improved their health as witnessed by "heightened immune function." While it may prove difficult to write about personal upheavals, and you should avoid writing too soon after an event, later the physical and emotional payoff is profound.

It Goes Deep in Search of Understanding

Recently I sat in a West Coast writing workshop, where I met quiet, beautiful, chestnut-haired Jessica Brown. On the last day of our workshop, she volunteered to read her story. Her story cut deep and would help her make sense of an experience that had caused her and her husband immeasurable pain. These are her words:

> "Yeah I'm free, free-falling" — Tom Petty bellowed through the speakers of my charcoal-gray Mini. I wanted to believe these words as I sang loudly along with Tom, with the wind swirling my loosely tied hair around my face, as I sped down the dark highway. I felt strong and powerful — free from the madness that had become my life. I flirted with the gas pedal a little more — and I thought about the lyrics. I wondered about free-falling and leaving this world for a while.
>
> What does it feel like to free-fall into nothing? Should I leave this world behind? Do I have the guts to turn hard to the right and do just that?
>
> My phone vibrated viciously in the cup holder. Would it be him? Would he be begging me to come back? I cranked up Tom Petty a few more notches and screamed, "Fuck him!" But I knew that fucking him was what got me into this mess in the first place.
>
> I had to figure out where I was going. I knew I could not go back there — and I could not go home and face

my husband. I had to find a hotel and lay low for a few days. Answer emails from work. Order eggs Benedict from room service. And drink a few beers.

But first I had to change my appearance. I couldn't walk into a hotel at 11 PM in paint-splattered clothes. I couldn't let them see the look of desperation in my face. They would look at my left hand and see the fading indentation of the ring on my finger, and I would be the gossip of the hotel staff. I could not face the shame. Not tonight.

What the fuck was I doing? Who had I become?

Jessica paused to wipe away her tears. This happens often in expressive writing workshops. By the time she wrote these words, her affair was long over. She had undergone therapy and come to accept herself as an alcoholic who had cheated on her husband. She had made important strides in rebuilding her life by working on her marriage and starting her own fulfilling business, a small yoga studio near the coast.

But Jessica also realized she had a story she needed to tell, and she wanted to come to grips with this difficult period in her life by writing it, hoping to turn it into a narrative she could move past and eventually share with others.

It Uses Words to Heal

If we want to write to heal, our words matter — especially our positive words. I witnessed this week after week at the veterans' writing group. While Sienna had lost some of her mental processes due to an overdose of anesthesia during a regular surgery, she eventually moved past her painful journal writings and discovered there was great value in what she called "positive writing." She would write about "hope," or make lists of "everything I am thankful for," and her outlook improved dramatically.

Initially Barbara Lee was not too receptive to positive writing. Instead she toyed with various metaphors to create her poems and simultaneously explore who she was. At first her metaphors proved gruesome, even shocking. As we saw, in "Emotional Autopsy," she described herself as "a bloodless cadaver… spread-eagled," and in "Wasted Potential" she viewed herself as "withered, dark misshaped fruit." But in time, Barbara was able to find words that would help her heal. In "The Measure of a Woman" she takes control of her life. She is the tailor "skillfully draping, tucking, and pinning the fabric of my being."

It Embraces the Writing Process

In one of my creative writing classes, Katie wrote about arriving home one day with hot pepperoni pizzas and sticky sodas that had leaked all over her car. Hands full, she banged on the door with her arms, but her husband failed to answer. Surprised, she kicked the door open with her high heels, yelling, "Josh! Where are you?" Later, when she saw the note on the kitchen counter, she was stunned into silence. After eighteen years of marriage, Josh had left her and their children.

In class, week by week, Katie inched forward with a story that explored her inner turmoil as she tried to understand why her husband had walked out, leaving her to manage their three children, their two dogs, and their home. As she wrote, bits of painful experiences surfaced in her memory. In telling the story she needed to tell, Katie began to unravel the knot in her stomach. Slowly she came to grips with a new understanding: her husband was trapped in serious depression and needed to get out from under the weight of his family.

When Katie started my fiction writing class, she said, "I want to write a bestseller." As the weeks passed, her story grew into a novel. As the semesters passed, Katie grew and changed. When she completed her certificate in the creative writing program, she wrote to me, "I came to the college to write a bestseller. But I leave here happy to have an understanding of a difficult period in my life. I am better for having done this." In the end she realized she was writing to survive the pain of losing her marriage, and she has done exactly that.

If a story is intended for publication, by all means publish it. But know that the process of writing to understand ourselves, of writing to heal, or writing to grow and become all we can, is a noble endeavor of its own.

Writing to heal from traumas and setbacks:

• opens us up
• goes deep in search of understanding
• uses words to heal
• embraces the writing process

Writing Prompts and Suggestions

If you remain troubled by a past experience or trauma, consider doing these exercises. The prompts are intended to be used either alone or in tandem with counseling. Choose the prompts that will help you tell your story, as well as the prompts that will best support your growth.

Important note: If you remain deeply troubled by your experience, seek out counseling and professional help.

 *Writing Prompt: Structured Writing on a Story You Need to Tell*

If you have not written about a difficult experience or trauma, you may want to approach it first by doing a structured writing adapted from the work of Kathleen Adams. By answering simple questions you can explore your experience and decide if you are ready to move forward with an in-depth exploration. Begin by completing each sentence starter, and follow it with a short paragraph of a few sentences. It should take about ten to twenty minutes.

- The story I would like to explore is...
- What comes to mind is...

- What bothers me about this experience is…
- What I would like to understand is…
- I am hopeful that…
- Perhaps it would help if…
- What I have learned is…

Later come back and review this writing. At this time ask yourself: What have I learned? Is this a story I need to explore in more depth? Decide on your next step.

 *Writing Prompt: Song Lyrics*

Our music and songs make it easy to explore hard events. Make a list of the songs you love. Then create a playlist or a mixed tape (these have evolved). When you play this music, choose the lines that connect to you. Then you may choose to write briefly about the lyrics you love, write a poem about a theme you found here, or create a collage that explores a few lines you love from these songs. You may want to share your music with a friend.

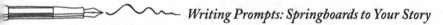 *Writing Prompts: Springboards to Your Story*

Here is a list of simple prompts that might help you tap into a story you need to tell. Try one or more of these ideas. Begin by freewriting, and see how one unfolds. If the writing takes off, continue with this prompt. If it stalls, choose another.

- I knew I was faced with a challenge when…
- I knew it was over when…
- The secret I harbor is…
- The scars I hide are…
- I am faced with the unknown because…
- I believe I have turned it around by…
- My hopes are…
- My dreams are…

*Writing Prompt: Questions about the
"Story You Need to Tell"*

If you continue to search for the story you need to tell, try to answer these questions with as much depth and honesty as you can. These stories *do not* have to be based on difficult experiences. Finding joyful and positive moments may well provide you your best story yet.

- What story do you want to tell? Why?
- What is unique about your story?
- What is painful about your story?
- What is joyful about this story?
- What is universal about your story?
- What have you learned from this story?

Remember, if your writing ever seems too painful, stop. If you are afraid someone will see what you have written, shred or burn it. The healing it has given you will remain a part of you.

CHAPTER EIGHTEEN

Writing to Heal from Illness and Injury

Writing has helped me heal.
Writing has changed my life. Writing has saved my life.
— **Louise DeSalvo**

When my surgeon called to tell me I was "done" with breast cancer, she asked me if I would meet with another patient, a young mother, who wanted to write her story for her child. In case.

"In case?" I asked stupidly, and then it hit. In case she died.

Two days later my cell phone rang. The connection was weak, and at first her words vibrated through my Bluetooth. I pulled forward into the drive-through, desperate for caffeine. "Cancer... stage four...I need to write," she said. "Jen." Her name was Jen. I scribbled it down on a Starbuck's napkin, along with a time and date for our meeting.

We met at her place, a refurbished ranch-style home on the north side of Phoenix — the kind with green grass, willowy eucalyptus trees, and a porch with those white Adirondack chairs you want to take a nap in, all just a block from the hubbub of downtown. An almost bald pixie met me at her door. Within minutes her voice, a silvery childlike song, charmed me as she heated green tea for us. In the coming weeks I would learn the story she needed to tell, and I would begin to write pieces of it — and encourage her to write as well. She had already embraced the idea in her own way.

Jen's story opens with the birth of Quinn. By now Quinn is nonstop energy, and you have to wonder how the petite Jen ever breast-fed this bundle of boy. "But I did," she explained. "And I like to get As on everything I do." She undertook breast-feeding as she undertakes life — with a can-do attitude. But when Quinn was only three months old, something odd happened. One day as Jen nursed, she found a hard lump on her right breast. She was troubled. She visited the doctor who had delivered Quinn, but he insisted it was nothing.

For a while Jen ignored it, but the lump expanded, growing quickly to the size of a large, hard walnut. Finally she sought a second opinion from a doctor who said, "It is probably nothing — but if you want to check it out, I know a fine surgeon."

As soon as possible Jen visited surgeon Linda Liu. After the examination, Dr. Liu sent Jen to another clinic to undergo immediate imaging. "They kept taking pictures, but I still didn't get it," explained Jen. "I thought they were going to find some weird cyst in there — with hair and teeth." She paused and we laughed. The radiologist just kept snapping pictures, and finally she turned and said, "This looks like cancer." Jen froze.

Darkness was creeping across the sky by the time Jen left the cancer clinic and wearily navigated the miles home. "Quinn was only five months old, and I had been diagnosed with cancer. I could feel the fear just creeping up all over me."

When Jen told her husband, he was equally stunned. Together they cried. Later that night, they began to do online research. "Chris is a scientist — and research is what he does," explained Jen. "We discovered that breast cancer is very curable and that most young women survive it, and we kept saying — *it's not like it has spread everywhere.*"

But it had spread. When the imaging came back, Jen learned from Dr. Liu that her cancer was stage four. The scan showed the disease inside her lungs and spleen, outside her liver, and in her chest wall.

"At first I couldn't even hear my diagnosis." Jen looked down. "Some people interpret stage four as a death sentence. But I couldn't — I just couldn't."

Blogging through Illness

Initially it can be hard to talk or write about cancer. Jen admitted she was overwhelmed by phone calls and text messages from family and friends. "When my sister-in-law, who had worked in public relations, asked if I needed someone to help with my PR, I realized I did." How can you juggle the onslaught of messages, Facebook notes, calls, and emails when you are immersed in figuring out how to save your own life? "And this is when I first realized that writing could help me," she explained.

"I decided I would start a blog," Jen added. "This would give everyone the chance to keep updated on my illness without feeling they had to call me all the time. And I didn't want to just keep dumping my story out. I have wonderful friends and family, but they are too busy to check on me every day." And Jen, who had to manage her surgeries and chemo while working full-time as a lawyer, was busy, too. The expressive blog writing allowed her to open up about her struggles while simultaneously keeping others informed.

"Computers do weird things when I enter a room. They turn on or off. I can't explain it." Jen joked about her lack of technology prowess, but she didn't let this get in her way. She went online, did the research, and launched www.boobyandthebeast .com. "And it worked," she explained. "Looking back, I realized I needed help on many levels, and I found the writing was completely cathartic. It gave me a powerful and needed release — and

I got a tremendous response to my blog. People kept asking if they could share it, and this has inspired me to keep writing."

On her blog Jen does not sugarcoat her experiences. Instead, she models how to write and even how to *rewrite* a painful life story. We can choose to succumb to or stand up to a chronic illness. And Jen is standing up. She has faced surgeries, radiation, chemo, insurance battles, and recurrences. And sometimes she wavers and cries, but mostly she focuses on those she loves, goes to yoga, finds her positive voice — and steadies herself with her words.

The average life span for a young woman with metastatic breast cancer is a little more than two years after diagnosis. Recently Jen finished her memoir, *The Fire Within*, on living with cancer. She researches, educates, and manages a life with this horrible disease. She is almost five years out.

Until recently Jen and I visited every third Monday at her chemo session. We shared our writing as well as the lessons we were learning from cancer. She taught me that we can choose our attitudes and find our words and *be healed* even when we face dying. Her courage continues to inspire me.

Once, as we munched nuts and sipped tea, I asked her, "How do you stay so upbeat?"

She pushed back in her chemo La-Z-Boy and looked up at the sky like the pensive Tinker Bell she is. "I tell myself, '*I may have cancer, but cancer does not have me.*'"

But though it helped Jen enormously, a blog, a very public form of writing, is not for everyone. When I first learned I had cancer, I could hardly speak about it, let alone blog about it. Our illnesses or setbacks may need privacy — at least for a while. And that is one of the huge advantages of writing. It can be private — or not. We can find our voice by following our own path, in poems, memoirs, scripts, blogs, journals, dictating our stories, or even scribbles on napkins. The important piece is finding your words — and that is more likely to happen if you *choose* your form of writing.

Once again my kitchen is cluttered with dozens of books — stories of healing, memoirs, novels, poems, and a couple of plays. When troubled, we need to burrow down in a comfy spot, find a form of words that works best for us, and write. It took me a while to realize how profoundly versatile writing to heal can be. My students have written essays, books, novels, plays, poems, journals, blogs, and several of these simultaneously. All these forms of writing help us to explore and heal ourselves from all types of setbacks. Write in the format that calls to you. Write in the format you love. And check out the models offered by established writers.

Stories Can Save Us

In a moving memoir, *A Three Dog Life*, Abigail Thomas writes about her struggle to build a new life after her husband, Rich, was hit by a car, leaving his skull shattered and his brain damaged. Rich lost his memory; only the present moment remained. Thomas moved from her beloved apartment in New York City to the small town of Woodstock near the nursing facility where Rich was eventually sent. Here Thomas found her way, learning to live close to a husband who experienced the rages, the hallucinations, and the deep-seated fears that can come with a traumatic head injury. This was a different man from the one she married, but Thomas graciously learned to love and understand him anew.

"I put a life together with my family and friends and dogs," she writes. "I learned to make use of the solitude I now had aplenty. I started writing, wanting to make something useful come from our catastrophe, and working hard, I began to be happy."

In *Writing as a Way of Healing*, Louise DeSalvo shares stories of several well-known writers who have navigated illness with the help of their writing. Flannery O'Connor, who had lupus, wrote these words even as she lay dying: "My my I do like to work. I et

[ate] up one hour like it was filet mignon." In his memoir, *Darkness Visible*, William Styron acknowledged that "he created suicidal characters in his fiction without realizing they were a way for him to manage his suicidal impulses." The author suffered from clinical depression, which he attributed to his mother's death, a traumatic experience for him at a young age. Styron's depression worsened when the author self-medicated with alcohol and later used Halcion, a dangerous drug that had been prescribed by his doctor. During therapy Styron realized how it was his writing that had helped him to cope with his trauma.

In 1892 Charlotte Perkins Gilman, author of the well-known story on madness, "The Yellow Wallpaper," explained why she wrote the story in an article. She said, "I suffered from a severe and continuous nervous breakdown tending to melancholia — and beyond." When Gilman consulted a doctor, she was told she needed to rest and to *avoid any writing*. This treatment was similar to the one she described in her story. After three months without writing, Gilman felt she would go over the edge. Ignoring the advice of her physician, she resumed her work and found renewed meaning and purpose. While she claimed to write "The Yellow Wallpaper" in order to save others from being driven crazy, Gilman no doubt saved herself by writing this cathartic story.

Writing Can Help Our Loved Ones, Too

Writing to heal can help our friends and companions as well. When I received my cancer diagnosis, my oldest friend, Jan, a nurse practitioner who lives outside Traverse City, Michigan, began to create and send me cards with heartfelt quotes and poems. The front of each card held a photo she had taken from her garden, a genuine Eden of hydrangea, delphinium, pansies, and iris blooms in a rainbow of colors — but mainly purple. A stunning purple.

After my surgeries were behind me, Jan came to visit me in Phoenix. We spent one morning hiking through the local botanical garden. Afterward we sat in the café, sipping iced tea and reminiscing as only dearest-oldest-best-friends can do.

It was then, while thanking her for the cards she had sent, I recalled the day I had waited well over an hour for a last-minute, presurgery MRI. I had to wait in another clinic in another huge, empty waiting room with stacks of *People* magazine on every table and *House Hunters* droning in the background. I was shaking, uncertain if it was the 60 degree temperatures or my nerves. To calm myself I pulled the cards Jan had made out of my book bag, as I often did. And I read them and reread them. Words of inspiration. And photos that could have come from Monet's garden. The images reminded me of how flowers can shimmer and dance and float their colors like scarves of silk in the wind. Perhaps it was nothing but a positive illusion, but when I fingered a certain photo of brilliant purple pansies with a small stone angel hovering over them, a warm and gentle vibration shot through me as if the universe wanted me to know that amid MRIs and surgery, there is still beauty in the world. And that I was loved by a friend. And that *it would be okay*. And, of course, it was.

Sitting outside the café with the cacti in bloom, I thanked her again. Surprised, she pulled back and stopped sipping her iced tea. "No. No," she insisted, "I should be thanking you. Creating the cards was a way for me to cope with your illness. Your cancer was difficult *for me*."

A Healing Family

Family and friends of those who are ill or injured suffer every bit as much as their loved ones. Perhaps more. And writing can support their journey. Nobel Prize–winning author Kenzaburo Oe sunk into a pit of despair when his first child was born with a growth on his brain so large he appeared to have two heads. Doctors explained that the child, named Hikari, would need surgery to live — and even with surgery the child would remain a human vegetable and require ongoing care. Oe was given the choice to allow the child to die or to have this serious brain operation.

The decision was hard for Oe. At first he hesitated, and although he consented to the surgery, he did so reluctantly. Now the author can look back and acknowledge that this operation saved not only his son's life but his own by giving him renewed meaning. Living with and raising a disabled child resulted in challenges that fueled much of Oe's writing. His first novel to appear in English, *A Personal Matter*, is an account of a man coping with the birth of a severely handicapped child, and in his memoir, *A Healing Family*, Oe recounts his family's real-life experiences while raising Hikari.

Every member of Oe's family learned to help Hikari live successfully, despite his ongoing seizures, autism, and poor vision. Eventually Hikari discovered he could share his emotions through his music. Over time his gift for music allowed him to become a composer and to produce two successful CDs. While Hikari learned how to communicate through his music, Oe learned to communicate both the pain and joy of these same experiences in his books.

Writing about Illness and Injury

In my work with cancer and hospital patients, I found that certain qualities surface in successful writing about an illness or injury. This kind of writing does the following:

It Accepts Our Story and Makes Sense of It

Kenzaburo Oe wrote to unravel his confusion and despair after the birth of his disabled son. He wrote and rewrote about his life with Hikari. In his memoir, Oe explained: "In the act of fictionalizing those events in the form of a novel, I was finally able to synthesize them, to make some kind of sense out of a senseless situation." And in making sense of his shattered story, in coming to peace with it, Oe had made his story manageable.

A story is, after all, a mirror of our psychological growth. We are peering into who we are and grounding ourselves as our story evolves. This is why Abigail Thomas wrote about her husband being hit by a car and ending up with a brain that no longer worked. It is why I wrote out my cancer journey. To understand it. To make sense of it. And when I opened up, I found others felt compelled to share their stories with me — and it helped.

It Explores Honest Feelings

Many well-known writers explore their honest feelings and painful experiences as they search to find themselves. Author Elizabeth Gilbert seemed to have all the hallmarks of success, with a husband, a country home, and a successful writing career — but she was miserable. After her divorce, she faced a crushing depression, and it was then she began her search for herself by writing *Eat, Pray, Love*. While most of us will never have a publisher, like Elizabeth Gilbert's, who will give us an advance to undertake a journey across the world and write a book, many readers were mesmerized by this honest search for self. In Rome, Gilbert delights in culinary experiences; on her visit to an ashram outside Mumbai, she emulates the yogis and struggles to quiet her mind; and in Bali, she seeks balance but finds love. While her search seems far from over, her words resonate because they seem to be drilling down in an honest quest to find the truth. Her truth. And that is what we hope our words will give to us.

Kenzaburo Oe was on the same search. He was only ten when the bombs fell on Hiroshima and Nagasaki. Ironically, it was the birth of his son that compelled him to research and study this tragedy. In 1963 he attended a conference in Hiroshima centered on the opposition to hydrogen bombs. "I recall...the intense feeling that the problem of my child could end up suffocating me if I couldn't get out into a larger arena, see things from a broader perspective," he explained. While in Hiroshima, Oe visited the Atomic Bomb Hospital. There he listened to the director, Dr. Shigeto, who explained that he had just taken up a post as assistant director and was on his way to the hospital when the bomb exploded, killing eighty thousand people and instantly wiping out 90 percent of the city. He described facing the countless dead, the disfigured and burned bodies in this hospital. In his gentle manner Shigeto explained that all he could do was move forward, trying his best to treat each victim. One at a time.

While listening to how the doctor handled the unbearable incident, Oe felt "profoundly consoled and encouraged." The author realized that with this piece of truth he, too, could survive his son's disabilities — one day at a time.

It Uses Words to Heal

While it is important to share our stories, the way we write and talk about our illness matters, too. Remember, we control how we understand our illnesses. And the words we use to interpret an illness impact how we face it. Jen viewed her stage four breast cancer as a challenge to be met — not as a death sentence. "In a support group I met a woman who repeatedly said, '*When I die*' as if the moment were imminent," said Jen. "She also talked about '*my terminal disease*.' This bothered me."

Often people take their illnesses — mental and physical — and elevate them to unnecessary heights. A problem evolves when the drama is dressed up, perhaps as a trauma, and the stories get stuck on replay. Most of us hate to hear stories that end up as a rerun without an end.

Andrew is a friend I know from teaching. A few months ago his daughter, Mia, suddenly lost her sight in one eye. Whenever we met friends for social gatherings, Andrew shared poor Mia's saga. First, he carefully detailed how Mia had a genetic disorder, which he described in WebMD detail. The eye muscle had suddenly slipped, which is what had left her blind in that one eye. In coming weeks the story escalated, and Andrew feared Mia would lose her job as a nurse at the hospital. He shared stories of Mia losing her balance, falling down, causing a car wreck because she could not see well.

A visit to the doctor confirmed that Mia might be blind in that eye forever. The family consulted a specialist, who predicted that as a genetic condition this disease was destined to strike the other eye, eventually leaving Mia completely blind. Andrew was terrified. Then, a brief respite — a miracle surgeon had been found. Surgery could be done. In the coming weeks Andrew was diagnosed with hearing problems, and a new set of illness stories surfaced. One day I turned to him and asked, "But how is Mia? You haven't mentioned her lately."

Andrew shrugged. "She's fine. The surgery worked." She regained her sight, which was something to celebrate — something Andrew had overlooked because he was trapped in his latest illness story.

We cannot deny an illness. We have to address and work to solve the problems it presents us. But the more we talk about and dramatize it, the more we impress a mind-set of illness on our brain. We can become too obsessed and create unhealthy thought patterns. Sadly, Andrew lives with them.

Jen, however, does not. "Unless a doctor tells me this darn disease is everywhere, then I am not going to view my illness as the end. I am going to keep living — to the fullest," said Jen. When she learned of her cancer recurrence, I was worried about her and texted to see how she was. "Oh, I went to NYC to see friends." Her Facebook page showed her in Central Park, where she was rolling in the grass, laughing with her pals.

It Embraces the Positive

Healing, of course, is not the same as being physically cured from a disease. Nonetheless, we can choose to heal our emotional, mental, and spiritual selves when faced with a terminal illness. A positive attitude shows up as an important key here.

Although Jen has returned to chemo, neither of us knows what this means. We cannot be sure if she will survive her cancer. But she is well versed in her odds, and she understands that life is a precious, tentative gift for all of us. She has scaled back on work, spends more time with her son, Quinn, and insists that her husband keep on schedule with his archaeological research in Kenya.

Jen marches forward bravely, keeping her illness at bay as she reintroduces chemo into her routine. She does not deny her illness. She talks about it, and she writes about it, but she makes every effort to find the upward path on the slippery slope she faces. But why not listen to Jen's own words for a minute. Here is one of her blog posts:

> Before my mastectomy, I had to get an EKG to test my heart, to make sure it would be strong enough for surgery. As I waited in the hospital lobby, I flipped through a *Good Housekeeping* magazine from last summer, with Michael J. Fox [who suffers from Parkinson's disease] on the cover; the feature article was about the actor turning 50. In his interview, he said that there's a motto in acting that he applies to his life: "*Don't act the end.*"
>
> I find myself thinking of that motto a lot lately, as I try to find my new normal. The pain of surgery is gone now, and at six weeks post-op, I've resumed most daily activities. What I'm struggling with now is getting beyond mere survival, getting to a point where I'm not constantly looking over my shoulder for the boogeyman, getting back to life.
>
> There's the fear that still rears its ugly head — less often now, but still ugly. A friend recently asked me how I live with fear without letting it get in the way of all the good moments. I admitted some nights I find myself crying just giving Quinn a bath, watching him splash and giggle and play with his plastic bath toys. Our lives are so fragile. And then I try to push that fear aside. I let it allow me to appreciate each moment with him even more than I might have before the cancer.
>
> In the *Good Housekeeping* article, Michael J. Fox

explained his motto this way: "If you know a bus is closing in on you as you stand in the middle of the road,
there's still a lot of space to fill between where you are
and the moment that bus hits you. In other words, don't
act like you've been hit by the bus until it happens."

My hair is returning slowly. Life goes on, and yet,
the axle around which my life spins has been knocked
off-kilter. I'm trying to find my new center of gravity, and
it's a strange, unbalanced space to occupy. I no longer feel
like that bus is closing in on me. And although there are
no guarantees in this life, between now and when that
bus does someday hit, I have a lot of enjoying my days
to get to.

Writing that heals:

• accepts our story and makes sense of it
• explores honest feelings
• uses words to heal
• embraces a positive outlook

Writing Prompts and Suggestions

These prompts focus on how writing can support us during an
illness or while we are recovering from an injury.

 *Writing Prompt: Dialogues*

When you are faced with an illness, disease, or injury, you need
to reach an understanding of what has happened. You can begin
by having a conversation with your body. A dialogue is a script
that bounces back and forth between you and another person,
pet, thing — or, in this case, your body. By talking you allow your
inner voice or wisdom to help you understand your illness, disease, or injury. Don't judge or criticize what you write. View this
as a search that might reveal some important insights.

It might start like this:

Self: Body, why are you so exhausted?
Body: You saw the test results.
Self: I did, and I didn't like them. I am afraid of my disease.
Body: I think we need to make some changes.
Self: What are you thinking? Maybe diet?

Play out your conversation with yourself to find answers that will help you get a handle on your situation.

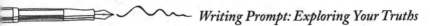 *Writing Prompt: Exploring Your Truths*

Choose one of these prompts, and freewrite for five minutes. If the topic takes off, stay with it until you reach a point of completion. If the writing seems stuck, choose another prompt. Revise it if needed:

- I have never talked about this...
- The hardest lie I ever told was...
- The way it really was...
- It is dangerous to...
- This story is hidden in a box in the back of my mind. It begins...

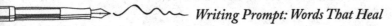 *Writing Prompt: Words That Heal*

Choose a word associated with healing: *hope, resilience, courage, endurance, patience, fortitude, tenacity, heroism, optimism, confidence,* or *strength*. (Choose a word not on the list if you think if fits.) Write a brief character description of one person you know who mirrors this word in the way she lives. Now choose a word that you want to embrace more fully in your life. Start with a statement like this:

- I want to be more hopeful...
- I want to be more patient...
- I want to be more...

Then write a brief character sketch looking into your future. Create a portrait of you as someone who is hopeful or patient or _____.

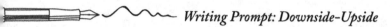 *Writing Prompt: Downside-Upside*

Make a list of all the difficult aspects of facing an illness, injury, or any difficult situation. Write first about what brings you down, what you hate, what isn't fair — the downside. Then scribble it out or draw *x*'s through it or rip it up. Now write about what you have learned, what you value, what you can build on from this experience. Draw a frame or stars around your upside. Write how you can live your upside more fully. Then go out and live it.

CHAPTER NINETEEN

Writing to Heal from Loss

Grief is in two parts. The first is loss.
The second is the remaking of life.

— Anne Roiphe

"It was my first death," Goldie Goldston explained. The twenty-six-year-old vet was seated facing the bar at the diner where we had first talked a few months before. "I need to see the bar," he reminded me as we slid into our booth. We both laughed. No one was going to get his back.

While Goldie remained clean shaven and placed the same order, for fries and a burger, he was more relaxed and easily launched into his painful story. We had agreed to talk about death.

"We were crossing a canal," he began. "My squad had been in a firefight, and the Taliban began to shoot at us unexpectedly. We returned the fire, but it was too late. They had already hit my good buddy — Nick." Goldie froze for just a moment, crawling back into his mental battlefield. He shook his head forlornly. "I reached out to him, but when I rolled Nick over, and he coughed up blood, I knew." He paused reverently. "Nick was gone. They shot him — *in the head*. And this experience sent a hard message through all of us. I cannot tell you how painful it is to watch someone you care about die — shot to death right in front of you."

Emma Bond knows the same shock of loss. But her story takes place far from a battlefield. I befriended her over lattes in her Albuquerque, New Mexico, home. Here she shared her writing with me — journals, letters, and her newest project, a children's book.

"I first began writing during my divorce," she explained. In her twenties, as a newly single mother, Emma had no immediate family nearby for support. "The writing allowed me to survive day to day." Emma moved ahead, building a wonderful life in Albuquerque and working her way up the corporate ladder as a human resources executive. Eventually she fell in love with and married a longtime friend, Paul.

After ten years of a high-powered corporate job, Emma decided she wanted to stay home with their two boys, and as many women who have traded in a corporate life do, she found this emotionally trying. Shortly after she quit, Emma attended a writing workshop.

"And I was forever changed," she explained. "My writing allowed me to honor my corporate accomplishment while opening me to this new chapter in my life." When Paul took a job in Portland, the couple used writing to help them prepare for the transition. "We hated leaving friends and the desert plains of Albuquerque," explained Emma. Initially, she admitted, their relocation to the Northwest was a bit bumpy, but the couple immersed themselves in Portland's culture and developed new friends and a new way of life. And Emma continued to write.

An Unexpected Death

Life was good for the couple. To celebrate their twenty-fifth wedding anniversary, Emma and Paul stole away to a remote beach resort near Puerto Vallarta, Mexico, where they enjoyed what they loved most — golf and quiet, relaxing time together on the beach. The first evening they kept staring at the stunning sunset over the coral reef. Paul snapped pictures of it with his iPhone. The week was a joyful, relaxing reprieve from their busy schedules.

Although the ocean was rough on the last day of their trip, Paul wanted to go snorkeling on that coral reef. After a leisurely lunch, they walked down the beach, holding hands. Paul squeezed Emma's hand, and looked at her intently. "This was a perfect vacation," he said, "and you are perfect for me." Emma spread her towel on the beach chair, pulled her book — *Awakening Joy*, a book the couple was reading together — from her bag, and settled in to wait. Paul handed her his glasses and shirt. He smiled at her and went into the water.

The afternoon was cloudy and wickedly windy. After a time Emma looked up from her reading and scanned the horizon, hoping to catch a glimpse of Paul. At first she was relieved to see he was making his way back to shore, but in a horrifying moment she realized he wasn't swimming but floating lifelessly. Simultaneously two men sitting at the resort bar realized what had happened and ran into the water.

Within minutes the men had carried Paul to the shore, and one of the men began to administer CPR. A woman on the beach drew near and hugged Emma gently. The kind stranger began offering prayers for a miracle. There were tears and more prayers, but the attempt to revive Paul failed.

Someone called the resort doctor. Since the beach was remote, it would be more than two hours before he would arrive. The men gently covered Paul's body with a beach towel. Eventually Emma would lift the towel from Paul's face to share her good-bye. "Any denial I might have experienced was taken care of at that time on that shoreline," said Emma softly. "I could not doubt that Paul had died...and I am thankful I had that time with him."

"I have faced many challenges in my life, but nothing as poignant as the death of my beloved husband," said Emma. While we all struggle with any number of losses, losing someone we love is the most painful loss. As Emma discovered, and as most of us will learn, an unexpected death is even harder. When someone who has been part of our daily life is suddenly missing, he or she leaves a hole — a huge abyss — inside us. When someone we love dies, all our intertwined associations, memories, hopes, fears, dreams, and plans shatter like pieces of glass. Tragically, our job, an extraordinarily difficult one, becomes to make sense of all these shards.

Happier Endings

While all of us will die, we rarely talk about death. Perhaps because we struggle with the idea of our own death, we choose to ignore it. Deny it. Before my brother died of complications from cancer, I knew he was going to die. When I visited him in the hospital, he held my hand tightly as if he knew it, too. We shared memories and talked about our love for each other, but we never whispered any words about death. Later I regretted that we had no conversations about the end of life. I decided then that I needed to find the courage to be more open to the deaths I would face, including my own.

Since death is another life story for us, an important one, why shouldn't we work on drafting, revising, and creating a vision of what is to come? Not obsessing. Not ruminating. Just setting a course we hope to follow. While usually we cannot predict when or how we will die, we can prepare. In our journals we can explore where we want to be buried or inurned, what rituals we would like, what gifts we want to leave our loved ones. Most important, we can have end-of-life discussions with those we love. In planning for death we give our loved ones — as well as ourselves — greater peace of mind.

Erica Brown titled her book on death *Happier Endings*. Perhaps this should be our goal — to make the experience of dying positive, whether it is our death or the death of someone we love.

Just as we have the power to rework or rewrite many of our life stories, we have the power to draft what we hope to experience in dying, and in reaching a peace with death, we can also help those we love to face death.

Grieving, Writing

By using our writing to explore death we can discover ways to make our losses meaningful. At first we may use our writing to supplant our tears. It may be a pouring forth of emotion and a breaking of our silence. But eventually our logic takes hold and provides guidance. Our words turn into stories. Our stories begin to light our paths. This grants us the wisdom to revise our understanding and to construct a new story that will help us make sense of our life beyond our loss. Indeed, Emma admits that a year later, grieving remains an ongoing process, but her writing continues to help her understand Paul's death and the changes she has had to face.

Journaling through the Death of a Spouse

Immediately after Paul's death, Emma sought help from a counselor, and she continued to journal. "By this point in my life, writing had become a part of who I was," she explained. Earlier she had been doing writing workshops to help others find their stories. By now she knew that in finding her own words, she was crafting her own healing.

Here are some entries she made shortly after Paul's death. While the writing mirrors Emma's intense emotional pain, it also shows she is already moving through difficult emotions, tapping into her logic, and making changes that will help her regain her balance after experiencing the vertigo of such a powerful loss.

First week. I'm impossibly overwhelmed. The world is crashing in. This hole is too dark. Breathe. So much has to be done — paperwork, death certificate, sell home — where is home?

Next Day. What am I good at? Organizing! Compartmentalize. I love compartments. Are there a million things to do? Or just a cluster of topics: Paul stuff, Oregon stuff, Albuquerque stuff, and Paperwork stuff? Just four subjects. Manageable.

Make lists. I love lists. Crossing out makes my accomplishments beautifully tangible. Something to feel good about. Damn... feeling good hasn't been my reality lately.

Several days later. Nothing will be as challenging once I get to the other side of this. Make lists. A-list = have to's; B-list = want to's. Enjoy watching this to-do list shrink.... My friends of fear and panic keep visiting. I need to put fear and panic on my C-list!

Grieving and Letters

Long before Paul's death, Emma had begun a series of lovely letters to save for her young grandchildren. After losing Paul the power of this undertaking became more important. "I wanted my grandkids to know what Paul was like, and I want them to know how much I loved them once I'm gone. I write these letters and keep them to give in the future as gifts." Mark Barden, who lost his young son during the Sandy Hook tragedy, has also learned the power that writing letters holds.

On the last day of his life, Daniel Barden watched the sunrise with his dad. When he noticed the reflection of the Christmas tree lights in the window, with the sunrise behind it, he was excited. "Isn't it beautiful?" he asked. His dad, Mark, took a picture of it. Mark has scanned that picture many times, hoping to see Daniel's shadow. Hoping for one last glimpse of the seven-year-old he loved.

That morning, on December 14, 2012, Daniel lost his life when in four torturous minutes, Adam Lanza stormed into Sandy Hook Elementary School in Newtown, Connecticut, killing six educators and twenty first graders, and then turning his gun on himself. Daniel was hiding in the closet of his classroom with his teacher and peers when he was shot to death.

"It's been god-awful," acknowledged Mark. "And yet, we have had so much love and support from our family, neighbors, and community." One kindness came from Mark's niece, who gave him a journal and encouraged him to write. "I began this writing as a way of holding onto my son — the stories of my son. It was a way I could keep from losing him."

Both Mark and his wife, Jacqueline, have been instrumental in the work of the Sandy Hook Promise, working for gun regulations that will prevent other parents from experiencing what they have had to endure. And the memories Mark has collected of Daniel are shared through letters he sends regularly to supporters of the group. Each letter is a powerful testament of a father's love.

Here is part of a letter I received from Mark on what would have been Daniel's ninth birthday:

Sandra,

Nine years ago today, our sweet little Daniel was born. Each and every day of his far-too-short life he inspired me — and he still does. He always will.

While it's tempting to spend the day hiding, mourning his absence even more than I do the other 364 days of the year, I'm instead writing you to celebrate Daniel — and all his life meant to us.

Many who knew Daniel called him "an old soul." He was more perceptive than many adults I know. He often went out of his way to speak to a special needs child at school – telling others, "She can't talk, but I know she can hear me." The child's mother was so moved by his kindheartedness she asked for her child and Daniel to be placed in the same class.

Daniel's perceptiveness was matched by his generosity. Just a few days before he was taken from us, Daniel asked if he could pour himself some milk, and then barely filled the glass. I asked why. He said, "Dad, you always have to leave enough for the next person."

Of course, these aren't just stories that make us smile through our tears. They help keep his memory alive and are valuable lessons about how we can — and should — all try our hardest, every day, to be generous, empathetic, and kind. Like Daniel.

So to anyone who will listen, we tell stories about Daniel. It's how we spread his many important life messages. It's how we share him: who he was, what he believed, and what he wanted for our world.

Mark Barden is creating a way of framing, remembering, and sharing Daniel's short but meaningful life. Most important, he has done all he can to take this terrible tragedy and work toward positive cultural change through the Sandy Hook Promise.

Grieving and Poems

Poems wrap words around our feelings. They often capture a glimmer, an insight. Perhaps magically. Sometimes powerfully. "Writing poems is the primary way that I grieved for my mother," poet Ellen Bass explained to me. "When she died, I thought I would come home and make an altar for her. To honor her. Instead I began writing poems, and I realized this is what I wanted to do."

From poet Ellen Bass I learned how words can help us hold and frame our pain. "When my mother died, my poems made a container for me," explained Bass. "Words allowed me to be with my feelings — with my sadness and my loss and my memories.

When we write, we are able to step back and remove ourselves from the unbearable. By taking a step back we give ourselves a space where we can manage it."

In the "The Muse of Work" Ellen artfully captures a portrait of her mother, who managed their family liquor store when the poet was a child:

> She knows the pale sherry you crave
> sliding it into a brown bag, sized precisely.
> There's the smell of newsprint and stale beer.
> The cash register rings its tiny cymbal.
> …
> Fifty years later, my mother dead,
> when I search for the words to describe
> a thing exactly — the smell of rain
> or the sound a glass makes
> when you set it down — then I'm back there
> standing in the corner of the store, watching her
> as she takes the worn bills,
> smooths them in her palm.

"When I finished writing the poems about my mother, I felt sad," said Ellen, her voice softening. "I felt so close to her as I wrote. She always seemed to be there. To be present." When we write about lost loved ones, we can touch their presence. We can be with them. At these moments we fully tap into our writing as a healing art.

Grieving and Tributes

Recently Edna, my ninety-year-old mother-in-law, told me she did not want a service when she died. "I am old and most of my friends are gone," she explained. "People do not need to get up and talk about me."

But we do need to talk and write and share our losses. I turned to her and said, "Mom, a service is not for you or for your friends who are gone. It is to help all of us who are left behind. We have to rewrite our stories to move forward without you. It will be hard for *us*." Funerals, celebrations of life, and memorials acknowledge those who die, but they are for the living. They help us accept and face our loss. For a moment Edna was silent. Then she nodded, reached out, and hugged me.

A eulogy or tribute is often written when a loved one dies, and it helps us with the process of adjusting to our loss. When my brother Les died, I wrote in my journal about communicating with him through dreams. Then I found a copy of a funny essay, "Junk Food Weekends," that my son Matt had written at age eight, talking about how he loved to spend weekends at his uncle's Tucson desert home. My family and I read it and reread it as if it were a treasure. It captured who my brother was — an uncle who would stay up half the night watching scary movies, like Hitchcock's *Psycho*. An uncle who would let the kids eat whole bags of Doritos. An uncle who pre-Internet could talk on ham radio to people all over the world and make them laugh with his fall-off-your-chair stories. Stories about coyotes and rattlesnakes and "pet tarantulas" who believed his desert home was their home.

My family loved this piece so much I read it at my brother's service. Afterward, at my home, where we toasted Les with his favorite drink, margaritas, one of his longtime friends, who had flown across the country to be with us, gave a heartwarming tribute about pranks and good times spent with Les. "He was a beautiful person, and I needed to do this," Dave explained when he hugged us good-bye.

Of course we understood.

Spirituality and Inspirational Death

As we write our way through loss, it helps to understand what we are experiencing — or what we will experience. Psychiatrist Elisabeth Kübler-Ross spent years studying how we die and how we grieve. Her five stages — denial, anger, bargaining, depression, and acceptance — have been chiseled into our modern-day under-standing of grief. For years experts have debated how we experi-ence these stages, and while we seem to experience all or most of them, they do not necessarily fall into this neat, predictable order.

Author Erica Brown argued that early in the grief cycle, we struggle with different forms of denial such as anger, bargaining, and depression. Eventually we reach acceptance, or "resignation." When we reach this point, we can move past the roller coaster of emotions and acknowledge that someone we love is dying. But Brown believes the final stage in the grief process can be "in-spiration." As a spiritual teacher, she has seen many individuals move beyond accepting a death to an understanding of death as a powerful, meaningful transition.

A number of studies show that spirituality, or the part of us that seeks meaning, purpose, and a connection to a transcendent presence, helps us face loss. My own experience confirmed this for me. When I finished writing an earlier draft of this chapter, I received one of those dreaded phone calls. My ninety-five-year-old dad lived a couple of blocks from my home. When Mom called, I learned that Dad was shaking violently and unable to stand. I phoned 911. Dad entered the hospital, mumbling inco-herently and with a fever of 104.

In the coming days I would sit with him for long hours at the hospital, delighted he was lucid again and thankful to have time with him. Often we found ourselves shivering in that freezer-cold room, waiting for more test results or a visit from another doctor. In those moments we shared family stories and sang ditties from my childhood, such as Cole Porter's "Friendship." Dad drifted in and out of sleep, and as he did I scrawled notes in my journal or prayed.

Sometimes the click…click…click of the hospital monitors carried me back to my childhood home in Indianapolis and to Saturday mornings, when we had pancakes for breakfast. Some-times Dad would burst into our bedrooms and wake us up saying,

"Have I remembered to tickle you today?" And my brothers and I would squeal with delight. And he would sing silly songs to us like "Mares Eat Oats." Later he would play the piano or play records by Sinatra or Edith Piaf. He loved music.

When the jolt of a buzzer or the banging of a hospital door awakened Dad, we would resume our talk as if nothing had interrupted us. I would share my latest memory. Then we would laugh — or cry. Sometimes we sang or prayed together. And unlike with my brother's death, I talked openly with Dad about dying. When I asked him about fear, he assured me he was not afraid. About prayer — he said prayer had been an amazing comfort for him throughout his life. And about God — he believed in a God, a spiritual presence who would reveal its mystery after we entered the portal of death. Since we had always shared music, I asked him if he would try to communicate with me through music once he passed away. He loved the idea.

Dad didn't want to die. He loved living, but three weeks after he entered the hospital, he realized his body could no longer support him, and he asked me to bring him home. And with the help of hospice, I did.

One day after we arrived home, my dad mouthed his last word to me, *Mom*. I promised to care for her. And she hobbled over to hold his hand. Two days after he made it home, my dad took his last breaths with his love, my mom, and his family gathered around him. In those moments he radiated serenity, a transcendent beauty. For long moments we stood in hushed awe around him.

After he passed, we sang and prayed. My brother recited Psalm 23, and then we stood reverently by his side. And in that holy moment — standing by my father and his soul — my head was filled with the joyful clanging of church bells. "Do you hear them?" I asked my family.

Just Ten Minutes

Healing comes from sharing our losses — in talking and in writing. While we need to share these experiences, the very thought of doing this can paralyze us. Before Dad died he explained to me that he saw the advantages to writing, especially after he first fell and broke his hip. "I see how it helps," he told me. "I just don't like to do it." In place of writing, I encouraged him to tell me his stories, and I bought a special "Dad journal." A week into my story-collecting adventure, Dad began to do his own writing. Perhaps because I found his stories worthwhile, he felt encouraged to share them. More likely, he was certain I was screwing up his stories! Either way, for a few days he was writing, and he was proud of it. "I am writing!" he would announce when I visited. And now I have a treasure — a few of the stories he loved and left me.

Even professionals acknowledge how difficult writing can be. Poet Mark Doty was losing his partner, Wally, to AIDS in 1998 when he wrote a memoir, *Heaven's Coast*. Doty explained, "To write was to court overwhelming feeling. Not to write was to avoid, but to avoid was to survive....And so I'd write, when I could, recording what approached like someone in a slow-moving but unstoppable accident, who must look and look away at once." Ultimately Doty's writing evolved into a beautiful tribute to his partner.

Remember, there may be no words for a while. I learned that when my student Lucas died and again when I lost my brother and my dad. After the death of her stepson, author Christina Baldwin wrote in her blog, "It has been five months since a midnight phone call pulled us into the emergency of our thirty-three-year-old son's dying. We were on our way to the airport by 3:00 AM and by 6:00 AM I had sent an email to extended family and friends asking for prayers...Exactly a week after his death I had four hours alone on a plane and I wrote in my journal. 'The story shatters…' I then documented moment by moment the four-hour passage. *I have hardly written since.*"

Doty wrote about his days of grieving for Wally as being "adrift in the sea-swirl of shock and loss." During grief we may wonder why our responses, our thoughts, and our writings are bizarre. I noticed this when I waded through my old journals. At the time of my brother's death, I rambled. I seemed a bit unbalanced as I tried to talk with his grief-stricken wife. Concerned about how odd it all sounded in my head, I made myself see a counselor. Looking back I realize that feeling off balance is the norm when facing a death.

Pain is a part of our grief. We have to accept and honor it. Grief demands we take the time for the sadness and sorrow. We can take long walks. Sit in parks. Meditate or pray. Soak in the tub. Read. Talk to a close friend. See a counselor. And, when the time is right, we can write.

Some forms of communication can occur in the moment, such as on Baldwin's four-hour plane ride home, and this is often a raw, unedited, chronological recounting that helps the mind find a place to hold a traumatic event, a sort of trauma parking lot. If that moment goes by, it may be hard to recapture. It's as though the brain is filing data and details with the imperative to get them down before life becomes overwhelming. And this outburst is often followed by long periods of inarticulate silence.

After traumatic experiences, words usually tiptoe back into our lives. When looking for my voice, I have learned to sit outside in the sun or curl up on a comfy sofa with my journal. Sometimes I simmer tea to sip as I write. "You only need to write for ten minutes," I promise myself at hard times. But usually I write more — and it always helps.

The "just-ten-minutes" trick is a wonderful way to invite our writing whenever it has stalled. In these few minutes our words may take over and begin rethreading our narrative. But not always. Sometimes we have to wait until a better day.

The Mind's Eye of Writing through Grief

About two dozen books on death and dying now clutter my writing space at the kitchen bar. As I flip through them, I am struck speechless yet again by our stories. The drowning. The car accident. The overdose. The brain tumor. The bullet to the head. The limp body of the child. The pain of loss is an abyss that we easily stumble into, but as I've said over and over now, writing is a proven navigational tool out of this void. These are some of the attributes of writing that lead to healing from our losses. This kind of writing does the following:

It Accepts the Loss

After Paul's death, Emma moved back to the Albuquerque plains she loves. During that time she sought solace both in her practice of writing and in yoga. Almost a year after Paul died, she needed to return to Oregon on business. While there Emma visited the ocean near her old home. It was here that she wrote copious notes in her journal. It was here that she began to reach a peace with the water that had taken Paul from her. In her journal she wrote of this acceptance:

> I stare at the ocean and wonder why. Why did my sunny tranquil book-reading, beach-sitting moment turn to terror? How is it that my partner left me — swallowed by the gentle rhythm of your pendulum waves? Now the waves mark time, painfully ticking off my memory wish list of things we planned to do. So now I sit. Sit here trying to make half-dreams whole.
>
> I have no choice. No choice but to move forward without him. These waves don't stop, even if my world did. Waves move forward — and so must I.

It Embraces the Need for Community

At a time of loss we especially need groups that give us a sense of belonging and connecting to something bigger than we are.

Something meaningful. Faith-based groups, volunteer service groups, cancer groups, environmental clubs, hiking clubs, book clubs and, of course, writing groups can help us find our stories as well as give us meaning and purpose.

Dr. Norma Bowe is an expert in understanding the power of community, especially how important it is when we face losses. I met her for lunch at New York's Omega Institute on a humid summer day. She teaches a well-known class at Kean University, the Death Class. Norma is a compassionate godmother-like teacher who swoops up her students each semester and carries them into worlds they never knew existed. They visit a cemetery and a prison, and they witness an autopsy. They talk and write about the physical aspects of dying, and they explore what it means to die. More important, they explore *what it is to live* by forming a support group to help others. They regularly serve meals at a homeless shelter, help rebuild houses, and share each other's pain when classmates face illnesses and deaths. And, of course, they write about their experiences. "Our writing helps ground us," explains Norma. "It allows us to make sense of what we are experiencing."

"And the service allows us to bond," Norma explained, sweeping her long, dark hair behind her back. "For example, last semester I had this lovely young girl in my class. Lindsay. She had been diagnosed with a brain tumor at age sixteen. She wanted to be in the class because she was dying and she simply needed to understand more about death. She was so engaged — and she asked such wonderful questions. On the day we visited the funeral home, she asked if she could lie in the casket to see what it would be like."

Dishes were clattering in the background of the Omega cafeteria, but I leaned forward, trapped in the web of this story. "What happened?" I asked.

Norma leaned close. "It was powerful. Lindsay went up where they hold the wake, and she climbed into the casket to try it out.

She was so funny and so brave and the class knew what she was facing — so we all felt a sense of unbelievable love for her.

"It is moments like this when the class becomes a community. At the end of that semester, I had a speaker who taught us about death dances." Norma closed her eyes for a long moment and sighed.

"Lindsay didn't feel well that day. She'd had a seizure just that morning, but she came to be with us. As everyone started to dance, she sat on the sidelines — too weak to participate." Norma's eyes peered intently into mine. "But then the coolest thing happened. A huge kid, a football player who was usually very quiet, went over to her and gently lifted her up and carried her piggy-back into the center of the circle, where he danced proudly with a smiling Lindsay on his back. All the students circled around him." Norma beamed.

"It is so important to find our sense of community and to tell about it and to write about these events. Don't underestimate the value of the writing. It helps to bring us together." Sharing our writing can help us build our sense of community and trust in a class or group.

It Finds Gratitude

When my Italian father-in-law died in 2000 after a stroke, there was a time of quiet and tears and grieving. A couple of weeks after his death we held a Catholic service to honor him, and back at his condo we gathered to drink wine and tell family stories. This became a time to share our gratitude. And we did. It started with stories and ended with the telling of joke after joke after joke, for Carmen was a consummate joke teller. A wild card. And we all loved this about him.

Carmen peppered all gatherings in his life with long hilarious jokes and short groaners, jokes that fit the occasion and ones he couldn't stop himself from telling whether or not they fit. There were dozens of pranks, too. A college professor, Carmen was famous for the phone he kept in his desk drawer. During class, a loud ring would pierce his lecture. Carmen would hurry to his desk, pull out his phone, answer it and cup the receiver secretively in his hand while starting a private conversation with the current president. His students would eavesdrop as Carmen would chastise President Ronald Reagan for calling during class, and then pretend to answer personal questions. *Nancy wants roses, red roses, for your anniversary.* He would never hesitate to offer his political advice. *Yes! You did the right thing by letting the air traffic controllers go. Let me call you back to talk about supply-side economics.* When Carmen hung up, his students responded with laughter and usually applause.

Just as Ellen Bass wrote poems to hold on to her mother, my family began to create Carmen's legacy by telling his stories and sharing his jokes at every family gathering. Because this is something that we all loved about Carmen, I found it helpful to record some of his irreverent lines and antics in my journal. This writing allowed me to grieve my loss and became a way to honor and appreciate him.

No wonder gratitude journals are popular. Recent studies show that when we write about our appreciation for someone else, there are significant benefits *for us*. We become more focused on the positive. One study even showed that the positive emotions released by our gratitude can reduce the frequency and the length of a depression.

It Embraces Wisdom

Writing that helps us face loss tries to make sense out of the senseless. It looks for meaning and wisdom. There is a Jewish tradition of trying to capture wisdom in an "ethical will." An ethical will is a spiritual legacy. It can be quite simple. One mother, an immigrant from Latvia who moved to Cleveland as a young child, left her three children a simple unedited note asking them to love one another and be good. Simple — but touching.

Words make it possible for our thoughts to travel through

time and survive us. Initially I began interviewing Jen because she had stage four cancer, and she wanted to leave her life story for her young child and for those of us who love her. But Jen has long outlived the projections for her death, and we joke that we will dance together when Quinn, her young son, marries. All the while Jen has been busy capturing her story and the wisdom she has gained in both a blog and in her memoir.

If we don't share our stories and our wisdom with our children — in blogs, books, or ethical wills — who will? Don't we want our loved ones to have whatever bits of wisdom we can claim? I want to hold on to the stories my dad shared with me shortly before he died. I want my father-in-law's jokes to continue to be a part of my family. I want our family stories to outlive me. By writing them down, I hope this might prove possible.

Thanks to a popular film of the same name, the *bucket list* has become a popular catchphrase in our culture. The message from the film resonates with us — we should seize the moment and try to accomplish what we dream of. And it makes good sense to capture our wisdom, too. To hold it — and give it to others.

How do we create a bucket list of wisdom? Both Mitch Albom and Randy Pausch did. In 1995 Mitch Albom was channel surfing when he discovered his former professor, Morrie Schwartz, talking with Ted Koppel on *Nightline*. As he watched, Albom realized that Morrie was dying of amyotrophic lateral sclerosis (ALS). Albom, a sportswriter, knew he needed to reconnect with his old professor. On Tuesdays he began to fly back to Boston and spend time talking with Morrie. Their conversations resulted in a treasure trove of Morrie's life wisdom and a book — *Tuesdays with Morrie.*

More recently, Randy Pausch, a professor at Carnegie Mellon, discovered he had ten tumors in his liver. While he appeared to be in fine physical shape, Pausch had pancreatic cancer and only a few months to live. Since he was a teacher, he decided to create an engaging lecture that would leave behind what he had learned from his life. This "last lecture" was delivered on

September 18, 2007, at Carnegie Mellon. The auditorium was packed. To defuse any sympathy from his audience, Pausch began by doing push-ups. With his audience fully engaged, he shared his life lessons, focusing on how he achieved his dreams and how he loved helping others realize their dreams. Before Pausch died, ten months later, his talk became a popular YouTube clip, and his wisdom was captured in a bestselling book.

One of the most important lessons for us to learn from Morrie and Randy is that *we can heal and die simultaneously —* and it is like no other experience. We are caught in the eye of the tornado, but we are choosing to live fully — and with grace. If we embrace this process, it is completely inspirational. It is how my dad chose to die. It is how we can best face our immortal life.

Writing that helps us face our losses:

• accepts loss
• embraces community
• finds gratitude
• embraces wisdom

Writing Prompts and Suggestions

Here are some prompts to help us face the pain of loss through our writing.

Writing Prompt: A Tribute or Eulogy

Write a poem or short speech that honors the person you have lost. As you write, work to capture the images, details, and one-of-a-kind actions that made this person special to you. If you can, read this at a memorial service, a celebration of life service, or a simple gathering of friends.

Writing Prompt: A Needed Conversation

Write a talk you need to have with someone you have lost. Before you begin to write, think about these questions: Is there a conversation you still need to have with this person? Is there a conversation you would like to have? Are there questions you wish you had asked? Are there topics you think would be important to explore together? Here is an example from a young woman who recently lost her mom to Parkinson's disease:

> You: Mom, I never had a chance to tell you how much I liked the blue dress.
> Mom: Blue dress?
> You: The one you made me last April. You were so sick and I was...
> Mom: Oh, that dress. I knew you liked it. Do you wear it?
> You: Yeah, but I was a bit of jerk. I didn't want you to spend your energy on me.
> Mom: I know. But I wanted to do something nice for you.

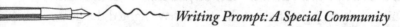 *Writing Prompt: A Special Community*

When we face a loss, we need the support of others. Choose a special group or community you are a part of — a book club, a church group, a work group, a golf team, a fishing club, a band, a choir, a yoga group, a group of close friends, a service organization, or a writing group. Then explore these questions: Why am I a part of this group? Why is this community important to me? What have we shared that has been important? What can I do to make this community more meaningful for other members as well as for me? How have the members of this group provided support for me? Have I been there for those who needed me? Am I there for these individuals at times of loss?

If you need more support, what groups should you consider joining?

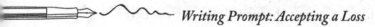 *Writing Prompt: Accepting a Loss*

Tell the story of a loss you have experienced — the loss of a pet, a classmate, a friend, or a family member — and how you came to terms with it. Before you write, get comfortable. If it will help, post photos of the one you have lost around your writing space. Then answer these questions: What happened? What precipitated this loss? What is hard about this loss? Who has helped you cope with the loss? What activities have helped you navigate your loss? What have you learned from the one you have lost?

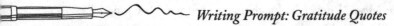 *Writing Prompt: Gratitude Quotes*

At times of loss it is critical to find ways to support your well-being. Finding and writing about positive quotes, especially ones that express our gratitude, will help. You might want to find or create your own gratitude quote. Then reflect on it and write about it. What does it mean, and why is it important to you?

Here is a quote by Albert Schweitzer. If this quote resonates within you, write about it: "At times our own light goes out and is rekindled by a spark from another person. Each of us has cause to think with deep gratitude of those who have lighted the flame within us." What does it mean? Who has lighted the flame within you? Why? How can you show your appreciation?

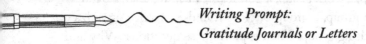 *Writing Prompt:*
Gratitude Journals or Letters

When you are grateful, positive emotions surface. After a loss, expressing your gratitude can help reground you by allowing positive feelings to resurface. Here are ideas for your writing:

- You might choose to write a letter of appreciation to the person you have lost. If you want, you could share it with others.
- You might choose to write "gratitude memories" or "gratitude poems" that allow you to reconnect with a few of the wonderful moments shared with the one you have lost.
- You may want to initiate a gratitude journal in which you can regularly express your thanks for the people and experiences you value.

Writing Prompt:
Create a Bucket List of Wisdom

This is where any past writings might prove helpful. You can re-read your old notes, journals, stories, poems, and essays and redis-cover your personal stories. Or simply begin anew. It is never too late to begin this search. Collect or write what you have learned. The goal will be to capture your wisdom. If you choose, this could begin as a collection of your favorite life stories.

Keep it. All of it. When you feel the time is right, share it with loved ones — or bequeath it to them.

Writing Prompt: Create a Bucket List
of Your Favorite Stories

This is similar to the last writing prompt, but it could be a shared family activity that helps in a time of loss — or at a time of family celebration. Pull together family stories and photos. Place them in a scrapbook, in a video, in a PowerPoint presentation, or in your own creative format. This bucket list of stories (or simply treasured family photos) can be shared at a family memorial, a celebration of life, or an appropriate family event: a graduation, a birthday, a wedding, or a retirement. Keep it, update it, and share it with loved ones at the right times.

PART SIX

WRITING TO TRANSFORM

CHAPTER TWENTY

Resilience

Your life is your story.
Write well. Edit often.
— **Susan Statham**

"Y ou can rewrite a story from your past, and you can change the ending," Chris Schnick explained. He paused to sip his latte. We had met at a café in Phoenix on a brisk Sunday morning in November. At one point I taught at the community college where Chris was the English faculty chair, well respected by both his colleagues and students. Often I saw him shooting across the campus with thin, wiry strands of hair bouncing in different directions.

But this Sunday morning was not about teaching or courses. Instead Chris was sharing a deeply personal story that completely changed my perception of him. I was discovering how he took pain and used writing to create something of profound beauty — a script honoring his sister, Jenny.

"My sister died last February 27 of pneumonia," Chris explained. "She had been homeless for more than a year. She was mentally ill, suffering from manic depression. And my family," he paused and swallowed hard, "my family is a large family, and we had a difficult time knowing what to do about Jenny. In the early nineties we had her committed because of her out-of-control thoughts. More recently she traveled around, and the family would talk about what to do — how do we find her? Do we get her committed again? None of us knew all the pieces of her story until later — and that made it hard to make sense of it."

When this tale began, Jenny lived in Baltimore, Maryland. She had stopped taking her medication and decided to take a trip. She drove north to New Hampshire to visit one brother before she began a long trek across country.

One day, at 2 AM, Jenny phoned Chris from New Mexico, and to this day he remains haunted by this call and his attempts to make sense of it. "What does it mean the last time you hear from your sister?" Chris asked. "What do those last words mean?"

Jenny never made it to Phoenix. After driving around the country for a while, she ended up in California, where eventually her car was impounded. About a year later she died on the steps of a small church outside Encinitas. Chris believes this church became Jenny's final community. "She went to that church because they accepted her," Chris explained. "The pastor told me she was gentle and kind, and for this reason they allowed her to sleep outside on the steps — even though they weren't supposed to. But she became ill." It is clearly a hard memory for Chris. "On the day Jenny died, one of the church workers came outside and held her hand for a while. Then she went back in to finish her work, and when she returned to check on Jenny, she had passed away."

"Writing this piece was about me trying to deal with this loss and not being able to," said Chris. "It's less about Jenny and more about me. Am I going to make it through the loss of Jenny?

"I started to write about Jenny even before she died. The last part was the hardest part to write. I stayed up all night working on it. I took it to my students and spent time discussing it with them." Chris spoke not only of anguish at Jenny's death but of the powerful guilt he experienced. "I kept thinking about it. How

could I have helped Jenny? What could I have done differently?"
he asked as we sipped our drinks. Here is an excerpt from his
script:

> [Chris alone on the stage speaks dead center.] She is not
> lying somewhere, dead. She is not. [look up] She is out
> there.
> 　　[A voice for Jenny answers.] *Chris. It's Jenny. I'm not
> going to make it.*
> 　　Where are you?
> 　　*New Mexico.*
> 　　*These trucks are crowding me.*
> 　　Where in New Mexico?
> 　　*I don't like to talk about my plans.*
> 　　Okay.
> 　　*I got to go.*
> 　　And she is gone.
> 　　[Chris turns in a chair, slowly, and faces the audi-
> ence] *Okay.* Yes. That's what I said. Lying there all night,
> "okay" can echo in your head until it is deadened by the
> dawn.
> 　　[stand up, center upstage] What did my okay even
> mean?

"There is a level of positive memories in my head, too," Chris
said, his head gently nodding to the jazzy music playing in the
background. "First, I remember her swimming. Jenny was always
in love with the water." Chris's eyes shined like brilliant topaz.
"She would stay out in the ocean — in the waves — forever. This
is such a beautiful memory I have of her." Here is how he shared
this memory in his script:

> [center stage] We used to bodysurf. When we were kids
> on vacation on the Atlantic seashore we would play in

the sand and in the water. We'd ride the waves in. I would take a big spill and slam in the hard sand, done. We were so little. She would topple end over end like a piece of driftwood in the surf and come up laughing, then dolphin back out through the waves. She could stay out there Forever…

"At the end of my script, I picked another memory that mattered. Jenny was going to swim the Chesapeake Bay. It was a benefit to raise money for diabetes. She wanted to do it, but it was the wrong month, and the weather was terrible. There were about seven hundred people trying to swim across the bay on this impossible day."

Suddenly it was as if a cloud had passed over Chris. The music continued pulsating through the coffeehouse, but Chris no longer moved to it. He ran his hands through his wiry hair, and his eyes seemed to be staring into the distance as he explained how Jenny undertook the challenge of this swim. The water was cold and the waves were choppy, with the bay emptying into the ocean at 2.5 miles an hour. But Jenny knew the ocean, and she understood she had to swim until the resistance dissipated. She was in her element — free and happy.

"But suddenly it was *all hands on deck*." With these words, Chris's voice took on a fast-paced urgency. "Midway through the event, the organizers determined the swim was too dangerous. Boats were summoned into the bay to pick up all the swimmers. There were police boats, fishing boats, sailboats, any and all available boats. They raced to the swimmers and pulled them out of the water — more than 680 swimmers." He looked down, shaking his head. "They pulled Jenny out of the water — against her will."

Later Jenny would tell Chris, "If they had let me be, I could have made it. *I know* I could have made it."

Rewriting Who We Are

"As I was writing this script about Jenny, there was this powerful *aha* moment," Chris explained. "Suddenly the whole story of Jenny came together for me. I realized some of this story had to be a fantasy. I explained this to my students — that I had to find a better outcome to this story to accept it. *To live with it.*"

This is where it becomes valuable to bring a positive spin to our interpretations of a painful event. Sometimes our positive interpretations, even positive illusions, allow us to take our shattered experiences and realign them into a new narrative, one we can bear. This is exactly what Chris did with the script he wrote about Jenny.

Chris stayed up all night reimagining and rewriting the last scene. "In the end my script goes back to the beginning and the questions I was originally struggling with. What could I do for my sister? What could anybody do? How could I accept this terrible loss? And suddenly I came to a new understanding of Jenny and what she wanted. And this gave me the ending I needed.

"The ending I created took place on the day Jenny swam the Chesapeake Bay. But in my ending, Jenny was not pulled out. She was allowed to finish — just as she had wished. In my new version I envisioned every boat going to a swimmer but not insisting on picking them up. *Just spot them. Be there for them — but let the swimmers choose their own paths.*" Here is the ending of Chris's script:

[Chris standing on a chair. To the audience, the boat captains] WAIT! Wait.

There's a new plan. Get a boat by each person. Spot the swimmers. [Clapping. To Jenny who is swimming] You are doing great! Jenny, just keep going. Keep going.

Chris. It's Jenny. I'm not going to make it.

{Where are you?} Chris asks.

[The lights on the stage go dark.]

"This was a hard experience for me — losing my sister." Our lattes are long gone and the music has gone silent. "I wrote about her death to help me accept it, and in writing about it I rewrote the story in a way I could live with it. Resolve it or end it. And, of course, the writing did help." We chatted for a few more minutes, and then Chris hugged me farewell and began to walk the few blocks to his home, where he would feed his chickens, play with his kids, and grade his papers before he faced writing students at the college again the next morning.

As I drove back to the other side of town, I thought of Jenny. And how Chris wanted to understand his homeless, mentally ill sister. And how her death split him open. And how by writing and struggling and reframing and rewriting Jenny's story, Chris did come to understand her. He still missed her. He still loved her. But in her death, and in writing about her death, Chris found her again and understood her more fully.

When I pulled into the garage, I was still thinking about Chris's experience. I sat there as if trapped in an NPR moment. Chris had needed a new story to face Jenny's death. Slowly he found the memories and scenes that allowed him to transform his understanding of his sister. Chris desperately wished he had found the words he needed in his last phone conversation with Jenny. He wished he could have spotted Jenny at her Chesapeake Bay race and helped her finish. But when she called early that morning, he wasn't awake enough to say more, and he couldn't have spotted her in the treacherous waves of her race. Instead his story turns to fantasy, a metaphor that will help him accept what happened: he became Jenny's supportive coach.

While he continues to grieve his loss, his new story has given him insight about Jenny and those who suffer from mental illness. *Be there for them. Spot them. Care for them. But let them be.* This is a lovely ending — one that has eased the pain of Chris's grief and helped him move forward.

Bolstering Resilience

In his struggle to redefine his sister's death, Chris turned to his personal stories and writing. His words proved he was resilient, able to face a difficult experience and recover and grow from it. I have seen such resilience in a number of the individuals I interviewed for this book. As they used their writing and worked through their difficulties, they came to believe in themselves and they learned they had no choice but to get unstuck from their pain. They rose up and refused to be defined by their troubles. Instead, if they needed help, they turned to others and asked for it. And their writing supported them. They wrote out lists of what they needed to do and spelled out new goals and ways to solve their problems. Then they acted on them. And I watched on the sidelines as the writing gave them the clarity to make these important changes.

A groundbreaking longitudinal study on resilience supported what I had discovered. Participants born into homes with abuse, alcoholism, and poverty who overcame their harsh circumstances demonstrated the same abilities — to transcend their difficulties, to solve their own problems, and to believe in themselves.

Equally important, those who overcame difficulties made connections with individuals who could help them. When they needed a support group, they found it. When a family was not helpful, they turned to trusted friends, or distant relatives, or teachers. In one case study, Kellen, a teen from a rough neighborhood, hung out at the nearby community center, where he made positive connections with adults who taught him to use the audio equipment as well as the digital recording studio in the music center. Here Kellen created a personal space and began writing songs expressing the troubles he faced — the loss of his dad, the imprisonment of his brother, and the ever-present battle with drugs and crime in his neighborhood. His songs were the stories he needed to tell. In finding this positive community, Kellen found himself. He became a respected songwriter.

Chris made me think back to the hard times I have faced — trying to juggle working and raising kids, the death of my brother, my cancer, my son's cancer, my mom's declining health, and my dad's recent death. I could flip through my journals and see I had learned the same survival skills that Chris practiced. When troubled, I wrote out my story. Toyed with it. And struggled with it until I reached a resolution or found a way to live with it. In writing this book, I realized, I was rewriting my story once again.

Our left brains can use our written words to rework the impossible emotions that tumble out of our right brains. Our words can be realigned with a new interpretation, a new metaphor, or a new narrative. Perhaps we will find an understanding of our own heroic struggle, centered on finding our path again and learning to live the best life we can live.

Maslow's well-known theory of motivation argues that we have basic needs, physical needs, and safety needs, and that these must be satisfied before we can live a fuller, happier life. When we are caught up in our suffering and our trauma, we expend energy on these basic needs and on our painful emotions. When we wage internal wars with mental illness or addictions or ruminate about money, a nasty boss, or a recent car wreck, it is hard to experience love or find meaning or tap into our creativity.

Living fully seems to center on adapting well to our circumstances, on accepting our reality, and working flexibly with what we have. If our needs are fulfilled, we can experience love and explore what we enjoy doing and expend more energy doing it. We can tap into our passions. And explore our creativity. Isn't this what most of us want?

One of the most rewarding aspects of working on this book has been watching how people move toward finding a better, fuller self. Often in the process of writing for their blogs, musing in their journals, creating their stories, or developing their new projects, they blossom. They redefine their pain and can use it constructively. They discover meaningful activities or new opportunities for service to others, and in these experiences their own creativity unfolds. Recently I met Emma Bond to celebrate the upcoming publication of her first children's book. As we clinked our wine glasses together, we both had tears in our eyes.

"Of course, I miss Paul every day," Emma said solemnly and paused. "But I don't think I could have had this profound personal growth without his death." And I understood, for I had watched her choose to channel her pain into new and positive adventures.

> *Writing is an act of resilience that can allow us to*
> *rewrite our story and re-create ourselves.*

Writing Prompts and Suggestions

This prompt encourages you to rewrite a story you need or choose to tell. Search for your new interpretation of the event.

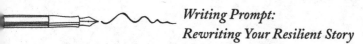

Writing Prompt:
Rewriting Your Resilient Story

Choose a current event in your life that has its share of challenges: An election? A move? A boss? A new baby? Maybe it is a setback — or maybe not. Plan to write a blog, a letter, a script, a poem, or a story about it. Before you begin writing, think about these questions: What is happening? Why do you want to write about this? Is there a problem that needs to be solved? If so, what are some actions you could take? Can you create a different way of looking at this event? How can you help yourself move forward? Do you need to create a different ending to this story? If so, how should it end?

- *Write a blog* to an audience who follows you. Share this experience and how you managed it. Share with your blog audience what you learned. What is the important take-away from this experience?

- *Write a letter* to a future "you" explaining how you managed a challenge. What did you do or can you do to turn this event into a positive experience, one that taught you something or helped you to grow, learn, and move forward?

- *Write a script,* as Chris did. In this script, share a memory (or memories) of a challenge you have faced or are facing. Work to see your story in a new way. Find the positive angle. Try to see it and write it in a way you can reinterpret and live with. Chris did this as he wrote his script on Jenny, fantasizing on how it "should" have ended.

- *Create a poem* by finding images that help you piece together, in new and positive ways, any challenge you have faced or are facing. Work toward creating a portrait of your resilience.

- *Write your best story* by sharing a challenging experience and finding a positive framework to understand it, reframe it, or end it. Know you can.

CHAPTER TWENTY-ONE

The Burst of Creativity

Imagination is everything.
It is the preview of life's coming attractions.
— Albert Einstein

Richard Serra had a rocky start. He studied painting at Yale, and after receiving a grant he headed to Florence to paint. While in Italy Serra took a trip to the Prado in Madrid, where he viewed a painting by Diego Velázquez called *Las Meninas* (1656). This work, a print of it hung in my high school classroom, focuses on a small Spanish princess, the Infanta Margarita, attended by her ladies. The painting haunts most viewers, as it did Serra. Why? Because Velázquez forces the viewers to step inside of it, to become part of the painting.

At the back of the room in this work, a mysterious man stands in the door staring at us. Is he entering or leaving the room? Then we see a mirror that reflects the images of the king and queen of Spain and they, too, are eerily watching us. If we scan the room, several sets of eyes study us, the viewers. Most striking is the painting of the painter, an actual portrait of Velázquez at work. He stands to the left with a palette in one hand and a brush in the other. His intense eyes peer through us, wondering if we

Las Meninas, 1656, by Diego Velázquez

will understand his message. He asks his viewers to climb inside his work and to be with him and in our moment, too. What an amazing feat for an artist to give to us in a work painted hundreds of years ago.

It took me a while to unravel the meaning of this work as it stared at me from the back of my classroom. But Richard Serra understood it on the spot. In recalling his visit to the Prado, Serra said, "I realized that Velázquez was looking at me.... There was a projection forward, where I was part of the painting. And I thought, 'I am the subject.'"

Starting Over with Words

The power of *Las Meninas* overwhelmed Serra, who realized he would never be able to paint anything this profound. Disappointed in his limitations, he returned to Florence, where he packed up all his paintings and dumped them into the Arno River.

Although Serra no longer saw himself as a painter, he didn't give up. Instead he worked on re-creating who he could be. He returned to New York, found a studio in Manhattan, and began to play with materials — rubber, wood, neon, molten lead, and eventually steel. He discovered he had an intense fascination with these materials and what they could do. Slowly the artist came to reflect on and change his story, and he began to see himself as a sculptor.

Since Serra had studied English literature, he had a fascination with words — similar to his fascination with materials and processes. He began to play with words that explored art possibilities. Serra tried a writing activity that is immensely simple but powerful, creating a list of more than a hundred verbs. Verbs that showed possibilities. Verbs that suggested ways of using these materials. Verbs that moved. *Action verbs.*

Inspired by words such as *roll*, *crease*, *bend*, and *fold*, Serra experimented with his materials to see what would happen. His excitement led him down a new path to what would become known as "process art." When he hit on the word *lift*, he took a large piece of rubber and lifted it up. He found it formed an intriguing topological form, like a sculpture. And he was onto something.

To Lift, created in 1967, sits in the Museum of Modern Art's collection in Manhattan today. The material rather magically lifts and lands in space. Today Serra's penciled list of words is held by the New York's MoMA as pivotal in guiding a new way of creating sculptures. The artist's unique minimalist sculptures can currently be seen in major cities throughout the world.

To Lift, 1967, by Richard Serra

Choosing to Live Creatively

Serra struggled to find his creative self. The artist understood his limitations and spent years reconfiguring who he was. Julie Burstein, author of *Spark: How Creativity Works*, explained that we must embrace four attributes in order to find our creativity: our experiences, our challenges, our limitations, and our losses. In following the pursuits of recent creative artists and thinkers, Burstein has helped us understand that the paths leading to creativity are covered in heartbreak, pain, and rejection.

"In order to create," Burstein said in her TED Talk, "we have to stand in that space between what we see in the world and what we hope for, looking squarely at rejection, at heartbreak, at war, at death. That is a tough space to stand in."

Let's return to what educator Parker Palmer called the "tragic gap." Again, this is the space that lies between the hard realities of our existence and the hopes and dreams we hold for our lives. It is tragic for us because of the difficulty of balancing these two different dimensions. Many artists, from Sylvia Plath to Kurt

Cobain, have been unable to navigate that gap, remaining trapped by despair. But if we reflect on our lives and rewrite our stories in ways that allow us to come to peace with our hardships, we can transmute our pain into creative works, and living will become more uplifting. We will love what we do.

While interviewing and researching writers for this book, I kept being called back to Maslow's theory of motivation and fulfillment. In his work he chose to study fulfilled individuals who loved what they were doing. They had found a purpose; they were living with meaning. By now we understand that our pain can take us to a new place. When we choose to rewrite our stories, we can find deep fulfillment. We might even experience a positive burst of creativity, a force that refuses to be framed in pain but reframes itself in a new way of seeing and experiencing our world. We not only produce something unique; *we can learn to live creatively*.

Finding Our Creative Flow

Let's return to the café on that cool November morning when I first interviewed Chris Schnick. Remember, Chris had been through a long bout of grief and pain. After he wrote a script about losing his mentally ill sister, a friend asked him to present it at a local theater house called Space 55. I remember Chris's description of his theater performance, probably because he lit up like a firefly in late spring as he discussed it. "That was hard, but I knew I had to do it," Chris said. "I made a commitment, and I understood that in performing you have to expend so much energy."

This was the coming together of the creative process for Chris. He had sat back and assimilated his memories of his sister in his writing, coming to an important insight about Jenny, and now he had a chance to share this newfound wisdom with others.

On the evening of his performance, the lights shined brightly in Chris's eyes and he couldn't really see the audience. As he talked with me, he blinked as if the lights were still distorting his vision.

"This presentation was the chance for me to put this story about my sister — as painful as it was — out there, to an audience. To tell it my way," Chris explained. "I was excited because I wanted people to understand what it was like to wrestle with the mental illness of a loved one, and it became important in that moment for me to share it.

"And as I presented it, something amazing happened. I felt something powerful pass through me that let me share this with others and also allowed me to stand back — and let go of this story — and even to let go of my pain and guilt." He paused and shrugged. "It seemed like the light on the stage was passing through me, and I was completely inside that light and that moment."

As Chris talked I kept thinking of flow. This word comes from the work of psychologist Mihaly Csikszentmihalyi, an expert on creativity. He found that what makes an experience genuinely satisfying is being in a state of consciousness where everything magically comes together for us. Csikszentmihalyi studied creative artists, athletes, scientists, and writers and discovered they described their most rewarding life experiences in the same way. At these moments these creative individuals were centered on doing something they loved for the sake of doing it. They lost track of time, dismissed any self-consciousness, and worked to meet whatever challenge had engaged them. This is what Csikszentmihalyi called *flow*. It is what Chris experienced on stage that night.

During my talk with Chris, I had my own "aha" moment: I realized that when the people I interviewed used writing to help them make sense of a difficult story, be it sexual abuse, war trauma, cancer, or grief, they often rediscovered themselves — *and* their creativity.

In other words, their writing had helped renew their energy. They were able to finish with a difficult chapter in their lives and head forward into a new story, often with a burst of creativity that allowed for new meaning. Perhaps they found a way to make a difference in the lives of others. Perhaps they just burst open in a new direction with a new passion. Often they bounded forward with joy.

While Robert, Barb, Jen, Emma, and Chris all had huge losses — of health, mental stability, a loved one — they were all able to re-create their stories by telling them, sometimes by sharing them in counseling, and always by writing them. When they were able to reflect and make sense of their story, they proved to be resilient and able to move forward in a positive direction. The biggest find here was that a positive change in their stories led to a positive burst of creativity.

Robert, Jen, and Emma wrote books. Barbara wrote poems, and Chris writes scripts and is working on a novel. Our creativity generates an explosion of positive energy that can sustain and help us live again. This is a powerful gift that can come out of suffering. Looking at Barbara I can see her life enriched by her new drive and her poems. She cheers me forward and wants to help me with my own creative explosion. Out of my pain came these pages and a drive to work with others on the power not just of rewriting our words — but of creatively rewriting our lives and living more fully.

Successfully writing our way through our hardships allows us to rediscover and fully experience our creativity.

Writing Prompts and Suggestions

These prompts will encourage you to tap into your creativity.

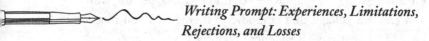 *Writing Prompt: Experiences, Limitations, Rejections, and Losses*

Creativity often surfaces from the pain of our experiences, limitations, rejections, and losses. Think back to your past. Then write for at least ten minutes on one of these topics:

- *An experience.* What experience opened you up and helped you discover or rediscover an ability you might not have explored or known you had? What new ability came from this experience? Dancing? Gardening? Running? Painting? Golfing? Writing? Cooking? Metalworking? Rock-climbing? Explore this.
- *A limitation.* When did you learn you had a limitation? How did you learn this? How did you feel? What came from this experience?
- *A rejection.* When have you experienced rejection? How did you feel? How did you handle this experience? What did you learn? Did it change you? How?
- *Losses.* Have you experienced a loss (a divorce, a death, a move, a retirement) that opened you up to a new aspect of your creativity? How did this happen? What did you learn from this experience?

Writing Prompt: Lists

Brainstorm a list of action verbs or phrases of possibility. Work to find the actions that you hope to take in coming weeks — perhaps plant a garden or write a poem. When you list all the action verbs or phrases you can find, re-create your list. But this time, make it a specific I-will-do-it list. What project do you need to undertake? What will you do to make this happen? Make your list detailed and clear. Post it on your bathroom mirror, tablet, smartphone, smartwatch, or computer. Begin acting on it. Now.

Writing Prompt: Create a Collage

Create drawings or graphics — or find pictures, photos, words — and create a collage that embodies a theme that you treasure in your life. Creativity? Resilience? Nature? Love? Hope?

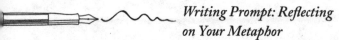

*Writing Prompt: Reflecting
on Your Metaphor*

Often as we work to understand and rewrite our story, it is helpful to find a metaphor or a symbol to represent us. Begin by making of list of twenty metaphors that connect to you. Could you be a balloon, a dancer, a storyteller, a coach, an acrobat, a teacher, a bird, a tree, a lotus flower, a bear, the sun? After making this list, choose one metaphor that fits you. It needs to be something that will allow you to open up and explore yourself in new ways. Reflect on your choice, and then answer these questions:

- What is your metaphor?
- Why did you choose it?
- How does it fit your story?

Epilogue

After the Gulf War and a number of years of struggling with PTSD and using alcohol as a coping mechanism, veteran Robert Serocki Jr. discovered writing. When he sent his second book to press, he visited with our writing group at the VA hospital. He wanted the vets to know how writing had helped him work through his post-traumatic stress disorder and move on. Since I interviewed him, he has published another book, *The Sword and the Anvil.* He continues to speak on the difficulty of coping with PTSD and to believe that writing helped him find his way back to himself. You can find out more about him at www.robertsercoki.com.

And there was Goldie Goldston, and his buddies Jeremy Lattimer and Todd Nicely, who shared their trials in Afghanistan. Although he doesn't write much now, I am especially grateful that Goldie trusted me with his war-worn diary when he returned home from his overseas stint. He continues to work his way through his PTSD. It is a difficult journey.

On a touching note, each November Goldie, along with Jeremy and Todd, gather with the rest of their squad in Leavenworth, Kansas, in the former home of Nick Hand, their friend who was killed in Afghanistan. In an act of healing they spend time with Nick's parents, visit Nick's gravesite, and reminisce. In my many interviews with them, I learned they all look out for each other as well as Momma Hand. As they say repeatedly, "*We are brothers.*"

And there's Barbara Lee, who suddenly took flight. She had lived for years claiming she had no meaning in her life and was wasting her God-given talents. One day she had the courage to share a poem she had written about the abuse she experienced and then to rewrite who she was. A couple of months later when we met for lunch, she proclaimed, "I am done with that old story. I am moving forward." Barbara has returned to school to study creative writing and yoga. She now understands herself as a poet. I still read her work, and I still love her metaphors.

Jen Campisano has continued with her blog and has finished a memoir that chronicles living with stage four cancer and surviving. She has been active in writing to legislators and participating in the annual Avon walk, raising thousands of dollars to support cancer research each year. She has appeared on the *Today Show* and at many events that support breast cancer research.

Jen and I remain friends, and in the past four years we have often talked about our writing during chemo sessions or at lunch. At one session she asked me if I had seen the blog that mentioned me. When I admitted I hadn't, she said, "I wrote that writing can help to heal you." She beamed. "Just look at me!"

And she may truly be healed. Recently her oncologist released her from a regular chemo regiment. Her scans are completely clear. Currently the discussion is ongoing: Was she misdiagnosed as stage four instead of stage three — or has she been healed? I want to believe in miracles.

When I last visited with Emma Bond, she was engaged in

her creative pursuits — excited about the publication of her children's book and preparing to teach a new class on "journaling for spiritual growth" at her church. Of course Emma misses Paul, but she has moved forward. In her words, "Gratitude for the life we had has made its way into my heart through the pages of my journals. Piece by piece, I am finding my peace."

Chris Schnick recently admitted that he still feels the painful loss of his sister, Jenny. He continues to support student learning at his community college, where he currently serves as the dean of Arts and Sciences. He is "slowly working on a novel." Occasionally he is able to squeeze in another presentation of his writing at Space 55. One of these writings highlighted conversations with his deceased father and with his son. I continue to follow his work.

Chris's enthusiasm and energy, indeed, the energy of all the writers who have partnered with me to create this book, gave me a renewed faith that we can shape our difficult stories, that we can get a handle on them by rewriting them and finding their meaning. And when we do this, we can become fuller and stronger individuals.

And my story? After college I wanted to write and teach. I believed I could do it all. I married my best friend, who was equally idealistic. I taught high school and college for thirty years. In the summers I labored away at my novels (they remain hidden in drawers) and wrote articles for teachers and teens.

And during this period Matt was born. Then Zach. While they brought unmatched joy into our lives, they also brought the pressures of parenting. Steve pursued his dream of an innovative business — working days at a job and nights at starting his engineering company. With parenting and teaching, I might have been swallowed whole if it had not been for good friends and a wonderful family — especially my mom, who stepped in to babysit.

During those hard-to-juggle years, the only writing I did was in my personal journals. And I am so grateful I did it. This practice taught me to move toward self-reflection and off the slippery slope of ruminations. It allowed me to walk the tightropes of parenting, of being married to a workaholic, and of surviving the ongoing challenges that life tossed, and continues to toss, at me. When I was diagnosed with cancer, writing helped me express my fears and leave teaching. It lit the path for rediscovering the writing experiences of my students, of vets, and of fellow cancer patients. I was entrusted with their wisdom, and I hold it in my heart and have attempted to share it here.

I learned that our writing can move us forward to more fulfilling, happier, creative lives. Writing helped me tap into this transformative power, and I didn't want that to be my secret — I needed to share it.

Write.

Acknowledgments

This book was woven together from the stories and kindnesses of many people. First, I have to thank the man who sat across from me in our kitchen every night, listening, asking important questions, and sharing honest insights — my best friend, my husband, Steve.

And I could not have given flight to a book without a lifelong friend like Billie Cox, who is generous, kind, and the only person on this planet who would be willing to read, edit, and cheer me through several drafts of this book.

When I was a new teacher, Christina Baldwin's book *One to One* carried the magic of personal writing into my life and then into the lives of my students. When I talked to Christina about my dream to carry this work forward in a book, she encouraged me. Thanks, Christina, for believing in this project and for serving as an inspirational mentor as I journeyed from book drafts to book to New World Library.

I am grateful to many writing groups, especially the Self as

Source writers who insisted I integrate my personal stories into this work. I struggled with this challenge, but I thank them for seeing that I had to walk through these pages, too.

Several outstanding writers influenced my work. While I cannot list them all here, I especially have to thank Ellen Bass and Cheryl Strayed. Ellen laid the groundwork, working and writing with those who have faced trauma. Her teaching, her poems, and our talks proved inspirational as I wrote and developed my theory of writing to heal. I appreciated Cheryl's wisdom about writing, her thoughtful answers to my questions, and her workshops at both the Omega and the Esalen Institutes. Cheryl's workshops inspired the book's title. I am also grateful for the willingness of many writers in these workshops to share their work with me.

I am indebted to the writers, veterans, and cancer patients who stepped forward to share their stories and help me create this book. While not all their stories could fit onto these pages, every story mattered. Also, I appreciate Rick Markson for helping me connect with veteran writers, and Dale Yavitt for arranging my writing groups at the Virginia G. Piper Cancer Center.

Friends matter — and I have some of the best. Several of them volunteered to read book drafts and were honest and helpful. Thanks go to Kirstin Thomas, Laurie Keefe, Margot McDonnell, Diana Sokol, Lois Bartholomew, Pam Davenport, and Marybeth Mason. When I needed psychotherapists to review the manuscript, both Kathleen Todd and Sara Harris graciously helped. And then there is my oldest-dearest-best-friend, Janis Frazee. When I needed a medical perspective, she was there, as always, to help.

New World Library truly brings books that change lives into the world. I am grateful to Jason Gardner, the executive editor. He embraced this project, and his gifts made this book much better. Barbara Fisher designed a lovely cover that captured the "glimmers," and Tona Pearce Myers designed the book's beautiful interior. Mimi Kusch proved what a difference a copyeditor extraordinaire can make. Kristen Cashman expertly prepared the manuscript for typesetting and coordinated the proofreading. As the book goes to press, Monique Muhlenkamp, Munro Magruder, and Kim Corbin are deftly guiding it into the world. I am honored to work with this amazing team!

I embrace my family with the biggest hug of thanks. I was lucky to have my parents, Lester and Betty Robinson, who gave me a life rich in learning, love, faith, and encouragement. And nothing has enriched my life more than my children, who love me and trust me to share our family stories. I thank Matt, Keely, Zach, Jordyn, and the biggest heartthrobs of my life, my grandchildren Macy, Harper, and Josiah. They have kept me hopeful, humble, and in the moment, even in the face of deadlines.

Finally, I appreciate my readers and writers. You inspire me. Let's keep finding our best paths — one story at a time.

Notes

Introduction

Page 4 *81 percent of us*: Epstein, "Think You Have a Book in You?"

Chapter One. Waving: Not Drowning

Page 12 *like a railway station*: from the film *Stevie*, directed by Robert Enders (United Artists, 1978).

Page 12 *"Not Waving but Drowning"*: Smith, *Collected Poems*, 303.

Page 13 *the tragic gap*: Palmer, "Standing in the Tragic Gap."

Page 15 *Paul McCartney must have*: "Hey Jude," *Wikipedia*, last modified December 6, 2016, en.wikipedia.org/wiki/Hey_Jude.

Page 16 *fourteen or more*: Smouse, "Phoenix-Area Drownings."

Chapter Two. Facing Trauma

Page 22 *Recent studies support*: Moran, "What Can the Organization of the Brain's Default Mode Network Tell Us about Self-Knowledge?" See also the American Psychological Association studies on silence, for example, www.apa.org/monitor/2011/07-08/silence.aspx.

Page 23 *After being liberated*: Winfrey, "Oprah Talks to Elie Wiesel."

Page 23 *I gained perspective*: "Biography," on Cheryl Strayed's official website, accessed December 8, 2016, www.cherylstrayed.com.

Page 24 *"Trough"*: Brown, *The Sea Accepts All Rivers and Other Poems*, 17–18.

Chapter Three: Writing

Page 30 *I felt I had lost all control*: Serocki, *Line in the Sand*, 99.
Page 30 *I remember being scared*: Serocki, *Line in the Sand*, 241.
Page 30 *I still had PTSD*: All quotations are from my interview with Robert Serocki Jr., Phoenix, Arizona, March 4, 2014.
Page 34 *who did not talk*: Pennebaker, *Writing to Heal*, 5.
Page 35 *had never been asked*: Pennebaker, *Writing to Heal*, 6.
Page 35 *profoundly important for them*: Pennebaker, *Writing to Heal*, 6.
Page 35 *students in the*: Pennebaker, *Writing to Heal*, 6.
Page 35 *who engage in expressive writing*: Pennebaker, *Writing to Heal*, 8.
Page 35 *more than two hundred*: Pennebaker, "Expressive Writing in a Clinical Setting," 23.

Chapter Four. A Room of Your Own

Page 50 *there's a kind of spiritual*: Dreifus, "Alice Walker," 30.

Chapter Five. Writing Down the Self

Page 56 *research on journaling*: Pennebaker, *Writing to Heal*, 13.
Page 58 *This is my place*: "Nora Roberts," video.
Page 58 *J. K. Rowling wrote*: Farr, "J. K. Rowling."
Page 59 *more than three hundred*: "Cumulative Total of Tumblr Blogs."
Page 59 *I have never been able*: Silverman, all quotes come from an interview with the author in Tempe, Arizona, December 1, 2016.
Page 60 *I've been keeping*: "Ask the Author Live: David Sedaris."
Page 61 *three stream-of-consciousness*: Cameron, *Artist's Way*, 10.
Page 61 *Morning pages map*: Cameron, *Artist's Way*, 15.
Page 62 *I am a binge writer*: Strayed, all quotes come from talks with the author at Omega Institute, Rhinebeck, New York, August 4–8, 2014.
Page 63 *Congress had to create*: Baldwin, *Storycatcher*, 40–42.
Page 64 *It has led to*: Baldwin, personal communication with the author, March 30, 2015.

Chapter Six. Stages of Writing and Healing

Page 71 *Allende had begun*: "Isabel Allende," *Contemporary Authors Online*.
Page 71 *My soul is choking*: Allende, *Paula*, 9.
Page 71 *Allende started this letter*: Allende, *Paula*, 15–16.
Page 71 *I had a choice*: Allende, *Paula*, 108; and DeSalvo, *Writing as a Way of Healing*, 39.
Page 74 *construct a complete story*: Pennebaker, *Writing to Heal*, 55–57.

Page 75 *I was fourteen*: Sebold, *Lovely Bones*, 5.

Page 75 *When she gave her account*: Sebold, *Lucky*, 3.

Page 76 *One of the things*: From *Fresh Air* interview of Alice Sebold by Terry Gross on NPR, July, 10, 2002.

Chapter Seven. The Magical Mystery Tour

Page 88 *When a neuron*: Doidge, *Brain That Changes Itself*, 54.

Page 88 *Neurons that fire together*: Doidge, *Brain That Changes Itself*, 63.

Page 88 *The more we use*: Damasio, *Self Comes to Mind*, 18.

Page 89 *our brain actually transforms*: Damasio, *Self Comes to Mind*, 18–19.

Page 90 *How we develop a sense of self*: Damasio, *Self Comes to Mind*, 24.

Page 91 *a narrative brain device*: Damasio, *Self Comes to Mind*, 25.

Page 93 *damaged brain can often reorganize*: Doidge, *Brain That Changes Itself*, xix.

Page 94 *One day overwhelmed*: Doyle Melton, *Love Warrior*, 111–13.

Page 94 *I'm going to*: McCarthy, "Her Marriage Was the Jewel in Her Blog Universe."

Page 94 *Writing will have to be*: Doyle Melton, *Love Warrior*, 138–140.

Page 95 *Yes! This is*: Silverman, interview with the author in Tempe, Arizona, December 1, 2016.

Page 95 *I morphed from*: Silverman, *My Heart Can't Even Believe It*, 5.

Chapter Eight. Stories

Page 98 *The problem of how*: Damasio, *Self Comes to Mind*, 311.

Page 99 *storytelling animals*: Gottschall, *Storytelling Animal*.

Page 99 *We have about two thousand daydreams*: Gottschall, *Storytelling Animal*, 11.

Page 100 *universal hero pattern*: Campbell, *Hero with a Thousand Faces*.

Page 100 *In writing* Wild: Strayed, all quotes come from talks with author at the Omega Institute, Rhinebeck, New York, August 4–8, 2014.

Page 105 *All my things are yours*: Parable of the prodigal son, Luke 15:11–12.

Page 107 *I don't go looking*: Rowling, *Harry Potter and the Prisoner of Azkaban*, 75.

Page 107 *This model acknowledges*: Burroway, *Imaginative Writing*, 165.

Page 107 *We mentally take notes*: Pinker, *How the Mind Works*, 541.

Page 109 *I think that the problem structure*: Gottschall, *Storytelling Animal*, 56.

Page 110 *flight simulators of human*: Oatley, quoted in Gottschall, *Storytelling Animal*, 58.

Page 110 *pilots internalize their*: Oatley, "Mind's Flight Simulator," 1030–32.

Chapter Nine: Finding Our Life-Defining Stories

Page 117 *far more likely*: "BRCA1 and BRCA2: Cancer Risk and Genetic Testing."

Page 118 *Guthrie had a 50 percent*: "Woody Guthrie Biography."

Page 118 *those with the bad prognosis*: Wilson, *Redirect*, 55–56; Wiggins, et al., "Psychological Consequences of Predictive Testing," 1401–5.

Page 122 *peak experiences*: McAdams, *Stories We Live By*, 256–64.

Page 122 *The Stepping-stones*: Progoff, *At a Journal Workshop*, 76–81.

Chapter Ten. Making Sense of Self with Stories

Page 125 *Distraught over her discovery*: White, *Maps of Narrative Practice*, 62–75.

Page 129 *Gazzaniga was able*: Gottschall, *Storytelling Animal*, 95–99. For more, see Gazzaniga, *Human*.

Page 130 *The shovel is needed*: Gazzaniga, *Tales from Both Sides*, 148–53.

Page 130 *It acts as an interpreter*: Gazzaniga, *Human*, 294–95.

Page 131 *The storytelling mind*: Gottschall, *Storytelling Animal*, 95–99; Gazzaniga, *Tales from Both Sides*.

Page 132 *Scotland Yard reopened*: Bradshaw, "World's Top 15 Conspiracy Theories."

Page 132 *"truthy"*: Gottschall, *Storytelling Animal*, 176.

Page 132 *When he appeared*: "Million Little Lies."

Page 132 *wholly fabricated*: "Million Little Lies." For more, see Gottschall, *Storytelling Animal*.

Page 137 *our life stories*: McAdams, *Stories We Live By*, 11.

Chapter Eleven. Writing to Heal

Page 150 *The Pennebaker Writing Process*: Pennebaker and Evans, *Expressive Writing*. For more, see Pennebaker, *Opening Up*; Pennebaker, *Writing to Heal*; and Adams, *The Write Way to Wellness*.

Chapter Twelve. Breaking the Silence

Page 160 *There is no portal*: Strayed, all quotes come from talks at Omega Institute, Rhinebeck, New York, August 4–8, 2014.

Chapter Thirteen. Getting Unstuck

Page 165 *asked people over seventy*: Brooks, "The Life Reports II."

Page 166 *People who remain fixated*: Nolen-Hoelsema, Wisco, and Lyubomirsky, "Rethinking Rumination," 400–424.

Page 167 *negative experiences were analyzed*: Kross, 35–40.

Page 167 *Step Back and Ask Why*: Wilson, *Redirect*, 72–73.

Chapter Fourteen. Embracing Other Perspectives

Page 171 *Some new research*: Pennebaker and Evans, *Expressive Writing*, 75.

Chapter Fifteen. Story Editing

Page 177 *The self-story*: Baldwin, *Storycatcher*, 128.
Page 178 *techniques designed to redirect*: Wilson, *Redirect*, 11.

Chapter Sixteen. Rewriting and Transforming

Page 185 *significantly better psychological adjustment*: Taylor, "Adjustment to Threatening Events," 1161–73.

Chapter Seventeen. Writing to Heal from Hardships and Trauma

Page 197 *news reports*: Lee, "The Missing Context."
Page 197 *It takes a period of disorder*: Baldwin, *Life's Companion*, 105.
Page 202 *This class seemed*: private phone conversation with student, 2013.
Page 202 *A significant number of studies*: Baikie and Wilhelm, "Emotional and Physical Health Benefits," 1–13.
Page 203 *wrote about their deepest*: Pennebaker, *Opening Up*, 37.
Page 203 *Yeah, I'm free*: Private writings of Jessica Brown shared with the author, 2014.
Page 205 *I want to write*: private phone conversation with student, 2014.
Page 206 *a structured writing*: Adams, adapted from *The Way of the Journal*.

Chapter Eighteen. Writing to Heal from Illness and Injury

Page 213 *I put a life together*: Thomas, *Three Dog Night*, 122.
Page 213 *I do like to work*: DeSalvo, *Writing as a Way of Healing*, 123.
Page 214 *he created*: DeSalvo, *Writing as a Way of Healing*, 173.
Page 214 *I suffered from*: De Salvo, 172–73.
Page 216 *Now the author*: Oe, *Healing Family*, 18.
Page 216 *In the act*: Oe, *Healing Family*, 28.
Page 217 *He was only ten*: Oe, *Healing Family*, 21–22.
Page 217 *I recall…the intense*: Oe, *Healing Family*, 21–24.
Page 218 *profoundly consoled and encouraged*: Oe, *Healing Family*, 25.
Page 220 *Before my mastectomy*: Campisano, "Motto" (blog).

Chapter Nineteen. Writing to Heal from Loss

Page 231 *It's been god-awful*: Baker, "One Year Later."
Page 231 *I began this writing*: Mark Barden, phone interview with the author, June 16, 2015.

Page 231 *Nine years ago today*: Mark Barden, personal letter to the author, September 27, 2014.

Page 233 *"The Muse of Work"*: Bass, *Like a Beggar*, 60.

Page 232 *Writing poems*: Ellen Bass, phone interview with the author, May 6, 2014.

Page 235 *argued that*: Brown, *Happier Endings*, 6–7.

Page 237 *Healing comes*: Pennebaker 1997, 20–23.

Page 237 *To write was*: Doty, *Heaven's Coast*, 205.

Page 238 *adrift in the sea-swirl*: Doty, *Heaven's Coast*, preface.

Page 240 *For example, last semester*: Norma Bowe, interview with the author at Omega Institute, Rhinebeck, New York, August 20, 2014.

Page 242 *Recent studies show*: Emmons, "Why Gratitude Is Good."

Page 242 *ethical will*: Riemer and Stampfer, *So That Your Values Live On*, xiv–xxv.

Page 243 *Their conversations*: Albom, *Tuesdays with Morrie*.

Page 243 *discovered he had ten tumors*: Pausch, *Last Lecture*," ix.

Page 244 *shared his life lessons*: "Randy Pausch's Last Lecture," Carnegie Mellon website.

Chapter Twenty. Resilience

Page 251 *You can rewrite*: Chris Schnick, all quotes come from an interview with the author in Phoenix, Arizona, November 17, 2013.

Page 257 *Participants born into homes with abuse*: Werner, "Resilience and Recovery," 11–14.

Page 257 *In one case study, Kellen*: Kinney, "Loops, Lyrics, and Literacy," 395–404.

Page 258 *theory of motivation*: Maslow, "Creativity in Self-Actualizing People."

Chapter Twenty-One. The Burst of Creativity

Page 262 *Las Meninas*: Diego Velázquez, *Las Meninas* (The-Ladies-in-Waiting), 1656 (Madrid, Museo del Prado).

Page 262 *I realized that Velázquez*: Burstein, *Spark*, 46-7.

Page 263 *creating a list*: Richard Serra, *Verb List*, 1967–68 (New York MoMA).

Page 263 *To Lift*: Richard Serra, 1967 (New York MoMA).

Page 264 *We have to stand in that space*: Burstein, "4 Lessons in Creativity."

Page 265 *I understood*: Burstein, "4 Lessons in Creativity."

Page 266 *What Csikszentmihalyi called* flow: Csikszentmihalyi, *Creativity*, 113.

References and
Suggested Reading

Adams, Kathleen. *Journal to the Self: Twenty-Two Paths to Personal Growth.* New York: Grand Central Publishing, 1990.

_____. *The Way of the Journal: A Journal Therapy Workbook for Healing.* Baltimore, MD: Sidran Press, 1998.

_____. *The Write Way to Wellness: A Workbook for Healing and Change.* Denver, CO: The Center for Journal Therapy, 2000.

Angelou, Maya. *I Know Why the Caged Bird Sings.* New York: Ballantine, 1969.

Albom, Mitch. *Tuesdays with Morrie: An Old Man, a Young Man, and Life's Greatest Lessons.* New York: Bantam, 1997.

Allende, Isabel. *The House of the Spirits.* New York: Knopf, 1993.

_____. *Paula: A Memoir.* New York: Harper Perennial, 1994.

"A Million Little Lies: Exposing James Frey's Fiction Addiction." *The Smoking Gun,* January 4, 2006. www.thesmokinggun.com/documents/celebrity/million-little-lies.

"Ask the Author Live: Davis Sedaris." *New Yorker,* August 14, 2009. www.newyorker.com/books/ask-the-author/ask-the-author-live-david-sedaris.

Baikie, A. and K. Wilhelm. "Emotional and Physical Health Benefits of Expressive Writing." *Advances in Psychiatric Treatment: Journal of Continuing Professional Development* 11 (2005): 338–46. Apt.rcpsych.org/content/11/5/338.

Baker, K. C. Newtown. "One Year Later: Honoring a 7-Year-Old's Kindness with Foundation in His Memory." *People,* December 11, 2013. People.com/human-interest/newtown-one-year-later-daniel-barden-honored-with-foundation-in-his-memory.

Baldwin, Christina. *Life's Companion: Journal Writing as a Spiritual Practice.* New York: Bantam, 1990.

_____. *Storycatcher: Making Sense of Our Lives through the Power and Practice of Story.* Novato, CA: New World Library, 2005.

Bass, Ellen. *Mules of Love.* Rochester, NY: BOA, 2002.

_____. *Like a Beggar.* Port Townsend, WA: Copper Canyon Press, 2014.

Bass, Ellen, and Laura Davis. *The Courage to Heal: A Guide for Women Survivors of Child Sexual Abuse.* New York: Harper and Row, 1988.

_____. *Beginning to Heal: A First Book for Men and Women Who Were Sexually Abused as Children.* New York: Harper Perennial, 2003.

Bradshaw, Derik. "The World's Top 15 Conspiracy Theories of All Time." *Guardian Liberty Voice,* March 22, 2014. www.guardianlv.com/2014/03/the-worlds-top-15-conspiracy-theories-of-all-time.

"BRCA1 and BRCA2: Cancer Risk and Genetic Testing." National Cancer Institute. www.cancer.gov/about-cancer/causes-prevention/genetics/brca-fact-sheet.

Brooks, David. "The Life Reports II." *New York Times.* November 28, 2011. www.nytimes.com/2011/11/29/opinion/brooks-the-life-reports-ii.

Brown, Erica. *Happier Endings: A Meditation on Life and Death.* New York: Simon and Schuster, 2013.

Brown, Judy Sorum. "Trough." *The Sea Accepts All Rivers and Other Poems.* Alexandria, VA: Miles River Press, 2000.

Burroway, Janet. *Imaginative Writing: The Elements of Craft.* 2nd ed. New York: Pearson, 2007.

Burstein, Julie. *Spark: How Creativity Works.* New York: HarperCollins, 2011.

_____. "4 Lessons in Creativity." TED Talk. Filmed in February 2012. www.ted.com/talks/julie_burstein_4_lessons_in_creativity?language-en.

Cameron, Julia. *The Artist's Way: A Spiritual Path to Higher Creativity.* London: Pan Books, 1993.

Campbell, Joseph. *The Hero with a Thousand Faces.* Princeton, NJ: Princeton University Press, 1968.

_____. *The Power of Myth.* New York: Doubleday, 1988.

Campisano, Jennifer. "Motto." *Booby and the Beast* (blog), March 2, 2012. www.boobyandthebeast.com.

Csikszentmihalyi, Mihaly. *Creativity: The Psychology of Discovery and Invention.* New York: Harper Perennial, 1996.

"Cumulative Total of Tumblr Blogs between May 2011 and October 2016 (in Millions)." *Statista: The Statistics Portal* (website). www.statista.com/statistics/256235/total-cumulative-number-of-tumblr-blogs.

Damasio, Antonio. *Self Comes to Mind: Constructing the Conscious Brain.* New York: Vintage, 2012.

DeSalvo, Louise. *Writing as a Way of Healing: How Telling Our Stories Transforms Our Lives.* Boston: Beacon Press, 1999.

Doidge, Norman. *The Brain That Changes Itself: Stories of Personal Triumphs from the Frontiers of Brain Science.* New York: Penguin, 2007.

Doty, Mark. *Heaven's Coast: A Memoir.* New York: Harper Perennial, 1996.

Doyle Melton, Glennon. *Carry On Warrior: The Power of Embracing Your Messy, Beautiful Life.* New York: Scribner, 2013.

_____. *Love Warrior: A Memoir.* New York: St. Martin's, 2016.

Dreifus, Claudia. "Alice Walker: Writing to Save My Life." *The Progressive,* August, 1989: 29–31.

Emmons, Robert. "Why Gratitude Is Good." *Greater Good the Science of a Meaningful Life,* November 16, 2010. greatergood.berkeley.edu/article /item/why_gratitude_is_good.

Epstein, Joseph. "Think You Have a Book in You? Think Again." *New York Times,* September 28, 2002. www.nytimes.com/2002/09/28/opinion /think-you-have-a-book-in-you-think-again.html.

Farr, Emma-Victoria. "J.K. Rowling: 10 Facts about the Writer." *Telegraph,* September 27, 2012. www.telegraph.co.uk/culture/books/booknews /9564894/JK-Rowling-10-facts-about-the-writer.html.

Frank, Anne. *The Diary of a Young Girl–the Definitive Edition.* New York: Bantam, 1997.

Frankl, E. Viktor. *Man's Search for Meaning.* Boston: Beacon, 2006.

Gazzaniga, Michael S. "Forty-Five Years of Split-Brain Research and Still Going Strong." *Nature Reviews Neuroscience,* 6 (August 2005). www .nature.com/nrn/journal/v6/n8/full/nrn1740.html.

_____. *Human: The Science behind What Makes Your Brain Unique.* New York: Harper Perennial, 2008.

_____. *Tales from Both Sides of the Brain: A Life in Neuroscience.* New York: HarperCollins, 2015.

Gilbert, Elizabeth. *Eat Pray Love: One Woman's Search for Everything across Italy, India, and Indonesia.* New York: Penguin, 2006.

Gottschal, Jonathan. *The Storytelling Animal.* New York: Houghton Mifflin Harcourt, 2012.

Hayasaki, Erika. *The Death Class: A True Story about Life.* New York: Simon and Schuster, 2014.

Hesse, Hermann. *Siddhartha.* New York: Bantam, 1981.

Joyce, James. *A Portrait of an Artist as a Young Man.* London: Penguin, 2003.

Karr, Mary. *The Art of Memoir.* New York: Harper Perennial, 2015.

King, Stephen. *On Writing: A Memoir of the Craft.* New York: Pocket Books, 2000.

Kinney, Angela. "Loops, Lyrics, and Literacy: Songwriting as a Site of

Resilience for an Urban Adolescent." *Journal of Adolescent and Adult Literacy* 55, no. 5 (2012): 395–404.

Kross, Ethan. "When the Self Becomes Other: Toward an Integrative Understanding of the Processes Distinguishing Adaptive Self-Reflection from Rumination." *Annals of the New York Academy of Sciences* 1167 (2009): 35–40.

"Isabel Allende." *Contemporary Authors Online*. Detroit: Gale, 2015. *Biography in Context*.

Lee, Michelle Ye Hee. "The Missing Context behind the Widely Cited Statistic That There Are 22 Veterans Suicides a Day." *Washington Post*, February 4, 2015. www.washingtonpost.com/news/fact-checker/wp/2015/02/04/the-missing-context-behind-a-widely-cited-statistic-that-there-are-22-veteran-suicides-a-day.

Love, Susan. *Dr. Susan Love's Breast Book*. 6th ed. Philadelphia: Da Capo, 2015.

Maslow, Abraham. "Creativity in Self-Actualizing People." In *Toward a Psychology of Being*. 3rd ed. New York: Wiley, 1999.

McAdams, Dan P. *The Stories We Live By: Personal Myths and the Making of the Self*. New York: William Morrow, 1993.

McCarthy, Ellen. "Her Marriage Was the Jewel in Her Blog Universe. Then She Found Out Her Husband Was Cheating." *Washington Post*, September 7, 2016. www.washingtonpost.com/lifestyle/her-marriage-was-the-jewel-in-her-mommy-blog-universe-then-she-found-out-her-husband-was-cheating/2016/09/07.

Moran, Joseph M., William M. Kelley, and Todd F. Heatherton. "What Can the Organization of the Brain's Default Mode Network Tell Us about Self-Knowledge?" *Frontiers in Human Neuroscience*, July 17, 2013. Doi.org/10.3389/fnhum.2013.00391.

Myers, Linda Joy. *The Power of Memoir: How to Write Your Healing Story*. San Francisco: Jossey-Bass, 2010.

Nolan-Hoeksema, Susan, Blair E. Wisco, and Sonja Lyubomirsky. "Rethinking Rumination." *Perspectives on Psychological Science* 5 (2008) 3: 400–24.

"Nora Roberts: As Engaging as Her Books" (video). *CBS Sunday Morning*, September 23, 2012. www.cbsnews.com/videos/nora-roberts-as-engaging-as-her-books.

Oatley, Keith. "The Mind's Flight Simulator." *Psychologist* 21 (2008): 1030–32.

O'Brien, Tim. *The Things They Carried*. Boston: Mariner Books, 1990.

Oe, Kenzaburo. *A Personal Matter*. New York: Grove Press, 1969.

_____. *A Healing Family*. Tokyo: Kodansha International, 1996.

Palmer, Parker. "Standing in the Tragic Gap." Center for Courage and Renewal, August 21, 2013. www.couragerenewal.org/723.

Pausch, Randy. *The Last Lecture*. New York: Hyperion, 2008.

Pennebaker, James W. "Writing in a Clinical Setting." *The Independent Practitioner* 30 (2010): 23–25.

_____. *Opening Up: The Healing Power of Expressing Emotions.* New York: Guildford, 1997.

_____. *Writing to Heal: A Guided Journal for Recovering from Trauma and Emotional Upheaval.* Oakland, CA: New Harbinger, 2004.

Pennebaker, J.W., and S.K. Beall. "Confronting a Traumatic Event: Toward an Understanding of Inhibition and Disease. *Journal of Abnormal Psychology* 95 (1986): 274–81. Doi=10.1037/0021-843X.95.3.274.

Pennebaker, James, and John Evans. *Expressive Writing: Words That Heal.* Enumclaw, WA: Idyll Arbor, 2014.

Pennebaker, James, and Joshua Smyth. *Opening Up by Writing It Down: How Expressive Writing Improves Health and Eases Emotional Pain.* New York: Guilford, 2016.

Pinker, Steven. *How the Mind Works.* New York: Norton, 1997.

Progoff, Ira. *At a Journal Workshop: Writing to Access the Power of the Unconscious and Evoke Creative Ability.* New York: Tarcher, 1992.

"Randy Pausch's Last Lecture." Carnegie Mellon University (website), September 18, 2007. www.cmu.edu/randyslecture.

Rainer, Tristine. *The New Diary.* New York: Tarcher/Penguin, 2004.

Reeves, Judy. *Wild Women, Wild Voices.* Novato: CA: New World Library, 2015.

Riemer, Jack, and Nathaniel Stampfer. *So That Your Values Live On: Ethical Wills and How to Prepare Them.* Woodstock, VT: Jewish Lights Publishing, 1991.

Rowling, J.K. *Harry Potter and the Prisoner of Azkaban.* New York: Arthur A. Levine, 1999.

Saint-Exupéry, Antoine de. *The Little Prince.* New York: Harcourt, Brace & Company, 1973.

Schwartz, Jeffrey M. *Brain Lock: Free Yourself from Obsessive-Compulsive Behavior.* New York: HarperCollins, 1996.

Sebold, Alice. *Lucky.* New York: Little Brown, 1999.

_____. *The Lovely Bones.* New York: Little Brown, 2002.

Serocki, Robert, Jr. *A Line in the Sand: The True Story of a Marine's Experience on the Front Line of the Gulf War.* Prescott, AZ: One World Press, 2006.

_____. *The Sword and the Anvil: A Definitive Guide for Natural, Healthy Healing from Post-Traumatic Stress and Trauma.* Chino Valley, AZ: One World Press, 2016.

_____. *Chrysalis: A Metamorphosis Has Begun.* Chino Valley, AZ: One World Press, 2014.

Silverman, Amy. *My Heart Can't Even Believe It: A Story of Science, Love, and Down Syndrome.* Bethesda: Woodbine House, 2016.

Smith, Stevie. *Collected Poems*. Edited by James MacGibbon. New York: New Directions, 1983.

Smouse, Rebecca. "Phoenix-Area Drownings Already Match 2013 Total." *Arizona Republic*, August 21, 2014. www.azcentral.com/story/news/local /phoenix/2014/06/29/phoenix-drownings-rise/11701583.

Sontag, Susan. *Reborn: Journals and Notebooks, 1947–1963*. New York: Picador, 2008.

Strayed, Cheryl. *Tiny Beautiful Things: Advice on Love and Life from Dear Sugar*. New York: Vintage, 2012.

_____. *Wild: From Lost to Found on the Pacific Crest Trail*. New York: Knopf, 2012.

Taylor, Shelley E. "Adjustment to Threatening Events: A Theory of Cognitive Adaptation." *American Psychologist*, 38 (1983): 1161–73.

Thomas, Abigail. *A Three Dog Life*. Orlando, FL: Harcourt, 2006.

Tolle, Eckhart. *The Power of Now*. Novato, CA: New World Library, 1999.

Werner, E. E. "Resilience and Recovery: Findings from the Kauai Longitudinal Study." *Focal Point: Research, Policy, and Practice in Children's Mental Health* 19, no. 1 (2005): 11–14.

White, Michael. *Maps of Narrative Practice*. New York: Norton, 2007.

Wiesel, Elie. *Night*. Translated by Stella Rodway. New York: Bantam, 1982.

Wiggins, Sandi, Patti Whyte, and Marlene Huggins. "The Psychological Consequences of Predictive Testing for Huntington's Disease." *New England Journal of Medicine* 327, no. 20 (1992): 1401–5.

Wilson, Timothy D. *Redirect: The Surprising New Science of Psychological Change*. New York: Little, Brown, 2011.

Winfrey, Oprah. "Oprah Talks to Elie Wiesel." *O*, November 2000. www .oprah.com/omagazine/Oprah-Interviews-Elie-Wiesel.

"Woody Guthrie Biography." *Bio* (newsletter). www.biography.com/people /woody-guthrie-9323949.

Permission Acknowledgments

G rateful acknowledgment is given to the following for permission to reprint quotations and reproductions of artworks. Every effort has been made to contact all rights holders of the material used in this book. If notified of errors, the publishers will correct any omissions or mistakes in future editions.

Page 12: "Not Waving but Drowning" (four-line excerpt) by Stevie Smith, from *Collected Poems of Stevie Smith*, copyright © 1957 Stevie Smith. Reprinted by permission of New Directions Publishing Corp.

Page 24: Judy Sorum Brown, "Trough," in *The Sea Accepts All Rivers and Other Poems* by Judy Sorum Brown, copyright © Judy Sorum Brown. Used with permission of the author.

Page 154: Barbara Lee, "Emotional Autopsy," copyright © Barbara Lee. Used with permission of the author.

Page 159: Barbara Lee, "Wasted Potential," copyright © Barbara Lee. Used with permission of the author.

Page 162: Ellen Bass, excerpt from "The Thing Is" from *Mules of Love*. Copyright 2002 © Ellen Bass. Reprinted with the permission of The Permissions Company, Inc. on behalf of BOA Editions Ltd., www.boaeditions.org.

Pages 192–93, 194, and 197: Matthew Goldston, all journal entries, copyright © Matthew Goldston. Used with permission of the author.

Page 200: Barbara Lee, "The Measure of a Woman," copyright © Barbara Lee. Used with permission of the author.

Index

About the Author

S andra Marinella is an award-winning teacher and writer from Phoenix, Arizona. For thirty years she taught high school and college writers. When she wasn't grading essays and short stories late at night, she wrote self-help articles for teens and recorded her life experiences in journals. She raised two wonderful sons, helped her husband found an innovative engineering company, made incredible lifelong friends, read stacks of books, and ate entirely too much dark chocolate.

When she faced and survived breast cancer, Sandra turned her focus from teaching to writing as a way to heal and change. She began volunteering with veterans and cancer patients. As she watched writing help them transform their lives, she discovered her new passion — sharing the power of their stories and the methods they used to heal their lives.

After writing *The Story You Need to Tell*, Sandra founded the Story You Need to Tell Project, which uses profits from the book to provide educational scholarships, writing workshops, and writing materials for those in need. Here Sandra helps writers find and transform their stories. She writes, speaks, and gives workshops on the power of our stories and personal writing to help us find our myths, metaphors, and meaning. Discover more at www.storyyoutell.com or follow her at www.facebook.com/storyyouneedtotell, www.instagram.com/sandramarinella, or www.twitter.com/sandramarinella.